Neo-Liberal Ideology

History, Concepts and Policies

Rachel S. Turner

Edinburgh University Press

For my mother

© Rachel S. Turner, 2008, 2011

First published in 2008 by

Edinburgh University Press Ltd
22 George Square, Edinburgh

This paperback edition 2011

Typeset in 11/13.5 pt Goudy by
Servis Filmsetting Ltd, Manchester, and
printed and bound in Great Britain by
CPI Antony Rowe, Chippenham and Eastbourne

A CIP record for this book is available from the British Library

ISBN 978 0 7486 4299 1 (paperback)

The right of Rachel S. Turner to be identified as author of this work has been asserted in accordance with the Copyright, Designs and Patents Act 1988.

Contents

Analytical Table of Contents   iv
Acknowledgements   vi

1   Introduction: Reinventing Liberal Ideology   1

Part I   Ideas in Context

2   Liberal Traditions   21
3   The 'Rebirth of Liberalism'   47
4   Reinventing the Liberal Agenda   80

Part II   Political Concepts

5   The Market: Against the State   115
6   Welfare: The Legitimacy of State Provision   140
7   The Constitution: Government and the Rule of Law   167
8   Property: Individualism and Ownership   192
9   Conclusion   216

Bibliography   227
Index   244

Analytical table of contents

Acknowledgements — vi

1 Introduction: Reinventing Liberal Ideology — 1
   Objectives of the Book — 2
   The Contours of Neo-Liberalism — 4
   Neo-Liberalism and Ideology — 9
   The Use of Concepts in Political Argument — 11
   Outline of the Book — 14

Part I Ideas in Context

2 Liberal Traditions — 21
   Introduction: History and Interpretation — 21
   Liberalism in National Contexts — 22
   The Challenge of Collectivism — 35
   Conclusion — 43

3 The 'Rebirth of Liberalism' — 47
   Introduction: Liberal Revival — 47
   Revising History — 48
   The Mont Pelerin Society — 69
   Conclusion — 74

4 Reinventing the Liberal Agenda — 80
   Introduction: Ideas and Action — 80
   Germany: The Social Market Economy — 81
   Britain: Retrieving Liberal Individualism — 89
   The United States: Conservative Capitalism — 98
   Conclusion — 107

Part II Political Concepts

5	The Market: Against the State	115
	Introduction: Market Values and Western Civilisation	115
	Classical Liberal Political Economy	117
	The Austrian Paradigm	121
	Imperfections of the Market Order	126
	National Market Capitalism	129
	Markets and the Global Economy	132
	Conclusion	136
6	Welfare: The Legitimacy of State Provision	140
	Introduction: Welfare and Ideology	140
	The Rise of the Modern Welfare State	141
	'The Fatal Conceit': Mistaken Ideas About Welfare	148
	Retrenching the Welfare State	155
	Conclusion	162
7	The Constitution: Government and the Rule of Law	167
	Introduction: Government, Liberty and Democracy	167
	Constitutional Traditions	169
	Law and Legislation	177
	'The Constitution of a Liberal State'	182
	Conclusion	188
8	Property: Individualism and Ownership	192
	Introduction: Private Property and the Market Order	192
	National Conceptions of Property	193
	Private Property and Government	201
	Property and the Modern Corporation	206
	Conclusion	212
9	Conclusion	216
	Varieties of Neo-Liberalism	219
	Future Directions	223
Bibliography		227
Index		244

Acknowledgements

During the research for this book I have accumulated many debts from the following individuals and institutions I would like to record here. The Political Economy Research Centre at Sheffield proved to be a very supportive intellectual environment within which to carry out the original research for this book, from 2001 to 2004. I am particularly grateful to Sylvia McColm for providing such a friendly work environment. The Department of Politics was my second home during my time at Sheffield and I would like to thank all the staff there (especially Sarah Cooke) for creating such a warm and congenial atmosphere. I would also like to thank the Economic and Social Research Council for the financial support it provided for my doctoral research.

I owe an enormous debt of gratitude to Prof. Andrew Gamble, who first interested me in neo-liberalism as a subject for research and provided invaluable support and advice during excellent supervision sessions. The most rewarding part of this research was the opportunity to work with him. I would like to thank him for his intellectual and emotional support. Special debts are also owed to Dr Duncan Kelly, Prof. Mike Kenny, Prof. James Meadowcroft and Prof. Raymond Plant. All have read drafts of the research on which this book is based and their insightful comments helped me to clarify my thinking. Similar thanks are due to Prof. Kenneth Minogue for giving me his time to discuss various aspects of neo-liberalism, and to Prof. John Henneberry for sharing with me his extensive knowledge of British property law. I have tried to do justice to the issues raised by all of the above. Any remaining errors, of course, are my own.

On a personal level, I would like to thank my family and friends for the support they have given me over the years; it has been invaluable. In particular, I would like to thank my partner, Philip, who has been an unfailing source of encouragement, solace and support. I would also like to thank Grace and Martha for the many welcomed distractions they provided from the pressures of academic research, and David, Gertie and Emma for their friendship and for making me feel a part of their family. Finally, I would like to express my deepest gratitude to my mother. She has helped me more than she will ever know. Without her unending love and encouragement, this book would not have been possible. It is to her that I dedicate it.

Chapter 1

Introduction: Reinventing liberal ideology

In one of liberalism's darkest hours in the immediate years after the Second World War, a new ideological movement met at Mont Pelerin in Switzerland to expose the dangers they felt were inherent in collectivism and to create an international forum for the rebirth of liberalism. Liberalism had since its conception regarded itself as the ideological force sustaining Western civilisation. However, in a vast programme of ideological readjustment stretching back as far as the late nineteenth century, liberalism in Western societies began to change its form, contours and emphasis. By the beginning of the twentieth century, the ideological dominance of classical liberal values – free trade and limited government – had given way to a pro-collectivist liberal creed embracing the principles of community, rational planning and institutional design.[1] In a statement of its aims, the Mont Pelerin Society (MPS) described its view of the prevailing crisis:

> Over large stretches of the earth's surface the essential conditions of human dignity and freedom have already disappeared. In others they are under constant menace from the development of current tendencies of policy. The position of the individual and the voluntary groups are progressively undermined by the extension of arbitrary power . . . The group believes that these developments have been fostered by the growth of a view of history which denies all absolute moral standards and by the growth of theories which question the desirability of the rule of law. It holds further that they have been fostered by the decline of belief in private property and the competitive market, for without the diffused power and initiative associated with these institutions it is difficult to imagine a society in which freedom may be effectively preserved.[2]

The MPS sought to secure the conditions for liberalism's survival. The society's principal aim was to influence the direction of post-war liberal thinking; a task that would involve 'purging traditional liberal theory of certain accretions which have become attached to it in the course of time'.[3] From its embryonic form in the MPS, this liberal movement has created a huge intellectual network of foundations, institutes, research centres, ideologues and scholars who relentlessly publish and package new ideas that would restore the liberal faith and redirect the course of Western civilisation.

Objectives of the book

The purpose of the present book is to determine the contours of this liberal movement, which has popularly become known in academic and policy debates as neo-liberalism. Its principal objective is to uncover the distinct elements of neo-liberalism in the national contexts of Germany, Britain and the United States during the second half of the twentieth century through contextual and conceptual analysis. Neo-liberalism is a term that has come to be used with a lack of precision in contemporary political debates. What it stands for and what it explains is both confused and confusing. Although the 'neo-liberal' label may be ubiquitous in contemporary political discourse, its exact ideological form remains unclear. For example, some accounts of neo-liberalism such as those put forward by Susan Watkins and David Harvey present it as an all-encompassing hegemonic ideology, without actually defining what the term 'neo-liberalism' stands for. Such interpretations suggest that, since the 1970s, a 'neo-liberal state' has been emerging in a global marketplace where state sovereignty is surrendered and personal and individual freedom can be guaranteed. While the 'neo-liberal turn' may have originated in Britain and the United States under Thatcher and Reagan, Harvey contends that it has become, in various shapes and forms, the central guiding principle of economic thought and management across the world, from New Zealand and Sweden to post-apartheid South Africa and contemporary China.[4] Other advocates of this view, most notably Alex Callinicos, maintain that neo-liberalism is synonymous with Anglo-American liberal capitalist values and with the Third Way, under which enterprise and justice can live in harmony.[5] The principal problem with these interpretations is that they isolate neo-liberalism at a governmental level and therefore fail to appreciate its ideological complexity.

This book does not adopt the popular hegemonic view of neo-liberalism, where, in relation to globalisation, the former is seen as the dominant paradigm of the twenty-first century. Instead, the book highlights the limited impact that neo-liberalism has had on government policy at the national level, and the contradictory obstacles that it faces to the realisation of its liberal programme at the global level. None of the accounts above attempts to trace the evolution of neo-liberalism and considers it in relation to other ideological trends, or unpacks the conceptual structure of neo-liberal thought. The central themes that this book addresses are how neo-liberalism has developed out of the traditions of liberalism, what its core concepts are, how they have been interpreted in different national contexts, and what makes neo-liberalism a distinctive ideology. The contention of the book is that understanding neo-liberalism as an ideology means deciphering the distinct elements typically combined in the term; indicating the variety of its uses in national contexts and the direction of the main path traced during the ideology's rich history. Indeed, from a consideration of the possible range of meanings which the term 'neo-liberal' has carried in Western political thought, it is possible to survey neo-liberalism's intellectual traditions and to isolate the distinct concepts which the ideology has come to conflate. The central aim of the present book is to identify this distinctiveness, to create a genealogy of neo-liberalism and a conceptual map of its core values. To achieve this, the book presents an inventory of the ideology's internal structure, content and shape. While neo-liberalism may not be wholly logical and consistent in its application of ideas and values, the book claims that it is possible to identify those concepts that map its distinctive discursive space as an ideology and give it its internal coherence.

The three countries that the book examines in depth are Germany, Britain and the United States. These countries have been selected because all three adopted, in some shape or form, key elements of the neo-liberal programme. At different stages during the second half of the twentieth century, all three were implacable opponents of state interventionism and supported many of the central tenets of neo-liberalism. The development of the different intellectual traditions in Germany, Britain and the United States has been assigned a prominent place within the body of the book in order to facilitate the reconstruction of the ways in which neo-liberalism drew on these traditions for inspiration and guidance and was in turn shaped by them. The book's intention is to bring to the fore the complex and varied nature of neo-liberal ideology through a comparative examination of these national contexts.

The Contours of Neo-liberalism

The term 'neo-liberalism' was coined in the 1930s by the German economist Alexander Rüstow, to indicate the distinction between the prevailing pro-collectivist liberal ethos and the principles of traditional liberalism. Neo-liberalism established itself as a variant of liberal ideology, driven by the constellation of threats it faced from rival political creeds to the realisation of its liberal project. In the post-war period many liberal thinkers supportive of 'old' liberal ideas began to push for a return to 'true' liberal values, which meant reconceptualising many of the principles liberalism stood for at the time. This required the recrudescence of an old intellectual tendency – classical liberalism – but with radically altered political dimensions, both to modernise liberalism as an ideology and to meet the economic and political demands of the era – hence the prefix 'neo'. The neo-liberal project strove for a new understanding of the state, economy and society within an ideological framework of traditional liberal tenets. This entailed a major intellectual process of reinvention. Classical liberal tenets were stripped of accretions associated with the past and reinterpreted on a new ideological terrain.[6]

In this book, neo-liberalism is defined by four generic principles or beliefs. In the first place, neo-liberalism places a stress on the importance of the market order as an indispensable mechanism for efficiently allocating resources and safeguarding individual freedom. Using the individualistic methodology of classical economics, neo-liberals maintain that unfettered markets produce a natural order in society from the voluntary exchange of goods and services, promoting productive efficiency, social prosperity and freedom. This system coordinates the plans of decentralised agents more expeditiously than central government by accommodating uncertainty, continuous change and scattered knowledge. While the existence of market failure is acknowledged by neo-liberals, the existence of government failure, they claim, is even more pronounced.[7]

The second generic principle of neo-liberal ideology is its commitment to a *Rechtsstaat* (rule of law–state). The *Rechtsstaat* is a legal state, limited by fundamental principles determined by the rule of law. Drawing on a Kantian view of freedom, law and reason, the *Rechtsstaat* is an instrument of law for the regulation of conflicting relations among autonomous individuals in a market society. The function of this state is to secure social cohesion and stability through the preservation of individual liberties.[8]

The third principle of neo-liberalism is its advocacy of minimal state intervention. Neo-liberals advocate that the liberal state should be strong but minimal: it should embody political authority but at the same time be constitutionally limited. Its roles and responsibilities should be determined by the public interest. Neo-liberalism has modified the principles of pure *laissez-faire* so as to afford the state the primary responsibilities of securing law and order, providing public goods and preserving the constitutional rules that safeguard the market order. What neo-liberals object to is an all-embracing corporate state of the kind found in Western societies in the post-war era. For instance, they do not deny the need for the existence of some form of welfare system, but they insist that a distinction has to be made between an institutional welfare state and a residual system of provision.[9]

The final dominant principle of neo-liberalism is private property. A system of full private ownership forms an indispensable part of a neo-liberal social order, reinforcing the irreplaceable value of the individual against the collective. To neo-liberals, the institution of private property and its corollary, the free market, act as a vehicle for decentralising decision-making and for placing it at the level of the individual. The concept goes to the heart of the public–private divide and, consequently, of liberalism itself, by conceptually delineating a sphere of private ownership and autonomy that no state institution may legitimately invade. As the Austrian economist Ludwig von Mises has commented: 'The Programme of Liberalism, if condensed into a single word, would have to read: property, that is, private ownership of the means of production. All the other demands of liberalism result from this fundamental demand.'[10]

While neo-liberals differ among themselves on the many details of a liberal system, they all support these basic principles. This is not to suggest that there is one 'pure' form of neo-liberalism. Intellectual tensions exist between different neo-liberal 'schools' of thought in different national contexts, which started from different intellectual and historical traditions.[11] Indeed, one of the central arguments of this book is that there are many strands within neo-liberalism, which makes it a complex and varied ideology. The book points out that the complexity of neo-liberal ideology arises not only from the tensions that exists between various liberal schools in different national contexts, but also from their connections with other ideologies on the same end of the political spectrum; in particular, with elements of New Right ideology in Anglo-America and of neo-conservatism and libertarianism in the United States. The overlaps that neo-liberalism has with other right-wing ideologies is discussed at length in the individual chapters. One of the most fundamental problems in applying the label 'neo-liberal' to specific individuals and movements is that most neo-liberals reject the term, preferring the label 'liberal' instead, or, in the case of the United States, 'neo-conservative' or 'libertarian'. Whilst not all neo-conservatives and libertarians are necessarily neo-liberal, this book recognises that many of their core beliefs overlap with those of neo-liberalism.

The book claims that, despite the differences that exist between particular strands of neo-liberal ideology, in many respects its various schools meet on common ground in terms of their aims, arguments and assumptions, which makes them constitute a coherent and distinctive ideology. Indeed, the book points out the differences that exist in the nature of neo-liberalism in specific national contexts, but the ideas pursued are essentially part of the same political project. For example, the differences between the various forms of liberal constitutionalism that define the German *Rechtsstaat*, the American Constitution and the British Constitution may be marked, yet all three constitutionalisms share the same reservations about unbridled state power and stress the need for its containment within a specified legal order. The book outlines the neo-liberal movement that arose in the post-war years, which generated political convergence around such core principles. The intellectual alliance of the MPS, the institutionalisation of its ideas in think-tanks and the accomplishments of political leaders and parties created an intellectual climate for transforming the nature of liberal ideology. The term 'liberal' subsequently shifted, from designating 'primarily a general attitude of mind' to designating the act of holding 'specific views about the proper function of government', defined within a definitive political programme.[12]

As with the new liberalism in the early twentieth century, there is some ambiguity as to who should be associated with neo-liberalism. A number of pre-eminent neo-liberal schools of thought and their associated thinkers stand out. Among the most powerful exponents of neo-liberalism were F. A. Hayek and Ludwig von Mises, representing the Austrian tradition; Lionel Robbins from the London School of Economics; Walter Eucken, Alexander Rüstow and Franz Böhm, from the Freiburg group; the German ordo-liberals, Wilhelm Röpke and Alfred Muller-Armack; Milton Friedman and Alan Walters, leaders of the monetarist camp; and James Buchanan and Gordon Tullock from the Virginia school of public choice theory. In addition, think-tanks such as the Institute for Economic Affairs and the Centre for Policy Studies in Britain and the Heritage Foundation and Cato Institute in the United States became a rich source of neo-liberal ideas.[13] Hayek observed that shaping public opinion in favour of the ideals held by the MPS would entail raising and training 'an army of fighters for freedom'.[14] This amalgam of thinkers and ideologues served that function: inside and outside of think-tanks, they both cultivated neo-liberal ideas and made them accessible to wider political audiences.

Throughout the book, various schools of liberal thought are discussed in depth in relation to neo-liberalism. Neo-liberals either have drawn some of their core principles from the ideas of these schools or have vehemently opposed and challenged their beliefs. The most prominent schools of thought discussed are classical liberalism, utilitarianism, the new liberalism, *Liberalismus* (German liberalism), Lockean liberalism, liberal progressivism and neo-liberalism. Table 1.1 distinguishes between these different variants of liberal ideology, outlined in the book. It is designed to make it easier for the reader to decipher the different stands of liberal thought under discussion.

An integral part of this book is the examination of the role that historical and intellectual traditions have played in the formation of neo-liberal ideology. Yet, while there may be an historical emphasis to the book, the book itself is not a study of the history of political thought, but rather of ideology. It outlines the historical and intellectual traditions that neo-liberals have drawn upon and examines how these traditions have been interpreted. The book is not concerned with presenting the ideas behind historical events like the American Revolution, or the ideas of political thinkers such as John Locke, Adam Smith and G. W. F. Hegel in their pure and unadulterated form, but rather in the neo-liberal reading or interpretation of these ideas. The book claims that neo-liberalism is an ideology of reinvention, which borrows ideas from the past and then reinterprets them on a new ideological terrain.

The present book does not present, therefore, a critique of neo-liberal ideas, but rather an analysis of the structure of neo-liberal ideology. Indeed, the term 'neo-liberalism' is not used in a pejorative sense, but to denote a tendency within liberal ideology. The book sees the events leading up to the rise of collectivist ideologies in the early twentieth century as neo-liberals perceived them. Thus it uses the term 'liberal' as a neo-liberal expression, although it recognises that the same term was also used by new liberals such as John Hobson, John Hobhouse and J. M. Keynes and by liberal progressives such as John Dewey, whose ideas neo-liberals

Table 1.1 Variants of Liberalism

School of thought	Geographical base	Approximate time frame	Key figures	Key principles and ideas
Classical liberalism	Britain/United States	1760s–1880s	Adam Smith, David Ricardo, Nassau Senior	free markets, minimal state, 'natural liberty'
Utilitarianism	Britain	1820s–1860s	Jeremy Bentham, James and John Stuart Mill	individualism, democracy, 'social liberty'
New liberalism	Britain	1890s–1940s	J. A. Hobson, L. T. Hobhouse, T. H. Green, William Beveridge	individualism, the common good, social responsibility
Liberalismus	Germany	1770s–1870s	Immanuel Kant, G. W. F. Hegel, Heinrich von Treitschke, Wilhelm von Humboldt	the *Rechtsstaat*, individual personality, law and reason
Lockean liberalism	United States	1770s–1800s	Tom Paine, Thomas Jefferson, John Adams	freedom, democracy, constitutionalism
Liberal progressivism	United States	1930s–1950s	Franklin D. Roosevelt, Lyndon B. Johnson, John Dewey	'social consciousness', rationality, self-development
Neo-liberalism	Britain/United States/Germany	1930s–1990s	F. A. Hayek, Ludwig von Mises, Milton Friedman, Wilhelm Röpke, Alan Walters, James Buchanan	the market order, entrepreneurship, the rule of law, private property, the 'social minimum'

vehemently opposed. It is, therefore, necessary to engage with the term 'liberal' in a contemporary analytical sense in order to discern the neo-liberals' opposition to its usage within this context. Expressions such as 'the rebirth of liberalism', 'reinventing the liberal agenda' and 'restoring the liberal faith' are, however, presented as explicitly neo-liberal ones, where the term 'liberal' refers to the classical liberal ideal of free markets and limited interventionism. The historical analysis presented in this book is explicitly made from a neo-liberal perspective. For example, the interpretation of Hegel presented in the following chapters is not an impartial academic one, designed to stand up to that type of scrutiny, but rather one that conforms to a neo-liberal interpretation of his ideas.

The remaining part of this chapter outlines the particular approach to ideology that the book adopts in relation to neo-liberalism. The theoretical apparatus of the book is outlined in a discussion of the relations between ideologies and political concepts. Finally, a synopsis of the structure of the work is given.

Neo-liberalism and ideology

This book adopts an approach to neo-liberalism which transcends Marxist theories of ideology by placing less emphasis on issues of truth and distortion; instead, it takes the ubiquity of political ideologies as the starting point of analysis. Drawing on Michael Freeden's approach, this book suggests that a contemporary evaluation of neo-liberalism as an ideology entails a threefold analysis: an analysis of the ideology's internal structure; a contextual analysis of the ideology's historical contingency; and an analysis of the ideology's core concepts.[15]

The first point is that the internal structure of an ideology should not be perceived as a static construction. Ideologies are evolving systems of ideas which interact on a number of ideatic dimensions. As W. H. Greenleaf observes, studies of ideology 'must reckon on and accept multiformity, overlap, divergence, inconsistency, obliquity and change as features intrinsic to their subject matter'.[16] Thus ideologies should be identified not just with similarities, but also with processes of change and adjustment. Freeden, however, makes it explicit that ideologies cannot develop in ways that transform their core concepts. The core is the unchanging part of an ideology, essential to its survival.[17] Seen from this perspective, it may be possible to map the conceptual boundaries of neo-liberalism. The general parameters of the ideology, however, remain fragile and elusive. As an ideology, neo-liberalism may not always be wholly logical or consistent in its position. As Stuart Hall observes, 'there are always loose ends, breaks in the logic, gaps between theory and practice, and internal contradictions in any current of thought'.[18] Therefore recombinations within an ideology – even within a variant of an ideology such as neo-liberalism – are normal and frequent. Boundaries may be traversed – either consciously or unconsciously – to broaden an ideology's appeal and to take account of what were peripheral issues and concerns. On this reading, neo-liberalism may be open to any number of possible future formulations. Attempting a grand narrative of neo-liberalism is therefore a futile endeavour. Ideological identity rests on its distinct and recurring ideological premises, which are fixed at its core.

If ideologies are changing entities, they are also historically contingent entities. Internally, ideologies may change their contours and emphasis, but these changes are contingent on beliefs and practices inherited from traditions of the past which may be modified to meet new political ends.[19] Indeed, for contemporary theorists such as Greenleaf, the study of political ideology is strictly an historical endeavour and must be understood in terms of categories of the past. Breaking down the dichotomy between events and ideas, Greenleaf claims that ideologies are best understood as traditions confined to certain periods of history. For example, he exhorts us to understand British political thought in the twentieth century in terms of the two opposing currents of libertarianism and collectivism. The value of Greenleaf's traditions is that they provide a tentative framework for organising a mass of material in a historically credible and coherent form.[20]

An historical approach to ideology, this book suggests, should identify neo-liberalism against the background of the thinkers and organisations that inherited ideas and practices from the past and modified them in line with new political practice. It should employ, for example, Michel Foucault's concept of genealogy as a method for investigating historical processes. For Foucault, genealogy is concerned with the exploration of what may not be evident, on the surface, in how social thought is produced. It is an analysis of descent 'situated within the articulation of history'.[21] It isolates the central components of political mechanisms and traces their development. Foucault, however, makes it clear that genealogy is in no way teleological. It does not attempt to identify the goal of a historical process and to describe how it emerged from its embryonic beginnings. Rather, it charts the continuities and discontinuities in the processes that, by contingent confluence, culminated in contemporary society. The historical development of neo-liberalism, from this perspective, can therefore be seen as a vast fabric of relations, meanings and values that represent the many confluences of past lines of descent. Its genealogy, this book suggests, exposes the motives, institutional pressures and anxieties which coalesced to make these lines of descent appear rational and necessary.

Structure, history and genealogy suggest that ideologies may be neither 'pure' in their boundaries nor linear in their descent. Internal consistency is maintained through the key propositions or core concepts that bind an ideology together and form a chain of interpretation and meaning. Together, these core concepts, to borrow Foucault's metaphor, constitute an ideology's 'regime of truth'. Working together, they 'form a distinct discursive space of meanings, and sustain a particular logic of thought'.[22]

The use of concepts in political argument

Mapping out and understanding the genealogy of ideas, however, is only half of the process of making sense of an ideology or system of thought. The context of political ideas must be accompanied by an understanding of the internal meaning of those central ideas or beliefs and of their role in creating a single ideological entity. The second half of the book, therefore, goes on to identify and examine the conceptual framework of neo-liberal thought – those core concepts that underpin neo-liberalism and give it identity as an ideology. Using Michael Freeden's morphological approach to the study of political ideologies, the book seeks to identify those core and accompanying adjacent and peripheral concepts that can be said to form a constituent part of neo-liberalism's 'idea environment' – the space which holds together a complex combination of political concepts in a sustainable pattern.[23] At the heart of Freeden's approach is his theory of 'decontestation'. Ideologies, he argues, decontest concepts by limiting the essential contestability and indeterminacy of political terms, by 'prioritising among options, accepting or ruling out paradigms that interpret political reality and competing over the legitimate meaning assigned to political language'.[24]

Freeden contends that the influence of these decontested concepts is affected by the specific morphological arrangements that place them in relation to each other. Structurally, ideologies consist of core, adjacent and peripheral concepts that exist in complex, dynamic internal relations with each other. Core concepts represent the unchanging part of an ideology.

They form a matrix of ideatic components that maintain the identity of an ideology. A number of important concepts exist adjacently to the core and are essential for the formation of an ideology.[25] Peripheral concepts are also an important part of the core of an ideology, but they are not essential to its survival. They attach meaning and relevance to the core and are responsible for updating and linking it to issues of contemporary concern. The peripheral concepts that exist within an ideology's perimeter relate to the ideology's cultural, historical and geographical setting; they 'straddle an interface between time and space'. These may be not fully-fledged concepts, but loose ideas or policy statements.[26]

It is clear from Freeden's complex morphological model that concepts within political ideologies can be distinguished by their core, adjacent and peripheral positions. Political concepts, however, do not exist in isolation from one another, but form the part of a larger whole. As Hall comments: 'They hang together. They mutually define and modify one another; they entail each other – they are interdependent.'[27] Indeed, at the heart of Freeden's approach is the idea of ideologies as 'multi-conceptual constructs' or 'conceptual configurations'. Freeden contends that it is from the ordering of core, adjacent and peripheral concepts in these configurations that ideological identity is ascertained. Ideologies, Freeden states, may develop and change over time; but, following Wittgenstein, Freeden states that they remain recognisable as ideologies from the 'family resemblances' they share with earlier variants.[28]

This book also adopts the conceptual–historical approach to neo-liberalism advocated by Terence Ball. Like Freeden, Ball sees political concepts as an integral part of the vocabulary of politics. However, whilst Freeden focuses on the configuration of political concepts, Ball's concern is not so much conceptual analysis as 'conceptual history' – 'that is, a concern with conceptual change and the construction of conceptual histories'.[29] Histories of political concepts, he contends, are histories of political argument and of conceptual contests. Unlike the meaning of words which are static, that of concepts, Ball suggests, changes over time as a result of political conflict. Therefore the deconstruction and reconstruction of the world of ideas, according to Ball, is determined by conceptual history. Conceptual change is brought about by concepts that transgress and leak across discursive boundaries. Ball states that it is the task of the 'critical conceptual historian' to describe how discourses have changed, in particular, to identify those concepts which have altered their meaning and to explain how these changes have been brought about.[30]

INTRODUCTION

Utilising the conceptual tools of Freeden and Ball, this book attempts to formulate a set of common denominators for neo-liberals. This is done at a contextual level by taking a conceptual–historical approach to the construction of neo-liberal discourse and by examining the ways in which liberal political concepts have been reconstructed by neo-liberals on a new political terrain. The purpose of this conceptual history is to put the neo-liberal interpretation of specific concepts into the context in which they were conceived. The book examines how neo-liberals have drawn on, or rejected, various interpretations of specific liberal concepts in order to find their own distinctive interpretation. Neo-liberalism, in this book, is also analysed at a high level of abstraction, using core neo-liberal concepts and a range of adjacent and peripheral concepts that sustain, interpret and operationalise the core. Indeed, this book sees neo-liberalism as a conceptual movement within liberalism that is made up of concepts such as 'the market' and 'the constitution' – which were previously adjacent or peripheral within liberal ideology but, with the rise of neo-liberalism, have moved to the core. The following table sets out the core, adjacent and peripheral concepts in neo-liberalism's conceptual configuration that are discussed in the second part of the book.

Table 1.2 Neo-Liberalism's Conceptual Configuration

Core concepts	Adjacent concepts	Peripheral concepts
The market	evolution, spontaneous order, limited knowledge, free exchange, individualism, self-interest, entrepreneurship	the enterprise culture, short-term profit motives, income-tax relief, privatisation, de-regulation, share-ownership
Welfare	minimal state, equality of opportunity, freedom, personal responsibility, self-reliance, negative rights	reduced social expenditure, education vouchers, private insurance, 'workfare', negative income tax
The constitution	freedom, private law, legal responsibility, abstract order, 'rules of just conduct', evolution	the legal state, a separation of powers, independent administrative courts, a 'fiscal constitution', balanced budgets, restrained democratic rule
Property	ownership, possessive individualism, legal privilege, individual initiative, negative justice, private associations	capital accumulation, voluntary savings, private inheritance, maximised shareholder profits

This book does not suggest that there can ever be an a priori definition of neo-liberalism, but claims that its conceptual arrangements can be identified from textual material and the perspectives of individual thinkers, which can be compared for overlaps and deviations. From this analysis, a clear profile of neo-liberal ideas and concepts can be created. These concepts may not be unique to neo-liberalism alone; what is unique is the way they are configured.

Outline of the book

From the above discussion it is apparent that neo-liberalism constitutes a complex set of thought-practices. These thought-practices can be analysed in three interconnected ways. First, they can be analysed through processes of conceptual change and adjustment within the internal structure of neo-liberalism. Secondly, they can be analysed through the historical context that shapes and sustains meaningful ideological expressions. Thirdly, they can be analysed through the ideational boundaries of neo-liberalism's core concepts.

The structure of the book reflects this theoretical approach. The first part adopts Foucault's genealogical approach and is devoted to the context of the historical ascendancy of neo-liberalism; it outlines and explains the fate of traditional liberal values in twentieth-century political thought. The second chapter explores liberal traditions in Germany, Britain and the United States. The chapter details unifying themes and varieties of thought in the history of German, British and American liberalism and notes the decline in traditional understandings of liberalism in the early part of the twentieth century. The purpose of the chapter is to outline, historically, the liberal traditions which neo-liberalism has both drawn upon and reacted against.

The third chapter examines the ideological context within which neo-liberal ideology evolved in the twentieth century. It set outs the historical and ideological context that witnessed the 'end of *laissez-faire*' and the rise of a new political creed in the form of collectivism. It goes on to explore the historical development of neo-liberal ideology in the post-war period: the founding of the Mont Pelerin Society and the growth of schools of thought and think-tanks that influenced the rise of neo-liberalism in this period. The chapter argues that the rise of neo-liberalism was not simply a revival of classical liberal doctrines in the twentieth century, but was predominantly a movement of reaction to the collectivist threat facing liberalism.

The fourth chapter deals with the impact of neo-liberal ideas on national policy agendas in Germany, Britain and the United States in the second half of the twentieth century. The chapter looks at the attempts made by think-tanks and politicians to overcome interventionism and to place liberal ideology at the heart of new policy proposals. In Germany, it details the nature of ordo-liberalism and the rise of the Social Market Economy in the 1950s; in Britain, it explores the grassroots opposition within the Conservative Party in the 1960s and 1970s and origins of the New Right; and, in the United States, it examines the impact of neo-conservatism on economic policy measures. The chapter's main contention is that neo-liberalism in the post-war years did not represent one single strand of thought, but rather a heterogeneous movement of ideas. Yet, whilst there are many strands of neo-liberalism, all exhibit similarities and represent a variation on a common doctrine, namely a distrust of the state.

The second part of the book concentrates on the ideas and assumptions explicit and implicit in neo-liberalism's core concepts. The four remaining chapters closely scrutinise four fundamental neo-liberal concepts: the market, the constitution, welfare and property. From a discussion of these concepts, the chapters examine comparatively the internal structuring of neo-liberal systems of thought in Germany, Britain and the United States.

The fifth chapter examines the concept of the market in relation to neo-liberalism. It allocates the market a core position in neo-liberalism's ideological configuration. It discusses the role of the market in classical liberal political economy, in neo-classical political economy and in the philosophy of the Austrian School of Economics. It goes on to detail some of the imperfections of the market, such as monopoly, bureaucracy, and regulation and state intervention, and it examines how neo-liberals overcome these obstacles. Finally, the chapter explores the role of markets in the global economy, outlining the neo-liberal vision of a globalised market order. The chapter contends that markets, for neo-liberals, are sacrosanct to the functioning of the economy; they are part of the natural spontaneous order of civilised values and mutual cooperation that sustains capitalism.

The sixth chapter focuses on the concept of welfare in neo-liberal ideology. The chapter outlines the differences and similarities between the welfare measures pursued in Germany, Britain and the United States in the post-war years. It then looks in depth at neo-liberalism's reaction to these forms of welfarism, and relates this reaction back to neo-liberalism's understanding of other liberal concepts such as freedom, individual rights and justice. The chapter then examines neo-liberal policy regimes in relation to welfare in Germany, Britain and the United States. The main point of the chapter is that neo-liberalism holds distinct conceptions of welfare – de-politicised conceptions – which form an integral part of its anti-collectivist value system.

The seventh chapter looks at the constitution and the rule of law. It sees the constitution as a fundamental concept for neo-liberalism, one through which the powers of government may be curtailed. The chapter explores national forms of constitutionalism, and identifies the different models of constitutional government that neo-liberalism draws upon to create its own ideal constitution. It sets out the neo-liberal ideal of a *Rechtsstaat* and the fundamental distinction between law and legislation. The chapter argues that the emphasis which neo-liberalism places on the constitution demonstrates that, far from being anti-political, neo-liberalism is rather an ideology with a serious doctrine about politics and government at its heart.

The eighth and final concept chapter is on property. The chapter focuses on the concept of private property in Germany, Britain and the United States, and on how different national strands of neo-liberalism draw on different intellectual traditions for their inspiration. The emphasis is placed on the concepts of liberty, individualism, law and justice in relation to the neo-liberal conception of private property. The chapter examines in detail neo-liberalism's interpretation of different forms of property ownership, in particular in relation to the modern corporation. The chapter claims that the concept of property is fundamental for neo-liberals as property forms the foundations of Western civilisation, acts as a basis for negative liberty by restraining the powers of government and encourages the individual initiative that leads to free market competition and economic efficiency.

Finally, the conclusion of the book uncovers neo-liberalism's specific conceptual pattern from a pool of virtually unlimited possible combinations. It identifies neo-liberalism's conceptual configuration and its distinctive identity as an ideology. The book contends that neo-liberalism represents much more than a simple commitment to unfettered free markets; it is a complex ideology with many individual strands, which come together to form a coherent movement in opposition to collectivism.

Notes

1. In some accounts, this strand of twentieth-century liberalism is referred to as socialism. However, to a large extent, policies that have been described as 'socialist' have often been left-wing liberal. Indeed, the differences between egalitarian liberalism and some theories of social justice are often difficult to discern.
2. The Mont Pelerin Society's statement of aims, republished in Max Hartwell, *A History of the Mont Pelerin Society* (Indianapolis: Liberty Fund Inc., 1995), pp. 7–11.
3. The opening address of the Mont Pelerin Society, republished in F. A. Hayek, *Studies in Philosophy, Politics and Economics* (London: Routledge, 1967) p. 149.
4. See Susan Watkins, 'New Labour: A weightless hegemony', *New Left Review*, 27 May/June 2004, pp. 1–28, and David Harvey, *A Brief History of Neo-Liberalism* (Oxford: Oxford University Press, 2005).
5. Alex Callinicos, *The New Mandarins of American Power* (Cambridge: Polity, 2003). See also his *Against the Third Way: An Anti-Capitalist Critique* (Cambridge: Polity, 2001).
6. The synthesis between old and new in so-called 'new' ideologies is explored by Andrew Vincent in his 'New ideologies for old?', *The Political Quarterly*, 69: 1 (1998), pp. 48–58.
7. The *locus classicus* of this argument is the work of the Austrian economist Ludwig von Mises. See his 'Economic calculation in the socialist commonwealth', in A. Nove and D. M. Nutti (eds), *Socialist Economics: Selected Readings* (Harmondsworth: Penguin, 1972).
8. F. A. Hayek endorses the *Rechtsstaat* state in his discussion of the legal and constitutional arrangements of a liberal society in his three-volume *Law, Legislation and Liberty* (London: Routledge, 1973, 1976, 1979).
9. The conception of a minimal state has historically been a central part of the liberal tradition and has been adopted, in different manifestations, by all neo-liberal thinkers. Yet conflicts exist over the exact grounds for state interference. Hayek, for instance, defines the public interest not in terms of some form of common good, but rather as those interests which are kept separate form individual private interests. See his *The Constitution of Liberty* (London: Routledge, 1960), pp. 204–6. The Virginia School, however, explicitly rejects the Hayekian notion of a 'public interest' separate from private interests. There is only self-interested behaviour, which, in the case of government actors – politicians and bureaucrats – must be constrained by precise constitutional specification. See James Buchanan, *The Limits of Liberty: Between Anarchy and Leviathan* (Chicago: University of Chicago Press, 1979).
10. Ludwig von Mises, *Liberalism: In the Classical Tradition* (New York: Foundation for Economic Education, 1985), p. 21.
11. For a discussion of these tensions, see Nigel Ashford's work, *Consensus and Conflict Within Neo-Liberalism* (Strathclyde Papers on Government and Politics, 1984).
12. F. A. Hayek, 'Liberalism', in his *New Studies in Philosophy, Politics, Economics and the History of Ideas* (London: Routledge and Kegan Paul, 1978), p. 147.
13. For a comprehensive discussion of British free-market think-tanks, see Richard Cockett, *Thinking the Unthinkable: Think-Tanks and the Economic Counter Revolution, 1931–1983* (London: HarperCollins, 1994). For the American context, see D. M. Ricci, *The Transformation of American Politics: The New Washington and the Rise of Think-Tanks* (New Haven: Yale University Press, 1993).

14. F. A. Hayek's paper on the 'The prospect of freedom', Mont Pelerin Society Archive, quoted in Cockett, p. 104.
15. See Michael Freeden, *Ideologies and Political Theory* (Oxford: Oxford University Press, 1996).
16. W. H. Greenleaf, *The British Political Tradition: The Ideological Heritage*, Vol. II (London: Methuen, 1983), p. 13.
17. Freeden, *Ideologies and Political Theory*, pp. 37–8.
18. Stuart Hall, 'Variants of liberalism', in James Donald and Stuart Hall (eds), *Politics and Ideology* (Milton Keynes: Open University Press, 1986), p. 36.
19. This approach follows Wittgenstein's model of rule-following, which suggests that no set of concepts contained within an ideology can fix or limit the ways they might be modified. See L. Wittgenstein, *Philosophical Investigations* (Oxford: Blackwell, 1972).
20. Greenleaf, *The Ideological Heritage*, pp. 17–18.
21. Michel Foucault, 'Nietzsche, genealogy and history', in Paul Rainbow (ed.), *The Foucault Reader: An Introduction to Foucault's Thought* (London: Penguin, 1991) p. 80.
22. Hall, 'Variants of liberalism', p. 38.
23. See Michael Freeden, 'Political concepts and ideological morphology', *The Journal of Political Philosophy*, 2: 2 (1994), pp. 145–61, and Freeden, *Ideologies and Political Theory*.
24. Freeden, *Ideologies and Political Theory*, p. 551.
25. Ibid., pp. 82–5.
25. Ibid., pp. 78–81.
27. Hall, 'Variants of liberalism', p. 39.
28. Freeden, *Ideologies and Political Theory*, pp. 90–1.
29. Terence Ball, 'Political theory and conceptual change', in Andrew Vincent (ed.), *Political Theory: Tradition and Diversity* (Cambridge: Cambridge University Press, 1997), p. 36.
30. Ibid., pp. 40–2.

Part I: Ideas in Context

Chapter 2

Liberal traditions

Introduction: History and interpretation

Liberalism as an intellectual movement of ideas has been a pre-eminent force in the history of political thought, establishing itself since its conception in the early nineteenth century as 'the outstanding doctrine of Western civilization'.[1] Liberalism, though, should not be identified with a single tradition; it does not constitute a clear-cut body of either doctrine or practice but comprises a number of conflicting historical forms. Ideologies, as Clifford Geertz has written, are cognitive maps 'of problematic social reality'.[2] This cartographical metaphor seems especially appropriate for describing the different and sometimes contradictory variants of liberal ideology. These variants, like maps, represent the historical landscape in their own ways, and for different purposes. Their representations can be accurate, but, like maps, are always incomplete, emphasising some features and neglecting others. Changes in the core features of these variants of liberalism are inevitable, as the variants themselves are constantly subjected to the forces of historical transformation.

This is one of the strongest arguments in favour of placing liberalism in its proper historical context. For it is only when liberalism is seen as an evolving, and therefore changing, ideology that historical differences fall into place. A hermeneutic approach, which explores the existential nature of understanding whilst recognising it as embedded in tradition, is one way of interpreting such changes in liberalism. The value of this approach is that it does not claim to present a systematic theory; rather, it recognises several overlapping but competing constructions of liberalism rooted in distinctive traditions. It attaches meaning to these traditions and to the associated practices that people inherit. These traditions are viewed as historically contingent; they are evolving and can be identified by tracing their historical connections back through time.[3]

Liberalism as a complex and pluralistic political ideology therefore has to be unpacked and clarified from within; it has to be understood as a number of internal variants in the form of traditions or phases. These traditions are composed of competing beliefs and practices, which form a part of the larger narrative that is history. These varied beliefs, languages and customs, which may be contradictory and often permeate into rival ideologies, stay within the boundaries of liberalism through the 'family resemblances' they share with those core concepts, expressions and values that can be labeled as fundamentally 'liberal'.[4]

It is only by outlining these family resemblances that neo-liberalism's place within the liberal creed can be identified. This chapter, therefore, traces the main strands of liberal traditions in Britain, Germany and United States which are relevant to neo-liberalism; it identifies unifying themes and conflicting tendencies. It examines the divergent nature of liberal thought-processes in the history of these three countries, revealing the historically contingent nature of liberalism's key concepts and propositions. Rather than presenting a straightforward history of liberal ideas, the intention of this chapter is to provide a historical narrative for assessing the impact of 'old' and 'new' liberal ideas on the neo-liberal ascendancy. Its concern is not to recount or analyse in any great detail a particular liberal perspective, but to provide a preliminary excavation of neo-liberal thought; to reconstruct the intellectual path by which neo-liberalism, by the 1970s, came to prominence as a distinctive ideology. National varieties of liberal ideology and the substance of their claims, the chapter argues, are of considerable significance in understanding and interpreting the general contours of neo-liberal thought, examined in the subsequent chapters.

Liberalism in National Contexts

Britain

Neo-liberalism has its roots in classical liberalism, which acquired authority in Britain in the late eighteenth century and provided the intellectual foundations for the Victorian era. This economic strand of the British liberal tradition centred on a reaction against the mercantilism of the early modern period, disseminated by the classical economists Adam Smith, Thomas Malthus and David Ricardo. Classical liberalism's advocacy of government constraint and its ideas on property were particularly suited to the development of a *laissez-faire* economy. Smith, in particular, is identified by contemporary neo-liberals as one of the true founders of modern liberalism.[5] Smith's free-market economy, first described in his *Wealth of Nations*, was later adopted by F. A. Hayek and the Austrian School and became an important founding principle of neo-liberal ideology. Smith's classical liberal position, encapsulated in his famous vision of the 'invisible hand', proclaimed that social well-being would unintentionally but efficiently be served by countless self-interested decisions in the daily activities of the free market. These individual interests, Smith asserted, are naturally harmonious; under a system of free competition, the operation of the market continually tends to produce prices as low as is consistent with supplying the product, whilst yielding a fair return on the effort expended in its production. This freedom of exchange would produce as much economic advantage for individuals as the circumstances permit, thus maximising both individual and social benefits. Smith never referred to this economic order as capitalism or as free enterprise, but rather as the 'natural system of perfect liberty and justice'.[6]

Smith stated that under this natural system of liberty government intervention should be severely curtailed. He argued that any attempt by central government to direct the 'industry of private people' would be quite superfluous, and, because it would require a degree of wisdom and knowledge which no government could possess, would in practice be damaging to the wealth of a nation. He proclaimed that government should restrict its activities in the economic sphere to enlarging the area of free trade and removing obstacles and disincentives to private enterprise.[7] It would be misleading, however, to describe Smith, without qualification, as a doctrinaire advocate of *laissez-faire*. His categories for intervention allow for a wider scope of state activity than the nineteenth century *laissez-faire* image suggests.[8] In the political sphere, Smith ascribed to government the right and duty of 'erecting and maintaining certain public works and certain public institutions, which it can never be in the interest of any individual or small number of individuals to erect and maintain'.[9] While Smith granted government an extensive range of roles in the provision of such public goods, he maintained that equality, liberty and justice are best achieved where politics is reduced to a minimum. In the political arena, however, a distorted conception of Smith's 'public goods', coupled with the growth in utilitarian philosophy, opened the way for much more extensive and fully considered acts of liberal interventionism after 1832 in policy areas that transcended the 'general good' – poor law, factories, shipping, banking, and company finance.[10]

To a large extent, utilitarianism overlapped with classical liberalism. Richard Leach points out that the utilitarians stemmed from a similar intellectual environment – the eighteenth-century Enlightenment – as the classical economists, and shared their strong belief in the individualist assumptions underpinning British liberalism.[11] In the same way the classical economists attacked monopoly, and especially the protection given to large landowners, the utilitarians attacked aristocratic government and renounced the concept of privilege. Jeremy Bentham and James and John Stuart Mill developed the utilitarian understanding of Smith's market society. Like Smith, they never advocated a harsh *laissez-faire*, but extended the principle of *laissez-faire* to rationalise or modernise liberal perceptions grounded in traditions of the past. Utilitarians held that the moral criterion for measuring the social good lies in the rationalistic calculation of what provides the 'greatest happiness of the greatest number' of individuals. Stuart Hall, for instance, states:

> Though Bentham believed that as much as possible the state's functions should be 'privatised' and was firmly committed to the principle of *laissez-faire*, he also believed in the active intervention of legislation to clear away the old encumbrances to liberty and the need for efficient administration to instil by intervention from above, if necessary, the conditions of free and unrestrained action.[12]

John Stuart Mill developed the Benthamite basis of utilitarianism further. Like Bentham, Mill opposed, in a liberal manner, all forms of government interference, yet his belief in representative government and his desire to see an educated democracy pushed him irrevocably towards a form of liberal interventionism. Mill's concept of 'social liberty' represented a compromise between a system of pure *laissez-faire* and unregulated state action; it involved a continuation of the strict tenets of individualism and an extension of individualism into taking account of the 'general welfare of the community'.[13] While the state, according to Mill, had no right to interfere within the inner sphere of any individual's life, it may have a conditional right to interfere in social affairs involving interactions between several persons where the principle of utility is the guiding principle. Thus Mill argued in favour of diffused, responsible and limited political power in a democratic system in order to provide for certain social ends, whilst respecting the private sphere of individual choice.[14]

For modern neo-liberals, however, the utility principle of the 'greatest happiness of the greatest number' involved a breach with *laissez-faire* principles and distorted true liberal faith by encouraging 'constructivist rationalism' and interventionism. Neo-liberals point out a fundamental distinction that exists in the liberal tradition between a distorted utilitarianism conception of British liberalism and the true values of classical liberalism.[15] Theoretically, however, this tension between utilitarianism and classical liberalism is somewhat overstated. It was the moral rationale for liberalism that had changed; the underlying premises of liberalism remained the same. Although there was an inveterate distrust of state power in both the utilitarian and the classical liberal schools, George Watson comments that 'liberals always accepted a role for government. They debated not whether it should exist, but what it should be'.[16]

Intellectually, the British liberal tradition was a product of both classical liberalism and utilitarianism, and it is these movements that set the ideological foundations of the Victorian period. Richard Bellamy places the growth of liberalism in the context of the historical development of British capitalism and of the moral order that it fostered. British industrial predominance, he writes, was attributed to a strong and coherent liberal tradition, endorsed by the middle and industrious classes. Although the principal originators of British liberalism – Adam Smith, John Stuart Mill and Herbert Spencer – held conflicting views over the exact interpretation of liberty, all tended to emphasise the self-creating power of the individual. Central to British liberal philosophy at the time was the idea of an economic and moral revolution that would free the individual from the constraints of the aristocratic order.[17] Liberalism became more ideologically demanding as it took on new ideas and represented different interests, in particular those of the middle class.

The most effective political expression of middle-class liberalism before the formation of the Liberal Party in the second half of the nineteenth century was the Anti-Corn Law League and its campaign for free trade. The intellectual basis of the mercantilist system had already been thrown into doubt by the publication of Smith's *Wealth of Nations*. The leaders of the league, Richard Cobden and John Bright, repelled by the landed aristocracy's monopoly over consumer markets, adopted Smith's ideas in a simple form and turned free trade into a popular moral crusade. Intellectually, they drew on the liberal principles held by the Manchester School, and were influenced by the French economist Frederic Bastiat's arguments on behalf of free trade. Free trade, Cobden and Bright claimed, would not only lead to peaceful political association, in contrast to the Machiavellian power politics associated with the old aristocratic order, but also bolster British economic power within the world system. It was hoped that the extension of free trade would encourage mutual commercial dependence and eliminate war between nations. This metaphysical idea, of a harmonious order of market transactions, was invariably based, in some form or another, on an almost religious belief. Indeed, E. Halevy has christened Manchester liberalism by the name 'non-conformist liberalism', indicating its commitment to free markets and non-intervention.[18]

The liberal ideal of a self-regulating market society also had a strong moral dimension. The Manchester liberal position of Cobden and Bright was built around the concept of the individual and the philosophy of independence and self-help. Supporters of the Manchester School saw industrial growth as a product of individual effort. The individual, freed from the constraints of the agrarian and hierarchical order of the old society, was encouraged to create a new way of life. The so-called 'age of *laissez-faire*' was defended by Herbert Spencer as a route to individual development and self-improvement. Spencer's greatest exposition of the liberal creed, Man Versus the State, defended the freedom of the individual and warned against the threat which an encroaching state power posed to individual liberty. Samuel Smiles echoed Spencer's concerns. His works, *Self-Help* and *Character*, captured the moral temper of the age, calling for individual self-discipline and initiative. Rejecting the social basis of Owenite socialism, Smiles claimed that attempts to shape and improve individual character through state action were futile: 'character is formed by the individual, not for him'.[19]

It is this current of thought that led A. V. Dicey famously to characterise the middle fifty years of nineteenth-century Britain as an 'age of individualism'. Despite the dramatic increase in the amount of state intervention during this period, the fundamental principles behind the intervention were not yet collectivist but were as, Dicey rightly claimed, impeccably individualist.[20] For many contemporary neo-liberals, therefore, this mid-Victorian era represented the high tide of British liberalism, with Cobden and Bright portrayed as the revered saviours of the liberal tradition.

After the success of the repeal of the Corn Laws in 1846, liberalism became established as a serious political movement in Britain; it was devoted to political argument rather than high theory, and in 1859 formed its own party. Associations such as the Liberty and Property Defence League, founded in 1882, were both political and educational in function and formed part of a larger liberal movement devoted to the cause of self-help versus help from the state. However, by the end of the nineteenth century, the British liberal tradition was irrevocably moving in another direction. The recognition of poverty and unemployment implied that individual self-development could not be automatically guaranteed through participation in the economic system. From the 1880s onwards, liberalism steadily transformed itself into a social philosophy committed to welfare reform, eroding the minimal state on which Victorian liberalism had based its identity.[21]

Germany

In Germany, the rich and vigorous intellectual and social developments of the Reformation consolidated a particular German tradition of liberty from its medieval roots, granting the individual 'the right to private judgement'.[22] The focal point of early German liberalism was religion as a symbol of individual experience, reason and conscience. Historically, however, Germany was much slower than Britain to develop the political dimension of its liberal tradition. The type of aristocratic liberalism that played so important a part in Britain, with the Whigs, was almost entirely absent from German politics. Nor did Germany possess a reform ideology like that of the Manchester School, which drove the liberal market model in Britain. German liberalism developed its own, distinct, if somewhat restricted path to political realisation.[23]

The general weakness of the liberal tradition in Germany is reflected in the nature of its *Weltanschauung*. Ideologically, German liberalism developed within the cultural and political context of the state. German liberalism was state liberalism: it 'regarded the state as the essential instrument to realise its liberal programme'.[24] The German liberal movement held a particular conception of the state that was far removed from the absolutism associated with the German principalities. The German liberal state was a legal and constitutional state. A *Rechtsstaat* (a constitutional state bound by the rule of law) was established in Germany as the embodiment of a constitutional dualism between the governors and the governed. The *Rechtsstaat* represents, as de Ruggerio observes, 'the legal tradition of the whole people; it is a 'civil juridical association'.[25] This liberal state is conceived so as to be limited by laws and by fundamental principles of legality, rather than as being a purely political organisation that can dispense law in the interests of polity. Indeed, it is paramount to the freedom of the individual that the state's functions are limited to the sphere of a legality compatible with the rule of law. It is this curtailment of state power through law and constitutional order which makes the *Rechtsstaat* the ideal state form for many neo-liberals. As discussed in Chapter 4, it was to form the constitutional basis of Germany's Social Market Economy in the post-war years, and has been widely endorsed by Austrian theorists such as F. A. Hayek, who have expressed support for the *Rechtsstaat's* separation of legislative and executive functions.

A Kantian conception of liberty, law and reason provided the philosophical background for the *Rechtsstaat*. Kant's system of thought was connected with Prussian-German reform liberalism. Kant was concerned with transforming the monarchic state into a constitutional state. He based his theory of the constitutional state on the fundamental distinction between morality and legality. In the sphere of morality, Kant held that individuals possess their own autonomous ground, with no limitations except those posed by individual conscience. The sphere of legality, in contrast, is controlled by the state. The state represents a legal order based on a coalition of the wills of private individuals – a public will – which provide the moral basis for rightful legislation. Adopting in substance, though with some modification, Rousseau's concept of the general will, Kant argued that law does not rest on individual consent, but on what would be chosen by free and rational individuals acting together. Jeremy Waldron states that, for Kant, '[t]he test of a just society is not whether the individuals who live in it have agreed to its terms, but whether its terms can be represented as the object of an agreement between them'.[26] It is these constitutional arrangements, Kant argued, that safeguard individual freedom. Freedom is not infringed by membership of that state, but is actually made possible by living under the state.

The Kantian conception of the state developed within the German idealist tradition and was carried further by Hegel. Hegel, drawing on Kant, developed a conception of the state as an abstract institution. In his *Philosophy of Right*, he acknowledged the importance of economic activity and individual freedom, but insisted that the state must be prepared to check the disruptive forces in society. The state, for Hegel, expressed a higher claim of rationality. It was a source of cohesion and social stability that built upon, and transcended, the individualist impulses at work in market society. Hegel clearly placed freedom in the sphere of politics. Unlike Kant, he saw no clear divide between morality and legality, between the individual and the state. Hegel reconciled the freedom of the individual to the authority of the state. Indeed, he made it explicit that the state is not an external despotic force in society, which is elevated to a status above its individual subjects, but a constitutional order that exists in the interests of society, as an institution of representation.[27]

Heinrich von Treitschke's political philosophy pushed the Hegelian tradition of state liberalism further. Following Aristotle, Treitschke considered the state as a natural institution. The state, for Treitschke, is a representation of power.[28] It is at the same time, however, a representation of freedom: the power of the state and the freedom of individuals are inseparably connected. Indeed, Treitschke is careful to point out that the state must secure personal liberty to its citizens and introduce order and justice in society. This fusion between the 'freedom of the people' and 'state power' was embodied in Treitschke's personal loyalty to the monarchical state of Prussia. As Krieger observes, '[t]he union in Prussia of the princely liberty of the past with the individual liberty of the future made it for Treitschke the German state, a rational reality upon which both kinds of freedom depended for their existence'.[29]

Treitschke's preoccupation with the power aspect of the state, however, invoked criticism from other liberal theorists of the time, and later from neo-liberals. While Hegel and Treitschke believed in freedom through the state, the German philosopher Wilhelm von Humboldt demanded freedom from the state. Humboldt pushed the neo-liberal ideal of a *Rechtsstaat* to its extreme form, limiting state activity to what is absolutely necessary – maintaining mutual security and removing obstacles that may impede citizens in the free exercise of their rights – without restricting the free actions of individuals. Hallowell points out that Humboldt is one of the few liberal theorists in German literature whose ideas can be closely identified with the classical liberalism of nineteenth-century Britain, and in particular with the anti-state ideas of Herbert Spencer.[30] Humboldt's *Essay on the Limits of State Action*, written in 1792 and published in 1851, warned against regulation by the state which overrides the natural order of individual association. His support for Bildung's beliefs – of the aesthetic development of individual initiative and ability – led him to attack state interventions designed to regulate the private lives of individuals. However, in the long-term, in a political atmosphere of state worship, Humboldt's liberal views proved to be fundamentally unproductive. Later German liberals realised that Humboldt's standpoint was untenable and abandoned such complete and uncompromising individualism.

A complementary concept to that of the state in German liberalism was the notion of the nation. In traditional German liberalism, the power of the state and the freedom of the individual were merged with the idea of nationhood. As the nineteenth century advanced, more liberals came to desire a state based on both law (*Rechtsstaat*) and nation (*Nationalstaat*). The fate of liberal values thus became intimately connected with the creation of a national state. De Ruggerio places these national sentiments within the historical formation of the German nation. In his history of European liberalism, he writes, the revolution in France 'aroused a powerful national consciousness in Germany. The idea of the Fatherland of the German nation was the new bond which replaced the broken fetters of the Empire.'[31] By the mid-nineteenth century, liberalism and nationalism were valid concepts for most of those who sought political change. The greatest campaign for national unification was fought during the 1848–9 Revolution.

The following decades were deeply coloured by the upsurge of German national feeling. While the revolution did little to alter the old power structures, it raised political awareness in middle-class circles of constitutional issues and the problem of national unification. The notion of an emancipated *Volk*, encapsulated within a strong German state, invoked a conception of common citizenship. German liberals conceived of the nation as a 'living and growing personality'.[32] Liberal theorists spoke to, and for, a universal entity. They gave the *Volk* a political function: within the context of their ideology, the *Volk* became the focus of their efforts and the source of their claim to set the course for the German future. Political unification, they believed, would be a culmination of German social, economic and cultural progress. This national dimension to German liberalism partly arose out of the industrial and commercial expansion of Germany in the mid-nineteenth century. William Carr comments that 'businessmen and professional people, increasingly irritated by restrictions on economic activity and convinced of the benefits . . . which would flow from unification, set out to create a groundswell of opinion favourable to the creation of a strong Reich'.[33] However, as Hans Vorländer observes, such a pro-national stance reflected the general weakness of liberal ideas both in German political discourse and in the political system in general. Liberalism became internally divided and eventually emptied of all substantive meaning through its associations with the state, nation and economy.[34]

Richard Bellamy argues that the peculiarities of German liberalism are reflected in the historical development of German capitalism. Social structures, he maintains, proved considerably less amenable to the liberal ethos than in countries like Britain. Late industrialisation meant that the German economy took on a pronounced corporate and statist form from an early stage.[35] For some liberals like Max Weber, the nature of capitalism was irrevocably moving Germany towards a *bürokratische Anstaltsstaat* (bureaucratic, rational and machine-like state). State paternalism, monopolistic practices and corporate power, Weber argued, were undermining the traditional philosophical and social bases of liberalism. Weber's analysis was not, however, intended to apply to Germany alone. His thought transcends its immediate national context, to address the fate of liberalism in a world characterised by competition between capitalist states.[36]

In Germany, the individual initiative and competitive spirit associated with the Protestant ethics and early entrepreneurial capitalism had been driven out by bureaucratic large-scale organisations. Weber did not deny the positive value of bureaucracy within the limits of its technical and administrative functions, but strongly opposed its extension to political life. The controlling power of the state, Weber claimed, with its policies of state enterprises, protectionism, and cartelisation, made it impossible for liberalism to retain a stronghold in political life. Beetham states that 'these developments Weber described somewhat dramatically as the "iron cage of modernity"'.[37] Germany could join the modern industrial world, Weber believed, only if it could overcome the authoritarian structure of its political institutions and create a pluralistic political system capable of providing responsible leadership.

The United States

In the United States, the liberal tradition developed along a different trajectory from Britain and Germany. Liberalism in the United States has a rich political heritage that has drawn on ideas which were not American in origin. These ideas were interpreted, adopted and modified to suit historical circumstances, and in the long term were moulded into a tradition that is characteristically American. Louis Hartz's study of American liberalism, *The Liberal Tradition in America*, argues that, unlike liberal traditions in other countries, the American political tradition lacked a feudal tradition limiting the boundaries of political thought. Liberalism, he asserts, was the only powerful and enduring tradition in America: it was the political equivalent of a civic religion. What Hartz calls 'Lockean liberalism' dominated American political ideology, creating, since the revolution, an atmosphere of consensus. Hartz is critical of those historians of the 1930s who saw the American past in terms of conflict. While regretting the Lockean dominance that he reports, Hartz maintains that systems of ideas in American history have traditionally been rigid and narrow, blurring the distinctions between liberal and conservative tendencies in American society. Historically, liberalism was never intended to be partisan, but a broad-spectrum ideology which highlighted the primacy of democracy as practised according to the Constitution.[38]

Bernard Bailyn applied Hartz's theory of liberal consensus to the intellectual context of the American Revolution. Bailyn's seminal study of the ideological origins of the American Revolution traces a complex labyrinth of ideas and identifies five major sources from which American colonists drew their political thinking: the writings of classical antiquity, the writings of Enlightenment rationalism, the tradition of English common law, the political and social theories of New England puritanism and the thinkers associated with the English civil war. According to Bailyn, this last group, the radical English Whigs, generated the liberal perspective that brought order to the other strands and, more than any other source, 'shaped the mind of the American Revolutionary generation'. Eighteenth-century America, Bailyn points out, was an ideological age; it was a liberal age.[39]

In the post-war years, Hartz's theory of liberal consensus was so singularly unchallenged as to constitute a hegemonic force in American academic discourse. For instance, Richard Hofstadter's classic study of the American political tradition found 'a kind of mute organic consistency' in the thoughts of all major statesmen from Jefferson to Hoover: liberal concepts of economic individualism and property bound Americans to the values of competitive capitalism and made America 'a democracy of capacity rather than a democracy of fraternity'.[40] In the latter part of the twentieth century, the dominance of this liberal strand of American political ideology was questioned. There has since been a continuing debate over whether the American founding was dominated by republican or liberal ideas, and various interpreters have posthumously rendered 'republican' what was widely assumed to be a liberal creed.[41] This sharp dichotomy between liberalism and republicanism in early American political thought does not, however, support the historical reality. Lance Banning points out that, although liberalism and classical republicanism may be analytically distinguishable as philosophies, 'eighteenth-century opposition thought was a complex blend of liberal and classical republican ideas'.[42]

This combination of liberalism and republicanism, Eric Foner contends, is reflected in the American revolutionaries' conception of freedom. Although liberalism and republicanism would eventually come to be seen as alternatives – two oppositional understandings of freedom – in the eighteenth century these ideologies 'overlapped and reinforced one another'.[43] Leaders of the revolution, Foner observes, were simultaneously republican in their concern for the public good and the citizens' obligations to the polity, and liberal in their preoccupation with individual rights and personal freedom. To revolutionary figures such as Thomas Jefferson and John Adams, there seemed to be no inherent contradiction between the individual freedom central to Lockean liberal philosophy and the public utility of the republican tradition.[44]

Locke was not the only English liberal to set forth the justification for revolution. Thomas Paine's *Common Sense* gave a radical edge to early American liberalism. In his pamphlet, Paine highlighted the tyranny inherent in the institution of monarchy, and argued in favour of representative government and a democratic constitutional order. Paine's political thought, John Keane observes, embodied the liberal–republican synthesis of the time. Paine founded his liberal theory on the concepts of rights, consent and the social contract, which brings into being the indefeasible sovereignty of the majority will.[45] Behind the radical interpretation of Whig principles, Paine's political theory was, however, 'vintage liberalism', combining sympathies for the manufacturing classes with a distrust of central government.[46] It is these sympathies that led Paine to set forth the political implications of economic liberalism. Like the expansion of political freedom, the expansion of commerce, Paine argued, rested on the capacity of the free market to integrate social tasks which had formerly been secured through the expansion of central authority. In an appraisal of the social relations produced by the market, Paine called for the commercial expansion of relations between democracies. He saw no dialectical confrontation between virtue and commerce in these relations. Rather, 'Paine believed that freeing all forms of enterprise from political control would usher in a moral revolution, for society could then govern itself simply by responding to the immanent laws of labour and market exchange'.[47]

Like the revolution, liberalism became the founding ideology behind the American Constitution. Eighteenth-century American constitutionalism gave institutional expression to a belief that a higher law existed which restricted the powers of government on behalf of the general welfare of the people. The Constitution created a federal government to replace a confederation of sovereign states, but it limited the power of national government through the enumeration of powers. As Paine had recommended, a distinction was made between civil society and government. The Constitution institutionalised this division by restricting the ambit of legislation and by protecting the domain of free association. Drawing on the ideas of David Hume, it asserted that in a commercial society the spread of wealth and luxury contributes to moral progress; the pursuit of self-interest leads to self-improvement and creates a productive citizenry.[48] Natural economic law and natural moral law were therefore coalesced under the rubric of the Constitution. The Constitution structured power in American political life, giving constitutional protection to private property rights through an elaborate system of checks and balances and divided sovereignty. 'Power and liberty', the architects of the Constitution proclaimed, 'were complementary, not antithetical'.[49]

In the nineteenth century, the United States moved into the liberal world of business, commerce and the open promotion of interests. Unlike European societies, the United States had neither a strong aristocracy to uphold virtue against commerce, nor a strong working class to uphold the ideals of socialism against the harsh realities of liberal individualism. An individualistic and acquisitive society of ordinary American citizens created liberal America.[50] A civic spirit in American society fervently extolled the dignity of labour. Alexis de Tocqueville thus came to state that the United States was a place where 'every man works to earn a living' and 'holds labour in honour'. It was a place where everyone was alike in working, 'never either high or low', and no one was 'humiliated by the notion of receiving pay'.[51] Tocqueville claimed that the attitudes and habits of people, through self-reliance and the habit of association and participation, would create a moralising process and enhance citizenship and local autonomy in a liberal society.

In the post-civil war period, American liberalism became closely allied with British liberalism. As the United States had borrowed from Britain the philosophical premises for its revolution, so it borrowed the ideas behind its commercial expansion. Benthamite utilitarianism and the classical liberal ideas of Smith and Ricardo found their way into American society, as the ideas of Locke, Paine and Hume had in the previous century. The fundamental issues in post-civil war liberal thought were economic. American liberals followed the natural laws of economics within a utilitarian framework, and set a new context for American political thought. Industrial capitalism and its associated values became the new frame of reference. 'The basic problem of the generation following the Civil War', Alan Grimes observes, 'was to find a system of thought which happily reconciled and related the accepted social norms of popular government and industrial capitalism'.[52]

What Grimes refers to as the *Nation* school of liberals, associated with the journal of the same name, became the representatives of nineteenth-century American liberalism. In line with twentieth-century neo-liberalism, these liberals accepted the classical view that liberty starts where coercive law ends, and that the functions of government should therefore be kept to a minimum.[53] Furthermore, they accepted the utilitarian belief that enlightened self-interest and the public interest are one and the same, and therefore the calculated pursuit of self-interest by rational individuals invariably promotes the greatest happiness for the greatest number. American liberalism rested on the fundamental assumption that the ethical basis for *laissez-faire* is that the public good is best achieved through competition between individuals to promote their own good. Grimes points out how this strand of liberalism became the dominant mode of thought in the United States in the nineteenth century. In the early days of classical liberalism, he contends, *laissez-faire* became a reform ideology associated with the rising class of tradesmen and entrepreneurs. In the Jacksonian era, it was used 'to open the area of freedom by restricting the area of privilege'. In the late nineteenth century, 'it became the conservative weapon against the new generation of social reformers'.[54]

American economic liberalism drew heavily on the British social theorist, Herbert Spencer. Spencer offered a powerful critique of all forms of state intervention in the 'natural' workings of society, stressing the sanctity of private property. Spencer's most important American disciple was William Graham Sumner. Sumner, following Spencer, joined *laissez-faire* to evolution, in order to attack all forms of social legislation. In a natural system of competition, Sumner proclaimed, survival is determined without state interference or privilege. Thus liberty, properly understood, means the 'abnegation of state power' and the frank acceptance of inequality.[55] In American capitalist society, Sumner's arguments were readily accepted by barons of industry and industrial concentrations were seen as part of the narrative of progress.

THE CHALLENGE OF COLLECTIVISM

The late nineteenth and early twentieth centuries were marked by a tension within the liberal traditions in Britain, Germany and the United

States. At the turn of the century, the social problems created by the West's rapid move towards industrialisation and the rising hostilities in Europe meant that liberals increasingly turned towards the state for new directions. It would be wrong to assert that there was a complete break with the liberal traditions of the past at this time. Classical liberal thinkers and movements still asserted independent ideas and reacted to alternative policies. For neo-liberalism, however, this period marked a fundamental break with the liberal traditions of the past and signalled the rise of collectivism. This period is crucial for putting into context neo-liberalism's genesis in the mid-twentieth century, discussed in Chapter 3.

The new liberalism

In Britain, in the years preceding the First World War, the basic tenets of liberalism were fundamentally transformed through a campaign of ideological adjustment. What came to be called the 'new liberalism', like all successful ideologies, reflected the intellectual atmosphere, responding to social concerns and anxieties with new directives for political action. A 'progressive tide' within liberalism 'shifted the centre of ideological gravity towards the left'.[56] The new liberalism of L. T. Hobhouse and John Hobson significantly changed the parameters of political debate within British liberalism by introducing new concepts and arguments concerning the structure of society and the role of the state. The rise of the new liberalism, however, did not represent a simple transition, from an age of liberal individualism, to one of 'quasi-socialist' collectivism. Liberalism, as Vincent maintains, was conceptually reconstructed from within as part of a wider process of ideological adjustment and change.[57] British liberals in the late nineteenth century were compelled to rethink economic liberalism in response to the great changes in economic, social and political circumstances, but without unduly compromising traditional liberal principles. While the ideological essence of classical liberalism may have been eclipsed by the rise of collectivism, individualism was not abandoned as an integral part of liberal theory. Rather, it became dissociated from *laissez-faire*, and the individual became an integral part of the collective.

The new liberals, drawing on Bentham's principle of 'social utility', Mill's concept of individual self-development and T. H. Green's idea of the 'common good', reconciled individual liberty with a conception of the 'social'. They realised that inequalities of economic power and the acuteness of the social and economic problems that the latter produced could constrain individual liberty as much as political power. Individual freedom, the new liberals argued, could only be realised within a social order. Personal liberty was reconciled with equality of opportunity, and redefined in a new relationship between state and the individual. The real challenge to liberalism was not tactical, but, as Hobson argued, it lay in its 'intellectual and moral ability to accept a positive progressive policy which involved a new conception of the state'.[58] A conception of the state as a positive and active institution came to occupy a central position in the new, social reform-orientated liberalism. The realisation of individual liberty was perceived as the provision of equal opportunities for self-development. This required a substantial increase in state activity in the name of what came to be called 'social justice'.

The new liberals were conscious that their position might be seen as little removed from that of the socialists. Indeed, Hobson expressed his concern that, 'once we admit that it is right for the state to interfere with economic freedom, we have advanced one step on the road which leads to nationalisation'.[59] The new liberals' commitment to individual liberty, however, meant that they were never socialists in a collectivist sense. Hobhouse made it clear that he supported neither the 'mechanical socialism' that attributed all value to labour, nor the 'official socialism' with its contempt for individual liberty.[60] Rather, the new liberals supported 'liberal socialism': they were both liberals and social democrats.[61] Liberal socialism, they proclaimed, must come from below rather than from above; it must be democratic. As Hobhouse stated, 'it must emerge from the efforts of society as a whole to secure a fuller measure of justice, and a better organisation of mutual aid'. Also it must be founded on liberty and self-maintenance, making 'its account with the human individual'.[62] The new liberals' political programme was based on achieving the appropriate balance of public and private enterprise. Hobhouse believed that it was possible through liberal means to organise economic expansion in the interests of common welfare without overriding the freedom of individuals or discouraging private initiative. For instance, he had confidence in the state's ability to contribute towards social well-being, but argued that it was to be 'left to the individual to build up by his own efforts the fabric of his independence, comfort and even wealth'.[63] New liberals thus retained the classical liberal conception of the market economy as an efficient engine for the creation of wealth, but at the same time, through social reform measures, purged it of those aberrations which had hitherto disfigured it. Their thought represented a rational and politically feasible middle ground that reconciled individual liberty and social control within a democratic polity – which, as Chapter 3 will point out, was so abhorrent to neo-liberalism.

The new liberalism had a substantial ideological impact on British politics in the twentieth century. The new liberals offered prescriptions for the renaissance of the Liberal Party at the beginning of the century, and, consequently, the years preceding the First World War were marked by intense debate about the fundamentals of social action. In the inter-war years, the new liberalism was not confined to the membership to, or outlook of, a single political party. Freeden notes how the new liberalism 'partially externalised the liberal tradition' by extending its base support to the socialist left, embracing R. H. Tawney, H. J. Laski and the *New Statesman*.[64] As part of a progressive tradition, the new liberalism also became the guiding ideology behind the achievements of the post-war Labour government. Indeed, the Beveridge Report and its recommendation to share responsibility between the public and private sphere clearly 'echoed no "essential sociability" doctrine of human nature'. Rather, the report was based on traditional liberal notions of contract and obligation. 'It introduced the community as a partner to the liberty and happiness of the individual, a partner whose concerted efforts were indispensable for realising individual interests and expressing individual variety'.[65] Liberal notions had become central components of socialist ideas.

National socialism

Until the last decades of the nineteenth century, German liberalism was perceived as an expression of the common good; it represented an optimistic vision of a 'harmonious social and political world based on a reconciliation of *Volk* and *Staat*', which became the embodiment of enlightened opinion.[66] By 1880 this vision had slipped from view. The Bismarckian state, strengthened by its success in achieving nationhood, turned the political tide against liberalism. A preoccupation with power, in particular with military power and the defence of national self-interest, created a period of ideological paralysis. The lessons of the Bismarckian years became increasingly apparent: 'nationalism was not an inherently liberal concept and national goals need not be part of a progressive political ideology'.[67]

When Germany entered the twentieth century, despite a short burst of reform-orientated left liberalism, liberalism lost ground further still. The economic concentration of the Weimar Republic and its subsequent disintegration, and ultimately the rise of National Socialism in Germany, discredited liberalism as a credible political creed. For John Hallowell, liberalism lost touch with its spiritual roots. Hallowell asserts that German liberals betrayed their own principles and beliefs long before the rise of Nazism. 'Traditional forms of liberalism, he writes, were perverted to purposes destructive of everything liberalism originally valued. Liberalism was not destroyed by the Nazis – rather the Nazis were the legitimate heirs of a system that committed suicide.'[68] This was a sentiment echoed by neo-liberal theorists in the immediate years after the Second World War. According to prominent neo-liberals, Germany from around 1870 became the great source of ideas favourable to socialism and economic planning. Hayek stated that intellectuals of the historical school in the last decades of the nineteenth century had turned the tide against the values and beliefs held by traditional German liberals, and 'by the time Hitler came to power liberalism was to all intents and purposes dead in Germany'.[69]

The shift in liberal values that Hallowell describes is reflected in the nature of the economic policies implemented in Germany during the late nineteenth and early twentieth centuries. In the years following the foundation of the German Empire in 1871, a strong belief in the self-operating mechanism of the market, the benefits of free trade and the virtues of a strict economy controlling public expenditure started to crumble. In 1879, under the strain of worldwide depression, German commercial policy switched from free trade to protectionism, introducing new tariff legislation for industrial duties. This move was followed by a period of comprehensive 'nationalisation'; participation in company management; social reform; and cartelisation in industry.[70] By the 1920s, a climate of national protectionism and the power of cartels had shifted the nature of German capitalism away from open free markets and towards a form of organised capitalism or 'high capitalism', as Weber called it. A. J. Nicholls maintains that 'economists', pessimistic about the international trading system, 'began to think in terms of national expediency rather than classical economic theory'.[71] The economic strength of the cartels was accepted by a large number of liberal theorists as making 'a necessary contribution to Germany's domestic prosperity and global power'.[72] The Democratic Party in the Weimar Republic, which was heavily influenced by industrial pressure groups, adopted a nationalistic stance towards economic growth, placing production before consumption. While liberals in the Democratic Party denied espousing socialism, a regulated economy with price-fixing and state arbitration in labour disputes was widely accepted.

By the early 1930s, the ground was prepared upon which the Nationalist Socialist system could build. The disintegration of the Weimar Republic marked the end of the liberal revival, underway since the turn of the century, and the promise of a bold new era in the history of the German liberal movement.[73] Free-market liberalism was intellectually bankrupt; the German liberal movement was socially and politically fragmented; and nationalism had become deeply engrained in the German mind. German intellectuals such as Carl Schmitt, Oswald Spengler and Ernst Jünger denounced liberalism's cultural associations with the West. National power, they claimed, could only be obtained by breaking free from liberal theories of democracy and the state. Schmitt, in particular, as a leading critic of parliamentary democracy, had long espoused the view that 'the end of all political activity is the acquisition of power for its own sake'.[74] The essential function of the state is to differentiate between friend and enemy. His model of the 'total state' led Hayek to denounce Schmitt as 'the leading Nazi theoretician of totalitarianism'.[75] Schmitt, however, never advocated totalitarianism. Renato Cristi contends that Schmitt was more opposed to democracy than liberalism. His thought represented what Cristi terms 'authoritarian liberalism', which embraced a strong state as a precondition for a free economy. Schmitt 'opposed what he took to be the totalitarian interventions of the state that sought to force civil society into conformity with democratic patterns'.[76]

The political climate of the 1930s gave the National Socialist Party the opportunity to rally support among liberal voters in favour of collectivism, corporatism and nationalist attitudes towards free trade. The struggle for nationhood that had always been a part of liberalism's historical development in Germany, both ideologically and institutionally, took on a fundamentally different form. The inevitable connection between unity and freedom was no longer apparent. A new kind of political order had superseded traditional liberal values and established itself as the ruling force in German politics.

Liberal progressivism

The changes in the contours of the liberal tradition in the United States in the early twentieth century closely followed those of the new liberalism in Britain. What came to be known as the 'progressive' era in the early twentieth century became a widespread liberal movement affecting every aspect of American political life. The stock market crash had ushered in the Great Depression, marking the end of the previous liberal era in American politics. The progressive movement ignited criticism, and change in response to social grievances and efforts to 'tame' capitalism became a central part of American reform ideology. Indeed, Richard Hofstadter's classic indictment of American progressivism, *The Age of Reform*, claims that the function of the liberal tradition in American politics had been 'first to broaden the numbers of those who could benefit from the great American bonanza and then to humanise its working and help heal its casualties'.[77]

Progressivism became the dominant public philosophy during the New Deal era. T. J. Lowi's *The End of the Republican Era* examines how in this era traditional understandings of liberalism became old liberalism, while the new liberalism emerged from one of the central premises of classical liberalism.[78] A minimalist conception of government to safeguard the rights of American citizens was pushed to its logical extremes by Franklin D. Roosevelt's New Deal programme, designed to accommodate the social needs of American citizens. Roosevelt consciously transformed liberalism, from 'a shorthand term for weak government and *laissez-faire* economics', into a belief in 'an activist, socially conscious state as an alternative to both socialism and unregulated capitalism'.[79] He persisted in his faith that human rationality and social experimentation could achieve a stable foundation for the freedom of the individual through social welfare provision. For critics of the New Deal, Roosevelt's social experiments involved substantive departures from the American liberal faith. Lowi, for example, argues that American liberal philosophy, through the New Deal, begot massive government expansion and undermined the very principles for which it had previously stood. Such a social experiment, he maintains, gave rise to an active federalist government and a new form of 'interest-group liberalism'.[80]

Hartz, however, claims that the progressive liberalism in American political life in the early twentieth century was in many ways, like in Britain, part of a 'socially consciousness' continuation of the liberal tradition of the past. The liberal reform programme championed during the New Deal era, he argues, was a movement within the framework of the liberal faith, which 'sought to extend the sphere of the state and at the same time retain the principles of Locke and Bentham'.[81] While the bold and persistent experimentalism of the New Deal may have been radical in its collective endeavours, the United States continued to cling to traditional liberal ideals. Behind the collective façade of the New Deal, there persisted a strong belief among liberal policy-makers that America was essentially a capitalist society committed to the principles of free enterprise. Thus Hartz points out that 'the New Deal left a lot of free enterprise standing, and much of its state action, from spending to trust-busting, was designed to fortify rather than weaken free enterprise'.[82]

This combination of old liberal principles and new social measures apparent in progressive ideology is reflected in the ideas of American liberal theorists of the time. The ideas of John Dewey, in particular, closely resembled the idealist philosophy of Green and Hobhouse in Britain. Dewey focused on moderate conceptions of the common good and on positive liberty in combining radicalism with pragmatism. He asserted that liberalism would have to adjust to the realisation that 'the liberty of the individuals' required planned action to 'socialise the forces of production'.[83] Dewey, with his faith in human rationality and in the power of creative intelligence, believed that a new conception of American liberalism, rather than socialism, offered the only comprehensive vision of a better future. As Alan Ryan comments, Dewey was not a 'simple collectivist'; he was a 'new individualist'. He accepted the traditional Lockean premise that liberalism must rest on the defense of the liberty of the individual, but rejected the 'rugged' individualism associated with the *laissez-faire* liberalism of the nineteenth century, which had isolated individuals from the social conditions for their full self-development.[84] Dewey's new individualism entailed a conception of the individual as a social entity; a conception which saw individuals as a united front represented by society. This new conception of the individual made him emphatic about the need for 'intelligent social action' to restore liberty. Dewey denied that the state should command the individual; the individual evolves in society not from political direction from above, but from social interaction and 'self-realisation'.[85]

The growth of progressive liberalism in American political culture was accompanied by a reworking of the old anti-statist liberalism of the nineteenth century under a new conservative guise. The reinterpretation of the term 'liberal' by the New Dealers had a lasting impact on politically terminology in American discourse. Supporters of the old liberalism saw a substantial departure from the core tenets of the American liberal creed. The conservative Herbert Hoover, despite his untiring avowals of liberalism, noted in 1963: 'Today the term liberal is claimed by every sect that would limit human freedom and stagnate the human soul.'[86] Alan Brinkley observes that 'the anti-statist liberal tradition of the nineteenth century increasingly became the property of those who in the twentieth century were generally known as conservative'.[87] It was this 'hijacking' of the label 'liberal' in the political vocabulary of the United States which was fundamental to neo-liberalism's defense of the term in the 1940s, discussed in the next chapter.

Conclusion

This chapter has traced the genealogy of the liberal traditions that have influenced the development of neo-liberal discourse. It has shown that liberalism is not an ideology with a secure and consistent internal structure; it is a cluster of related and sometimes contradictory beliefs and notions, which prioritises different ideas at different times. As this chapter has indicated, what underpins these different liberal variants is the broad acceptance of several core conceptual components, which form an integrated and mutually supportive value structure. Liberalism as a series of traditions has followed established patterns of thought stemming from thinkers such as Locke, Kant and Mill. It has affirmed the moral sovereignty of individuals, highlighted the rational basis of self-determination leading to self-development, and stressed the importance of responsible power as the main institutional corollary of liberty. Throughout its history liberalism has reconstructed these core beliefs in response to changing circumstances, taking on new or revised ideological forms. As a multifaceted ideology, liberalism has steered its course somewhere in that vast uncharted area between the radical left on the one hand and the conservatism of the right on the other. By the early twentieth century, liberalism in Western societies had moved towards the shoreline of the left. For neo-liberals, the left incorporated not just the new or progressive liberalism of Britain and the United States, but also the fascism of Nazi Germany. Their clear-cut ideological confrontation between 'true' liberalism and collectivist socialism makes little or no distinction between socialism and social democracy, communism and fascism. As the next chapter will demonstrate, however, old liberal ideas did not disappear completely from the conceptual map. Neo-liberalism as a new political phenomenon arose during the second half of the twentieth century from the liberal traditions of the past, born out of frustrations of political exile since the beginning of the century.

Notes

1. Harold J. Laski, *The Rise of European Liberalism: An Essay in Interpretation* (London: Allen and Unwin, 1936), p. 9.

2. Clifford Geertz, 'Ideology as a cultural system', in his *Interpretation of Cultures: Selected Essays* (New York: Frank Cass, 1973), p. 218.
3. For a lucid discussion of the study of traditions and history in politics, see the 'interpretive' approach of Mark Bevir in his *Logic of the History of Ideas* (Cambridge: Cambridge University Press, 1999).
4. Michael Freeden, 'The family of liberalisms: A morphological analysis', in James Meadowcroft (ed.), *The Liberal Political Tradition: Contemporary Reappraisals* (Cheltenham: Edward Elgar, 1996), pp. 14–39.
5. Smith, however, never regarded himself as a 'liberal'. Smith can be more readily ascribed to the tradition of the Scottish Enlightenment than to the liberal one.
6. Adam Smith, *The Wealth of Nations* (Oxford: Clarendon Press, 1976), p. 651.
7. Ibid., p. 454.
8. See J. Viner, 'The intellectual history of *laissez-faire*', *Journal of Law and Economics*, Vol. 3 (1960), pp. 45–69.
9. Smith, *Wealth of Nations*, p. 534.
10. See J. B. Brebner, '*Laissez-faire* and state intervention in nineteenth-century Britain', *The Journal of Economic History*, Vol. 8 (1948), pp. 59–73, and A. J. Taylor, *Laissez-Faire and State Intervention in Nineteenth-Century Britain* (Basingstoke: Macmillan, 1972).
11. Richard Leach, *British Political Ideologies* (Hemel Hempstead: Philip Allan, 1991), p. 67.
12. Stuart Hall, 'Variants of liberalism', in J. Donald and S. Hall (eds), *Politics and Ideology* (Milton Keynes: Open University Press, 1986), pp. 58–9.
13. John Stuart Mill, *On Liberty* (Harmondsworth: Penguin, 1982), p. 126.
14. Ibid., pp. 129–31.
15. See, in particular, F. A. Hayek, 'Liberalism', in his *New Studies in Philosophy, Politics, Economics and the History of Ideas* (London: Routledge and Kegan Paul, 1978).
16. George Watson, *The English Ideology: Studies in the Language of Victorian Politics* (London: Allen Lane, 1973), p. 75.
17. Richard Bellamy, *Liberalism and Modern Society: An Historical Argument* (Cambridge: Polity, 1992), pp. 9–47.
18. E. Halevy, *A History of the English People in the Nineteenth Century* (London: Macmillan, 1961), p. 184, quoted in W. H. Greenleaf, *The British Political Tradition: The Ideological Heritage* (London: Routledge, 1983), p. 25.
19. Watson, *The English Ideology*, pp. 88–9.
20. A. V. Dicey, *Lectures on the Relation Between Law and Public Opinion in England during the Nineteenth Century* (London: Macmillan, 1905).
21. G. Dangerfield, *The Strange Death of Liberal England* (New York: Capricorn, 1935).
22. John H. Hallowell, *The Decline of Liberalism as an Ideology: With Particular Reference to Germany* (London: Kegan Paul, 1946), p. 26.
23. Hans Vorländer, 'Is there a liberal political tradition in Germany?', in J. Meadowcroft (ed.), *The Liberal Political Tradition: Contemporary Reappraisals* (Cheltenham: Edward Elgar, 1996) pp. 87–109.
24. Ibid., p. 103.
25. Guido de Ruggerio, *The History of European Liberalism* (Oxford: Oxford University Press, 1927) p. 253–4.
26. Jeremy Waldron, 'Theoretical foundations of liberalism', *Philosophical Quarterly*, 37: 147 (1987), p. 112.
27. G. W. F. Hegel, *The Philosophy of Right* (Oxford: Clarendon Press, 1941).

28. Edward N. Megay, 'Treitschke reconsidered: The Hegelian tradition of German liberalism', *Midwest Journal of Political Science*, 2: 3 (1958) p. 300.
29. Leonard Krieger, *The German Idea of Freedom: The History of a Political Tradition* (Boston, MA: Beacon Press, 1957), p. 370.
30. Hallowell, *The Decline of Liberalism as an Ideology*, p. 40.
31. De Ruggerio, *The History of European Liberalism*, p. 212.
32. Krieger, *The German Idea of Freedom*, p. 401.
33. William Carr, *The Origins of the Wars of German Unification* (London: Longman, 1991), p. 27.
34. Vorländer, 'Is there a liberal political tradition in Germany?', p. 103.
35. Bellamy, *Liberalism and Modern Society*, pp. 157–216.
36. David Beetham, *Max Weber and the Theory of Modern Politics* (London: Allen and Unwin, 1974).
37. Ibid., p. 56.
38. Louis Hartz, *The Liberal Tradition in America: An Interpretation of American Political Thought Since the Revolution* (New York: Harcourt, Brace and World, 1955).
39. Bernard Bailyn, *The Ideological Origins of the American Revolution* (Cambridge, MA: Harvard University Press, 1967), pp. 59–60.
40. Richard Hofstadter, *The American Political Tradition* (London: Jonathan Cape, 1962), p. 47.
41. See J. G. A. Pocock, *The Machiavellian Movement: Florentine Political Thought and the Atlantic Republican Tradition* (Princeton: Princeton University Press, 1975), and Joyce Appleby, *Liberalism and Republicanism in the Historical Imagination* (Cambridge, MA: Harvard University Press, 1992).
42. Lance Banning, 'Jeffersonian ideology revisited: Liberal and classical ideas in the new American Republic', *William and Mary Quarterly*, Vol. 43 (1986), p. 12.
43. Eric Foner, *The Story of American Freedom* (Basingstoke: Macmillan, 1998), p. 8.
44. Ibid., p. 9.
45. John Keane, *Tom Paine: A Political Life* (London: Bloomsbury, 1995), p. xx.
46. Michael Foot and Isaac Kramnick, *Thomas Paine Reader* (Harmondsworth: Penguin, 1987), p. 22.
47. John Patrick Diggins, *The Lost Soul of American Politics: Virtue, Self-Interest, and the Foundations of Liberalism* (New York: Basic Books, 1984), p. 38.
48. See Iain Hampsher-Monk, 'British and European background to the ideas of the constitution', in Joseph Smith (ed.), *The American Constitution: The First 200 Years* (Exeter: Exeter University Publications, 1992), pp. 1–16.
49. Foner, *The Story of American Freedom*, p. 24.
50. See Gordon S. Wood, 'Ideology and the origins of liberal America', *William and Mary Quarterly*, 44: 3 (1987), pp. 636–8.
51. Alexis de Tocqueville, *Democracy in America* (New York: Basic Books, 1956), pp. 152–3.
52. Alan P. Grimes, *American Political Thought* (New York: Holt, Rinehart and Winston, 1955), p. 291.
53. Ibid., p. 293.
54. Ibid., p. 301.
55. William Graham Sumner, *What Social Classes Owe to Each Other* (New York: 1883), p. 24, quoted in Foner, *Story of American Freedom*, p. 122.
56. Michael Freeden, *The New Liberalism: An Ideology of Social Reform* (Oxford: Clarendon Press, 1978), p. 3.

57. Andrew Vincent, 'Classical liberalism and its crisis of identity', *History of Political Thought*, 11: 1 (1990), pp. 143–61.
58. J. A. Hobson, *The Crisis of Liberalism* (London: King, 1909), p. xi.
59. Ibid., p. 133.
60. L. T. Hobhouse, *Liberalism and Other Writings*, edited by James Meadowcroft (Cambridge: Cambridge: University Press, 1994), pp. 81–2.
61. Peter Clarke, *Liberals and Social Democrats* (Cambridge: Cambridge University Press, 1978).
62. Hobhouse, *Liberalism*, p. 69.
63. Ibid., p. 71.
64. Michael Freeden, *Liberalism Divided: A Study in British Political Thought 1914–1939* (Oxford: Clarendon Press, 1986), p. 16.
65. Ibid., p. 370.
66. James J. Sheehan, *German Liberalism in the Nineteenth Century* (Chicago: University of Chicago Press, 1978), p. 272.
67. Ibid., p. 274.
68. Hallowell, *The Decline of Liberalism as an Ideology*, p. 108.
69. F. A. Hayek, *The Road to Serfdom* (London: Routledge, 1944), p. 30.
70. Gustav Stolper, *The German Economy 1870 to the Present* (London: Weidenfeld and Nicolson, 1967), pp. 34–46.
71. A. J. Nicholls, *Freedom with Responsibility: The German Social Market Economy 1916–1968* (Oxford: Oxford University Press, 1994), p. 19.
72. J. J. Sheehan, *German Liberalism in the Nineteenth Century* (Chicago: University of Chicago Press, 1978), p. 395.
73. L. E. Jones, *German Liberalism and the Dissolution of the Weimar Party System 1918–1933* (London: Chapel Hill, 1988).
74. Hallowell, *The Decline of Liberalism*, p. 104.
75. Hayek, *The Road to Serfdom*, p. 187.
76. Renato Cristi, *Carl Schmitt and Authoritarian Liberalism* (Cardiff: The University of Wales Press, 1998), p. 27.
77. Richard Hofstadter, *The Age of Reform* (New York: Vintage Books, 1955), p. 5.
78. T. J. Lowi, *The End of the Republican Era* (Norman: University of Oklahoma Press, 1995).
79. Fonder, *The Story of American Freedom*, p. 204.
80. T. J. Lowi, *The End of Liberalism* (New York: Fontana, 1979).
81. Hartz, *The Liberal Political Tradition in America*, p. 259.
82. Ibid., p. 263.
83. Quoted in Fonder, *The Story of American Freedom*, p. 211.
84. Alan Ryan, *John Dewey and the High Tide of American Liberalism* (New York: Norton and Company, 1995), p. 31.
85. Ibid., p. 323.
86. Quoted in Grimes, *American Political Thought*, p. 406.
87. Alan Brinkley, 'The problem of American conservatism', in his *Liberalism and its Discontents* (Cambridge, MA: Harvard University Press, 1998), p. 283.

Chapter 3

The 'rebirth of liberalism'

Introduction: Liberal revival

As the previous chapter has demonstrated, liberal ideas are seldom static and never uniform. The beliefs held by liberals in 1945 displayed, as they had in the past, considerable diversity. They continued to change and continued to produce internecine debates in the years that followed. A new liberal framework, clearly visible in the immediate years after the Second World War, while significantly different from the old, drew on the liberal traditions of the past as a source of guidance for establishing a new liberal discourse and a new liberal agenda.

The collectivist liberalism evident during the war and in the years of its aftermath was accompanied by the growth of a powerful counter-movement encapsulated within this framework. Economists, philosophers and social scientists of the 'old' liberal school became an important voice on behalf of old liberalism in modern society and bitter critics of the collectivism they saw sweeping through Germany, Britain and the United States since the 1930s. Neo-liberalism emerged in the late1940s as a revered symbol of anti-socialism and a powerful voice of liberal hopes. This happened after it became evident to many liberals that liberalism had ceased to bear any clear relation to the ideological rationales that had supported its creation. This revival of liberal thought occurred slowly, at times almost imperceptibly, coming together from innumerable small adaptations which accumulated gradually but decisively.

It is the intention of this chapter to trace the path by which neo-liberalism since 1930s articulated an important and serious critique of contemporary liberal culture. This path was awash in ideas – ideas of significant range and diversity, but which somehow managed to coexist and form a coherent ideology. The revival of liberalism, the chapter will argue, was the product of a period of fundamental adjustment. This period occurred during the 1930s and 1940s, culminating in the immediate postwar years, and formed the early intellectual life of neo-liberalism. It became associated with a backlash against the prevailing collectivist ideologies of the age and with the formation of the Mont Pelerin Society, through which early neo-liberals sought to distinguish their ideas and beliefs from those associated with the prevailing collectivist liberal ethos. This period established the basis of an effective political movement, creating a vast network of scholars, publications and think-tanks to rival and outperform liberal opponents.

The purpose of this chapter is therefore to explore the intellectual and historical context within which neo-liberal ideology evolved in the 1930s and 1940s. First it will set out the intellectual context within which the seeds of neo-liberalism germinated, by highlighting the apparent decline of *laissez-faire* liberalism during the first half of the twentieth century – with particular reference to the works of J. M. Keynes, Joseph Schumpeter and Karl Polyani; it will then examine the different forms of collectivism that emerged in Germany, Britain and the United States in the twentieth century and assess neo-liberalism's backlash against these variants; finally, it will turn to the formation of the Mont Pelerin Society in the immediate years after the Second World War, which was integral to the ideological genesis of neo-liberalism.

Revising history

At the heart of the neo-liberal counter-attack in the post-war period was the claim, made by F. A. Hayek and others, that a socialist account of liberal capitalism had become the dominant strand of historical interpretation. Hayek argued that, since the early decades of the twentieth century, there had been a movement away from the liberal ideas on which Western civilisation had been built. Liberalism in the old sense had been driven out by socialism, which was irrevocably pushing Western civilisation towards totalitarianism. Hayek claimed that a particular historical interpretation, used as 'propaganda', was responsible for some of these illiberal trends in the world. In particular, it was the direct influence of certain economic historians over public opinion that had partially led to the present discredited status of economic liberalism. Classical liberalism had not only been ravaged by world war and a severe worldwide depression, but had also been the victim of misrepresentation.[1]

In the 1940s, Hayek expressed a strong desire to re-examine recent events and the beliefs held by socialist and new liberal intellectuals. If the course of history is ultimately determined by the life and death of ideas, Hayek believed that liberalism could be recaptured only if the prevailing collectivist ideas could be discredited in the face of recent trends.[2] In 1946, while at the London School of Economics, he wrote that not only would 'the whole relation between governmental coercion and individual freedom require re-examination', but also current views of history would have to be revised, 'if the dominant beliefs and misconceptions are not to drive us even further in a totalitarian direction'.[3]

Epitaph for laissez-faire

Hayek's desire to re-examine the history of the early twentieth century stemmed from his belief that the ideals of liberalism had been driven out of history by a chain of events which had slowly transformed the ideological precepts of the previous political era. In particular, the end of the First World War and the onset of depression had produced an excessive worship of collective consciousness. This is not to suggest that these events alone produced that advance of collectivist ideologies. In Britain, for example, on the eve of the First World War, there had already been long-running debate about the role of government. Rather, these major events, for many liberal theorists, helped to clarify the inadequacies of classical liberal ideology in the modern world. The subsequent advance of collectivist ideologies and the alternative economic strategies in the first half of the twentieth century meant that liberalism in the old sense was no longer regarded as a mainstream ideology. This movement, away from the *laissez-faire* liberalism of the nineteenth century, is reflected in a series of publications that captured the declining faith in the ability of the market system of liberal capitalism to cope with the economic problems of the twentieth century.

J. M. Keynes's celebrated lecture 'The end of *laissez-faire*', in 1926, can be seen as one of the first works signaling the paradigm-shift, from the liberal world of nineteenth century to the managed world of the twentieth. It was A. V. Dicey, rather than Keynes, who was the first to write about the movement from individualism to collectivism in the late nineteenth century.[4] The significance of Keynes's work, however, is that, while Dicey acknowledged that a period of transition was occurring in the late nineteenth century towards collectivism, Keynes, writing in the 1920s, was making an actual judgement that a watershed had been passed – a judgement which was later ratified by Joseph Schumpeter and Karl Polanyi in the 1940s. In Keynes's view there was no going back to the classical liberal world of the nineteenth century – liberal collectivism was the future.

Keynes shared Hayek's belief in the power of ideas in history. For Keynes, though, the difficulty was not so much in developing new ideas as in escaping from the old ones. Keynes, fearing for the survival of the capitalist system, became a sharp critic of classical economic liberalism – the 'natural liberty' of individuals, balanced budgets, *laissez-faire* government, the gold standard and the virtue of thrift. In his lecture on the decline of *laissez-faire*, he emphasised the fragility of the economic order that others took to be 'natural' and 'automatic' and challenged the notion that the system could continue to work in a self-adjusting manner. Classical economic liberalism, he claimed, was not a long-run theory, but just one among many possible states of equilibrium in the history of economic evolution. Keynes argued that the state should step in to do what private enterprise claimed it was doing, but in reality was not doing. The old outmoded nineteenth-century dichotomy between state and society, he maintained, had to be rejected, to give way to a new theory of political economy.[5] Drawing on the work of Joan Robinson and other young Cambridge economists' theory of imperfect competition, Keynes held the view that *laissez-faire* capitalism did not offer the appropriate solutions for the economy of the twentieth century.[6]

As early as 1924, Keynes had proclaimed the end of *laissez-faire* – 'not enthusiastically, not from contempt of that good old doctrine, but because, whether we like it or not, the conditions for its success have disappeared'.[7] At the core of Keynes's rejection of classical liberalism was his belief in the need to create a new agenda in politics. This meant clearing the decks of the old liberal accretions of the past to make way for 'a reformed and remodelled liberalism'.[8] He envisaged a transition from the individualism and anarchy of *laissez-faire* capitalism to the order and social stability of a system of managed capitalism. Keynes, in an epoch-making phrase, advocated 'capitalism by the agency of collective action'.[9] This meant encouraging the experimental use of state apparatus to achieve social and economic ends. Semi-autonomous corporations working within the state, Keynes claimed, must be made responsible for those decisions which fall outside the ambit of the individual. By attacking Say's Law that, in the long-run, the amount of production would equal that of consumption, Keynes shifted the debate on state intervention from the supply side to the demand side of the economy. Keynes argued that, in reality, an economic equilibrium of production and consumption did not exist, and that unemployment represented more than a temporary dislocation until production and consumption could find a new balance. He went on to show, in his *General Theory of Employment, Interest and Money*, how economic slumps and inflationary booms could be avoided if governments controlled and manipulated the economy.[10] Macro-economic, rather than micro-economic, government intervention, as Robert Skidelsky observes, was to be 'indirect' and 'general', as opposed to 'direct' and detailed'; it was to be 'a managed rather than a commanded economy'.[11] This type of government intervention Keynes justified on the grounds that its purpose is to save, rather than destroy, both capitalism and liberal democracy.

Keynes's economic theories led to sharp criticism from within old liberal ranks. Hayek, in particular, claimed that, through his interventionist approach, Keynes had vitiated the theoretical purity of liberalism by introducing alien and contradictory elements of socialism. Indeed, Hayek explicitly rejected Keynes's entire approach as 'conceptual realism'. Keynes, he claimed, was a political opportunist, and the *General Theory* was 'a tract for the times', which was characteristic of a man who was 'more of an artist and politician than a scholar or a student'.[12] Keynes himself, however, never looked for salvation in socialism, but saw his ideas as a necessary extension of liberalism, designed to meet economic challenges posed by capitalism in the twentieth century. Socialism for Keynes was just as outmoded as *laissez-faire*. Indeed, in 'The end of *laissez-faire*', he famously described socialism as 'little better than a dusty survival of a plan to meet the problems of fifty years ago, based on a misunderstanding of what someone had said a hundred years ago'.[13] Keynes' interest lay in developing new methods and new ideas for managing capitalism, ones which would 'promote economic and social justice, whilst at the same time respect and protect the individual – his freedom of choice, his enterprise and his property'.[14] In the tradition of Hobhouse and Hobson, Keynes remained 'a believer in state intervention, but an equally dedicated individualist',[15] and specifically described his own aspirations as 'the true destiny of the new liberalism'.[16]

Joseph Schumpeter shared Keynes's conviction that the era of *laissez-faire* liberalism had come to an end. Although a conservative theoretician, Schumpeter 'spoke not of the problems of maximum production under the perfectly equilibrated competitive balances of classical economics, but of the concrete, social institution of capitalism, operating in historical time'.[17] Unlike Keynes, who operated within a static framework of the contemporary context, Schumpeter examined both sociologically and historically the conditions of capitalism's emergence, growth and decline. Indeed he perceived capitalism as a social organism evolving and changing rapidly with technological innovation. Periods of prolonged recession, Schumpeter argued, where not to be taken as faults in the capitalist machinery, but where to be seen as parts of a natural and inevitable restructuring of the economy. It was during the Nazi era in Germany that he envisaged the transformations that would occur in the capitalist system. In his *Capitalism, Socialism and Democracy*, Schumpeter detailed the institutional changes in capitalism and determined how these affected its economic mechanisms. In this work Schumpeter presented the paradox of capitalism – the theory that capitalism would be destroyed by its own success. He emphasised the great strength of liberal capitalism – a system which 'appeals to, and reinforces, a schema of motives that is unsurpassed in its simplicity and force' – but observed how modern developments had reduced the competitiveness of the system.[18]

Schumpeter shared Marx's vision of the evolutionary process of the destruction of capitalism, a process generated by the capitalist system itself; but he argued that transformation would not take place in the way Marx envisaged. There would be no economic crisis, but, instead, a growing crisis of legitimacy due to a Weberian process of rationalisation. Capitalism, Schumpeter held, would decompose because its mentality would create a social atmosphere hostile to its functioning.[19] But not only would liberal capitalism be menaced from without, it would also be menaced from within. Schumpeter believed that, as innovation became routinised and thus the economy became autonomised and ultimately bureaucratised, the system would 'inevitably' breakdown. As techniques of production reached perfection, the challenge of the entrepreneur would be eliminated. The large corporation manager would have little in common with the old type of entrepreneur and would become 'just another office worker'.[20] Further, the progress of capitalism and the growth of the corporation would reduce the importance of the small producer and trader, thereby eroding the meaning of 'property' and 'free contract'.

Schumpeter famously described this undermining of capitalism as the process of 'creative destruction'. For Schumpeter, it was not capitalism itself, but the forces contained within it, 'that incessantly revolutionize the economic structure from within, incessantly destroying the old one, incessantly creating a new one'.[21] He maintained that the actions of entrepreneurs and the processes of rationalisation would inevitably produce these destructive effects. Schumpeter consequently drew a line under the liberal capitalism of the nineteenth century. The organisation of the modern world would require an alternative economic system, which is a negation of the creative destruction of the former economic order. This alternative to liberal capitalism, for Schumpeter, was socialism. Schumpeter argued that, when classical liberalism had exhausted itself, capitalist civilisation would inevitably be replaced by socialism or by some form of collectivism. While he maintained that free-market liberalism may be the best form of social and economic organisation, he explicitly rejected the core beliefs of neo-liberal economists such as Ludwig von Mises by stating that it was also possible to envisage a socialist system of rational economic organisation. Schumpeter claimed that the state, aided by the bureaucracies of huge corporations, would have a crucial role in maintaining the efficiency of a socialist economy – by correcting fluctuations in business cycles and by eliminating an atmosphere of 'uncertainty'. As Daniel Bell reflects, 'Schumpeter was too much of a European to believe that government could be an auxiliary or mediating body. For him, the state would be an autonomous force taking over the direction of society for its own bureaucratic impulses.'[22]

Both Keynes and Schumpeter, therefore, saw major defects in *laissez-faire* capitalism. While Keynes remained optimistic that the most serious defects, such as unemployment and severe inequality, could be rectified through judicious and effective government intervention, Schumpeter's work represented a lament for the passing away of liberal capitalism. Another theorist, Karl Polanyi, pointed out that these defects had always been an important part of *laissez-faire*. In his *Great Transformation*, Polanyi attempted to undo the foundations of classical liberal economics. He explained how the self-regulating market system had always relied on unnatural social controls. He claimed that *laissez-faire* liberalism in nineteenth-century Britain had given rise to the conscious directing of social forces. John Stuart Mill and William Townsend and other well-known advocates of *laissez-faire*, Polanyi pointed out, were social activists. There was nothing natural about the market system. Markets, for Polanyi, were institutionalised; they were socially and culturally embedded. Indeed he maintained that market capitalism required a correspondent social system to support it and to surround it with meaning. 'The road to the free market', he wrote, 'was opened and kept open by an enormous increase in centrally organised and controlled interventionism'.[23] Protective legislation and administrative instruments were fashioned by the state to make the system work. However, while the competitive market was the product of intentional creation, Polanyi contended that its regulation was to be left to its own internal devices.

Polanyi went on to explain the subsequent collapse of the old liberal order in the 1930s in terms of the destructive nature of markets. Like Schumpeter, Polanyi saw the disintegration of *laissez-faire* capitalism as stemming from the market system itself. He reflected that 'the origins of the cataclysm (of the 1920s and 1930s) lay in the utopian endeavour of economic liberalism to set up a self-regulating market system'.[24] He observed how the institutions of liberal capitalist states became unstable following the breakdown of the gold standard in the early 1930s, and he rejected classical liberalism as the cornerstone of economic policy. The instability of the business cycle and its associated unemployment were inevitable outcomes of the capitalist system in the twentieth century. Polanyi observed that capitalist states reacted to this collapse of classical liberalism by re-embedding the market. He thus foresaw a post-war 'embedded liberal' order, where governments 'could and should take control of the national economy by active market manipulation since the private economy as a whole was perceived as inherently unstable and incapable of delivering socially optimal outcomes'.[25]

For Polanyi, creating such an order entailed progressive institutional change. Classical liberalism had finally succumbed to what he referred to as the 'double movement' of two institutional motivators – the self-regulating market economy and the protective social response from the state – which had started in the nineteenth century. An interventionist drift underpinned the social foundations of the democratic capitalist economy of the twentieth century. The classical liberal notion that only piecemeal and reactive intervention was necessary to maintain the operation of an otherwise autonomous market economy was abandoned from the 1870s onwards. As Polanyi observed, 'liberals themselves regularly called for compulsory action on the part of the state as in the case of trade union law and anti-trust laws'.[26] The congenital defects of *laissez-faire* capitalism, therefore, for Polanyi spawned a substantial interventionist response and unconsciously returned the economy to its traditional place in society – as a politically administered and socially embedded institution.

The road to planning

Keynes, Schumpeter and Polanyi all shared a conviction that the so-called 'age of *laissez-faire*' was over and that collectivism was paving the way for the future. Their work provided the intellectual climate within which neo-liberalism evolved in the mid-twentieth century. In addition to this, liberal policy-makers in the immediate post-war years reinforced the trend towards intervention in Western democracies. They viewed classical liberalism as an inappropriate ideological framework from which to approach the major questions of the post-war world. Governments in advanced industrial societies accepted collectivism or planning as the proper framework within which specific economic policies could be developed and employed, both for long-term and for short-term economic management. They argued that, if economic planning could be used during the war to defeat National Socialism, it could equally serve to defeat poverty and unemployment and to meet national aims after the war.

In Britain, the United States and Germany, governments adopted different attitudes to collectivism. While in all three countries central involvement was ultimately invited, the nature and scale of this involvement differed significantly. As W. H. Greenleaf comments, 'collectivism can be applied in small doses as well as large; it can come by imperceptible steps as well as revolutionary cataclysms; there is such a thing as conservative as well as radical collectivism'.[27] The different roads to planning that Britain, the United States and Germany embarked on are briefly outlined here, as they are fundamental to understanding the origins of neo-liberalism as a movement in opposition to collectivism, and its distinct interpretation of the core concepts discussed in the second part of the book.

In Britain, the road to planning was first documented by A. V. Dicey. Dicey noted how collectivism and the idea of positive government were developed in Britain in the late nineteenth century as part of a piecemeal process intended to rectify the defects of the market system and to provide for social or 'public' needs.[28] This notion of a 'public good' was promoted in Britain by, amongst others, the Fabian Society. The virtues of the free market came under sustained challenge in the 1880s from the society's socialist opinions. The state, for the Fabians, represented 'the local and national agent of collective determination'.[29] Solutions to an array of social and economic problems – from the quality of social life to the orderliness of public behaviour; from the competitiveness of British industry to the military competence of the nation – were firmly placed in the hands of the state rather than the market. The new emphasis on the role of the state was not confined to socialist opinion. As discussed in chapter 2, new liberals such as L. T. Hobhouse and J. A. Hobson attempted to reconcile traditional liberal principles with a commitment to extended state activity. These liberals frequently pointed out that they were not advocating 'planning' in the socialist terms of state ownership, regulation and control, but liberty and political and economic equality, in line with the 'necessary responsibilities of the state'.[30]

Conservative and liberal parties, in the name of 'social welfare', national efficiency or industrial rationalisation, passed an array of legislation during the fourteen years leading up to the First World War.[31] The demands of the war itself led to taking unprecedented steps in the central control of the economy during and immediately after the war, which were supported by all parties. Tariff reform, the proposed nationalisation of the coal industry, the creation of state monopolies and increased state spending were measures that constituted conscious steps in the direction of a systematic management of the economy as a whole. The steady march of collectivism in Britain was accelerated by the impact of the world economic crisis of 1929–32 and by the events leading up to the Second World War. These events were widely perceived as the death-throes of *laissez-faire* capitalism. Planning, rather than *laissez-faire*, became the dominant theme in economic policy debates in the inter-war years. Planning and the degree of collectivism it implied, however, invariably meant different things to different groups of intellectuals and politicians.[32]

The apparent breakdown of market capitalism in the inter-war years led to the creation of a progressive planning movement, comprising of 'middle opinion', to reinterpret capitalist principles within a framework of national planning. The Next Five Years Group, which covered a wide spectrum of political opinion, from the left of the Conservative Party to the right of the Labour Party, attempted to harness the concept of planning to traditional socialist gradualism. The group advocated a centralist interpretation of planning, which, it claimed, could serve as an 'ideological bridge' between the parties.[33] For other socialist planners like Barbara Wootton and Herbert Morrison, technocratic planning represented the one possibility of genuine agreement in the planning debate. Wootton's and Morrison's planning model rested on the Fabian faith in the virtues of technocratic expertise. They claimed that, if management was freed from the irrational constraints of the profit motive and placed in the hands of state administrators, then industry would become more efficient and equitable. Morrison was convinced that this goal of 'sound public business' would naturally advance other socialist goals of equality, full employment and economic growth.[34] Other socialist theorists like Harold Laski identified the technocratic planning of Wootton and Morrison with 'capitalist planning', claiming it had only tenuous connections to socialism. Planning, for Laski, meant a complete overhaul of private ownership and freedom of enterprise and the setting-up of a centrally planned economy supervised by a national authority; there could be no half-way house between the two.[35]

The Second World War drew together these hitherto disparate strands of the planning movement and enabled the collectivists to seize power. The collectivists rejected communist-style central planning and adopted a policy of 'liberal socialism' or the 'middle way', which subsequently became the foundation of the Butskellite post-war consensus. William Beveridge noted in 1942 how the 'former methods of peace' were unlikely to accomplish both national goals and social justice, and that 'adjustment of resources to needs' would have to be 'carried out by complete state planning'.[36] In this regard Greenleaf points out that 'the wartime coalition was probably the most radical reforming administration since the Liberal governments of the years before 1914', introducing, by 1943, a scheme of social security, family allowances and a universal free health service, as well as commitments to educational change, full employment, closer ties between government and industry, and Keynesian budgetary techniques.[37]

In 1945, all parties entered the general election being committed to the principles of social and economic reconstruction. In the spirit of the new liberalism, the Beveridge Report, published in 1942, made the case for a compulsory, contributory, state-backed system of provision. Responsibility was to be held in both the private and public spheres through interaction between the community and its members. The post-war state in Britain was also made responsible for managing the nation's currency and economic resources instead of entrusting those matters to the impersonal forces of the market. Robert Skidelsky refers to this post-war state as 'the corporate state'; the role of government was no longer merely to consult but also to supervise those actors involved in economic life.[38] By the late 1940s, however, the idea of a socially controlled economy was abandoned in favour of a mixed economy where the emphasis was placed upon Keynesian demand management. This Keynesian social democratic consensus dominated the post-war era in Britain until the economic crisis of the 1970s.

Like Britain, the United States in the late nineteenth century embarked on its road to planning. An American reform ideology developed at this time, and efforts to 'tame' capitalism became a central feature of its programme. A progressive movement around which liberals could coalesce became a permanent feature of American political life in the early twentieth century. The movement held a reasonably coherent creed; most fundamentally, it claimed that the state was an administrative institution which should be able to exercise some level of authority over the structure and behaviour of private capitalist institutions. The First World War marked a watershed in the progressive movement's efforts, reinforcing liberal hopes of creating an 'enlightened state' under which government, capital and labour could learn to cooperate with one another. Alan Brinkley observes that one of the most prominent American progressives, Walter Lippmann, 'hoped for many things from the war', in particular a state which could replace 'clash' with 'plan' and 'disorder' with 'purpose'.[39] An ordered economy, and even larger visions of a planned economy, became the model for American progressives in the early twentieth century.

The 1920s saw a continuation of this vision and the creation of associational arrangements. Rational organisation and scientific planning in economic affairs became the hallmark of the 'associational' ideal.[40] During this republican period, the state underwent significant expansion and a degree of rationalisation. The associationalists asserted that the ordered economic world characteristic of the war years would have to be maintained in peace time, to facilitate efficiency within the industrial world. In particular, the government would need to harmonise its relations with the business community in order to achieve economic rationalisation and to rectify the destructive effects of the market.[41] This forceful federal role in the management of the economy served as a model, in 1933, for the creation of the New Deal's National Recovery administration following the Great Depression. Indeed, Brinkley argues that, by following Herbert Hoover's programme of unprecedented federal activism to deal with the Great Depression, 'the New Deal was not a sharp and decisive break with a conservative past. It was the culmination of political forces that had been gathering strength for at least a decade before'.[42] Franklin D. Roosevelt's administration was focused on economic regulation aimed at spurring industrial expansion and social reform. The function of the state was to work with business and labour so as to regulate wages and prices and stabilise various industries. In 1935, new standards were set for labour and social insurance with the National Labour Relations Act and Social Security Act.[43]

The New Dealers of the late 1930s used an array of different labels to describe their visions of reform: 'antimonopoly', 'regulation', 'planning'. Together, these 'described a common vision of government – a vision of capable, committed administrators who would seize control of state institutions, invigorate them, expand their powers when necessary, and make them permanent actors in the workings of the marketplace'.[44] During Roosevelt's second administration, American liberals, reacting to the 1937–8 recession, urged 'additional social reform, supported a re-organised executive branch with enhanced national planning and administrative capability, and turned to the "new economics" of compensatory fiscal policy'.[45] At the heart of this new approach to liberal economic policy was the increasing acceptance of the ideas of Keynes. During the years of the Second World War, Keynesian policy prescriptions for an expanding mixed economy with government–business cooperation, full employment, rising living standards and economic security constituted a significant landmark in the evolution of American liberalism. The role of the American state was not to 'manage' capitalism directly, but to work in partnership with the private sector towards redressing weaknesses and imbalances in the private economy and towards sustaining prosperity and stability.[46] For some historians, the strength of this relationship between government and business during the years of war created a powerful 'corporate liberalism' in post-war America.[47] Brinkley, however, suggests that the war, in the long run, did not increase federal control of corporate behaviour, but contributed instead to 'a government commitment to indirect management of the economy through Keynesian tools', and the United States began to construct a 'compensatory state'.[48]

In post-war American society, a national consensus was established in economic and political thought in relation to the era of national prosperity. While Harry Truman's administration sustained the New Deal legacy of using federal government to stabilise the economy, expand welfare provision and help the disadvantaged, the nature of the progressive ideology changed after 1945. Liberals rejected excessive state expansion, showed sensitivity to the partnerships that were created between the corporate world and the state and worked to preserve individualism, tolerance and the welfare state. Consumption rather than production became the principal priority of the American economy and came to define the concept of the 'American dream'.[49] In the Keynesian tradition, American liberals argued that it was possible to conceive of a socially responsible capitalism; an economic system in which 'the state compensated for capitalism's remaining flaws through aggressive fiscal policies and through expanded welfare and social insurance'.[50] The task of post-war American governments was not to construct a corporate state, but to work towards creating this 'compensatory state' through which capitalism could be managed without the extensive state regulation of corporate behaviour in the pre-war era.

In Germany, the rise of collectivism came from changes in the nature of corporatism in German politics. As the previous chapter observed, compared with both Britain and the United States, the classical liberal market model was marginal to German economic thought in the nineteenth century. Germany had instead a long tradition of sectoral corporatist regulation and coordination and of tripartite concentration. Collectivism developed in Germany in the 1870s from a particular model of 'societal corporatism'.[51] This was not the face of corporatism later found in fascist Italy and Nazi Germany. Rather, this model focused on the reciprocal relationships between the state and organised interests. A system of 'collective capitalism' or 'societal corporatism' embodied labour, big business, organised interest groups and other social groups within a non-competitive, associational framework of relations. Cooperation between these groups and state administrators in the formulation of national economy and policy created a consensus in German society around fundamental issues.[52]

The year 1879 proved to be a turning point in the advance of corporatism in Germany. Fundamental changes gradually emerged in the economy that exerted a deep influence over German history. Societal corporatism was superseded by a system of state corporatism, which later became the defining element of the National Socialist authoritarian state. In the German federal states – especially Prussia – the state and local authorities acquired new responsibilities and powers in sectoral economic policy. Under the Bismarkian state, co-operation between labour and capital started to be replaced by uncompromising control and central allocation for the economy. Both business and industry were subjected to the primacy of the politics of the state. Under the strain of worldwide depression, free trade was uprooted in favour of protectionism. At the same time, competition was being restricted by the growth of cartels. Furthermore, the state's control of the German economy was extended with the transfer of major industrial sectors to public ownership. The era of 'municipal socialism' was marked first by the nationalisation of the railroads, and then by the transfer of mines, iron works, water works, gas works and other industries under state and municipal control.⁵³ Historians have noted this movement, away from the previous 'pluralist' era of free exchange among social groups. In a widely influential article, Hans Rosenberg argued that the 1873 crash and ensuing Great Depression led to the rise of illiberal trends in German politics. He cited the rise of 'neo-mercantilism', 'collective protectionism', interest group organisation, mass parties and 'modern anti-Semitism and pre-fascist currents'.⁵⁴ By the end of the nineteenth century, Werner Abelshauser contends that Germany, 'while overcoming her economic backwardness', was 'almost predestined to become the first post-liberal nation' through the setting-up of market regulations and restrictive economic practices.⁵⁵

These illiberal tendencies in Germany were greatly strengthened by the experience of the First World War. Measures of economic mobilisation were enforced with little regard for market forces. The war gave the state the opportunity to seize direct control of production and prices within a framework of cartels extending over nearly the whole of the manufacturing and heavy industry. In order to stabilise industrial relations, organised labour was integrated into the system and given equal rights in managing the economy. Consequently, unions made remarkable gains in social policy, wage policy and labour legislation.⁵⁶ Organised labour continued to achieve gains in Weimar Germany, with significant increases in public expenditure for housing, the expansion of health, disability and social insurance, as well as with legislation which restored the eight-hour day and procured employment. This early period of the Weimar Republic was not, however, one of binding state arbitration, but was rooted in the German tradition of corporatist social thought. Larry Jones observes that 'the social and economic turmoil following the war had done much to stimulate a revival of corporatist sentiment among those social groups that felt most directly threatened by the demise of the old order'.⁵⁷ In particular, trade unions, the German artisanry and other business groups and the government acted as formal associational units of representation, which in the short term helped to restore some form of social framework and to stabilise the German state politically and socially. In the long term, however, conflict and dissolution rather than cooperation and stabilisation were to become the enduring legacy of the Weimar Republic. While some form of corporatism may have survived the political and economic ravages of the First World War, liberal pluralist interest policy was never truly resurrected during the Weimar period. By its end, interest groups were no longer part of a tripartite corporatist interest policy characterised by consensus and class collaboration, but part of a repressive state regime dominated by a network of 'big business'–'big labour' economic power relations.[58]

Following the dissolution of the Weimar Republic in 1933, the long transition from 'societal' corporatism to 'state' corporatism in Germany was finally completed under the Third Reich. After 1933, the Nazi Party established an authoritarian variant of corporatism in response to the problems facing the German economy: extreme state corporatism. Adolf Hitler was extremely critical of free market economics, blaming economic liberalism's stress upon the importance of private-sector ownership and control of the economy for Germany's weak position in the world economy. The solution to Germany's economic ills, he maintained, lay in a substantial increase in the regulation and direction of economic life by the state. This strand of state corporatism was accompanied by nationalist and imperialist ideology. 'Economic statism', for German nationalists, became an important means of achieving unity, nationalism and economic and military success. The Nazis favoured the introduction of protective tariffs, foreign debt reduction and 'import substitution to remove what they regarded as debilitating dependence on the world economy'.[59] The introduction of central planning, embodied in Hitler's Four Year Plan of 1936, was nothing short of a complete transformation of the structure of the German economy. Preparations for a 'total war economy' entailed substantial increases in military expenditure and the proportion of the economy devoted to military purposes in general; the creation of a large state-owned and state-operated industrial structure; and state command over the direction of economic resources – over labour and goods, and by methods of taxation, credit regulation, and price and wage determination.[60] During the years of the Second World War, the neo-liberal economists Walter Eucken and Alfred Müller-Armack pointed towards the economic failings of the centrally administrated economy of the Third Reich – in particular, its tendency towards economic policies that encouraged uncontrollable inflation; its inflexibility in response to consumer requirements; and its inability to stimulate production. They argued that there would have to be a return to the merits of free enterprise and private ownership of the means of production, and hence to autonomy of investment, liberty of contracts concerning prices, wages and interest, and private production for private consumption. The rise of this variant of German neo-liberalism is discussed at length in Chapter 4.

The critics of collectivism

Collectivism, from the 1930s onwards, became an increasingly dominant ideology in the world, which was fundamental for the rise of neo-liberalism. Neo-liberals such as Hayek, Milton Freedom and Alexander Rüstow identified Nazism, fascism, Soviet communism, New Deal social reform and Keynesianism as part of a larger collectivist impulse, which was threatening to devour the philosophy of individual freedom. All countries, even those with strong liberal traditions and opposed to extreme forms of collectivism – Britain and the United States – were pursuing collectivist programmes. Liberal values had not only been destroyed in Germany under the central direction of Hitler's Nazi state, but were steadily being eroded in democracies like Britain by advocates of planning such as Barbara Wootton.[61] For neo-liberals like Hayek and Mises, therefore, it was not the means of collectivist planning which were so objectionable, but the ends. In his *Collectivist Economic Planning*, published in 1935, Hayek observed that collectivism in all its guises invariably meant collective ownership of the means of production and collective direction and control of their use. He claimed that the assumptions of planners involved a rational belief in the deliberate management of all social affairs.[62] Mises, however, was quick to point out that the dilemma for policy-makers was not a simple one of choosing between economic planning and no planning. As he stated:

> The alternative is not plan or no plan. The question is: whose planning? Should each member of society plan for himself or should the paternal government alone plan for all? The issue is spontaneous action of each individual versus the exclusive action of the government. It is freedom versus government omnipotence.[63]

Hayek observed with alarm that this supposition of the primary competence of the state that economic planning entailed had, in the first half of the twentieth century, 'gained a ground until today there is hardly a political group anywhere in the in the world which does not want central direction of most human activities in the service of one aim or another'.[64]

The American columnist Walter Lippmann, in his account of the collectivist mind-set of the 1930s, *The Good Society*, outlined the intellectual drift towards collectivism and totalitarianism. Lippmann's work was the most influential among several liberal-minded defenses of freedom in the mid-1930s. He wrote:

> Throughout the world in the name of progress, men who call themselves communists, socialists, fascists, nationalists, progressives, and even liberals, are unanimous

in holding that government with its instruments of coercion must, by commanding the people how they shall live, direct the course of civilization and fix the shape of things to come.[65]

Lippmann thus referred to collectivism as the 'dominant dogma of the age'.[66] In his work, he made an eloquent liberal defense of personal, political and economic freedom against the riding tide of market regulation and socialist planning. A perfectly free economy, he argued, that indulged the vagaries of the individual, was a better regulator of human energy than a centrally planned authority could ever be. Lippmann, however, proclaimed that, in the face of the growing threat of fascism and communism, it was unlikely that there could ever be a return to the previous liberal era. Liberalism, he stated, had been stagnating since the late nineteenth century, allowing collectivism to become the new intellectual orthodoxy throughout the world. Liberalism, in effect, had become an endangered species.

Lippmann's pessimistic stance caught the attention of liberals in Europe, many of whom had been displaced from their own countries. Indeed, there was something of an exile culture building up among liberal thinkers throughout Europe at this time: Isaiah Berlin was forced to flee Russia; in Germany, Alexander Rüstow spent the mid-1930s in exile in Turkey and, later, in Geneva; and Hayek, who had anticipated that throughout the 1930s his permanent home would be Austria, spent the years preceding and during the war in retreat, in London and Cambridge. These liberals were alarmed by the apparent inexorable decline of liberal ideas in Europe throughout the 1930s, but, unlike Lippmann, they kept alive a belief that the future belonged to liberalism. In August 1938, an international conference was organised in Paris by the French philosopher, Louis Rougier, to honour the publication of Lippmann's *The Good Society* and to foster a discussion of liberalism's revival. The conference was attended by twenty-six liberal sympathisers from Europe and America, including Hayek and Mises from Austria; Raymond Aron and Jacques Rueff representing France; Wilhelm Röpke and Alexander Rüstow from Germany; and, of course, Lippmann himself, representing America.[67] Richard Cockett states that 'the Paris conference represented a drawing together of the disparate threads of Western economic liberal thinking, and of those united by their opposition not just to totalitarian collectivism, but, more specifically, also [by] their opposition to Keynesianism'.[68]

The Paris conference had a significant influence over the future course of liberal thinking. It represented the first coherent attempt to bring together the leading proponents of freedom and liberty in the world for a reconsideration of the legacy of liberalism. Attempts were made to develop a 'new', revitalised interpretation of liberalism that both moved beyond the outmoded nineteenth-century conception of *laissez-faire* liberalism and challenged existing collectivist streams of thought: an interpretation that would involve 'the combination of a working competition not only with the corresponding legal and institutional framework but also with a re-integrated society of freely co-operating and vitally satisfied men as the only alternative to *laissez-faire* and to totalitarianism'.[69] It was out of this struggle at the conference to create a constructive alternative to prevailing ideologies, to find a 'third way' between *laissez-faire* liberalism and collectivism, that, as A. J. Nicholls states, the term 'neo-liberalism' was coined by the German economist Alexander Rüstow. However, as Nicholls points out, 'it was never popular with those whom it described'.[70]

The liberals in exile, as well those individuals who simply valued the fundamentals of a liberal society, managed to keep alive the anti-collectivism movement during the years of the Second World War. Individuals and groups in different countries pushed forward the intellectual counter-revolution against collectivism that had started at the Paris conference. Eucken and Rüstow, operating from Switzerland, supported the German League for Free Economic Policy, dedicated to the furtherance of the free market.[71] In Britain, the Individualist Group, later the Society of Individual Freedom, chaired by Ernest Benn and composed of businessmen, lawyers and anti-statist writers, was united in its 'desire to restore to British public life that spirit of individual liberty and responsibility which characterised its period of greatness and which is today gravely threatened'.[72] While in the United States, influenced by Hayek, there was strong conservative opposition to the New Deal and to wartime industrial planning. Anti-New Deal groups pointed out the similarities between the powerful tide of interventionism supported by the American government and the central planning pushed forward by the Nazis.[73]

The link between planning and dictatorship became the dominant theme of the leading critiques of collectivism published during the war years. Hayek's extensive discussion of this link, published in *The Road to Serfdom*, was perhaps the most profound analysis of the shortcomings of the collectivist position to come out of the 1940s. Hayek, in dedicating the book to 'The Socialists of all Parties', set forth his polemic on economic planning, which was directed at the aspiring collectivists he saw in all the political parties in Britain – Labour, Liberal and Conservative. *The*

Road to Serfdom was intended as a populist tract on the mediation between human freedom and government authority. The central theme of the book was that all forms of socialism were on a par with National Socialism and fascism. For Hayek, democratic planning was an illusion. Government ownership of the means of production in democracies, he claimed, would, in the end, lead to coercion and dictatorship, because partial planning creates problems which, to the planner, appear soluble only by more extensive planning. Hayek therefore saw the proposals in Britain for post-war Keynesian demand-management of the economy as a staging post to the complete collectivisation of the economy. As he wrote:

> Both competition and central direction become poor and inefficient tools if they are incomplete; they are alternative principles used to solve the same problem, and a mixture of the two means that neither will really work and that the result will be worse than if either system had been consistently relied upon.[74]

The *Road to Serfdom* was thus a defense of economic freedom of the market order rather than of the political freedom of the democratic order. For Hayek, a defense of capitalism was more important than that of democracy, because 'only capitalism makes democracy possible'.[75]

Hayek was not alone in pointing out the dangers inherent in socialism. Michael Polanyi, for instance, in his review of *The Road to Serfdom*, was in agreement with Hayek that 'National Socialism was not a reaction against socialism, but an outcome of it'.[76] Similarly, George Orwell expressed concern over the political unrest between 1930 and 1950 and the despotism he saw creeping over Western civilisation. Orwell had first-hand experiences of totalitarianism during his time in service during the Spanish civil war, chronicled in his *Homage to Catalonia*. In many ways, Hayek's *Road to Serfdom* was a precursor to Orwell's 1945 fable, *Animal Farm*, about the horrors of the Marxist state. Both works were published in the heyday of collectivist enthusiasm. Orwell was thus in agreement with many of the underlying themes of *The Road to Serfdom* and reviewed Hayek's book favourably:

> In the negative part of Hayek's thesis there is a great deal of truth . . . collectivism is not inherently democratic, but, on the contrary, gives rise to a tyrannical minority of such powers as the Spanish Inquisitors never dreamed of . . . Hayek is probably also right in saying that in this country (Britain) the intellectuals are more totalitarian minded than the common people.

Orwell, however, expressed concern that Hayek's faith in 'free' competition would create for the great mass of people a tyranny probably worse, because more irresponsible, than that of the state.[77]

Competitions, Orwell pointed out, inevitably lead to dictatorship by monopoly. Free-market capitalism of the kind supported by Hayek, he contended, would, in the end, lead to a return to the conditions of slump and unemployment in which the seeds of communism could germinate. The most negative response to *The Road to Serfdom* came from Herman Finer's *The Road to Reaction*, published in 1946. Like Orwell, Finer identified the authoritarianism implicit in Hayek's work, in particular its attitude towards democratic government. Finer fumed that Hayek's book 'constitutes the most inopportune offensive against democracy to emerge from a democratic country for many decades'.[78] Reflecting the collectivist orthodoxy of his time, he argued that capitalism, in particular during the Great Depression, was not capable of preserving democratic government. He wrote that, during the 1930s, 'the sense of desperation produced by the downward tug of economic ruin subjected political systems throughout the world to tremendous strain'. In particular, he observed that in Germany Nazism was not a product of 'socialist ideas', but a reaction to the 'the chronic deficiencies of unbridled competition as the governor of the modern economic system'.[79] In a vitriolic attack on Hayek's defence of the liberal market order, Finer concluded that '[i]t is not property that gives liberty . . . liberty is the fruit of democracy . . . The true alternative to dictatorship is not economic individualism and competition, but democracy.'[80]

A book that was more sympathetic to Hayek's political leanings was Karl Popper's *The Open Society and its Enemies*. There are important parallels between the backgrounds and belief systems of Popper and Hayek. Popper, like Hayek, was a product of *fin de siècle* Vienna; he abandoned an early inclination towards socialism; he distinguished between different forms of rationalism; he saw human freedom and well-being as being of the greatest importance; and he constructed a critique of the totalitarian tendencies of a planned society.[81] Popper's critique of Marxism in *The Open Society* was undoubtedly influenced by Hayek's ideas and by 'the same fear of the intellectual allure of totalitarian ideology that motivated Hayek'.[82] Indeed, on reading *The Road to Serfdom* in May 1944, Popper wrote to Hayek:

> When I came to the passage in the Preface in which you described the writing of the book as 'a duty I must not evade', I felt that you were driven by fundamentally the same experience which made me write my book and which made me describe it . . . as a War effort.[83]

Both Popper and Hayek were fighting collectivism in their own ways: for Hayek, it was in the form of a populist tract; for Popper, it was in the shape of scholarly critique of three of the main exponents of collectivist ideas – Plato, Marx and Hegel.[84] Popper's critique, written during the years of the Second World War, claimed that the ideas of Plato, Marx and Hegel were hostile to the Open Society, because they held false theories of knowledge and of history. For Popper, this argument had wider implications for the political context in which he was writing. He maintained that the most fundamental issue after the war had ended would be a defense of the ideals of a free society against those anti-liberals from the left and right who called them into question. The significance of Popper's contribution to the 'Camp for Freedom' was in his scholarly and complementary critique of the impetus of large-scale planning which was rampant in the years during and after the Second World War, and his defense of liberal individualism.[85]

Another thinker who was critical of the collectivist tendencies Western societies were adopting after the war was John Jewkes. Jewkes's *Ordeal by Planning*, published later than both *The Road to Serfdom* and *The Open Society* in 1948, became one of the most celebrated critiques of planning in post-war Britain. Like Hayek and Popper, Jewkes, while admitting that he might 'offend' many people, considered it a 'duty' to expose the shortcomings of collectivism to the majority. Jewkes contended that the wartime planning system, which many in the post-war world wished to maintain and to develop, condemned Britain to poverty and failure. In complete agreement with Hayek, Jewkes wrote: 'At the root of our troubles lies the fallacy that the best way of ordering economic affairs is to place the responsibility for all crucial decisions in the hands of the state.'[86] In the tradition of classical liberalism, Jewkes made the case for 'the free economy; institution of private ownership of property (including ownership of the means of production); the sovereignty of the consumer; the freedom of contracts of service; independent parties; and free economic intercourse between nations'.[87] The 'mixed' Keynesian economy of post-war Britain, Jewkes argued, was as equally destructive of these liberal principles as the centrally planned one of the Soviet Union. For Jewkes, there was no distinction between 'good' planning and 'bad' planning. All planning, Jewkes argued,

> ultimately turns every individual into a cipher and every economic decision into blind fumbling, destroys the incentives through which economic progress arises, renders the economic system as unstable as the whims of the few who ultimately control it, and creates a system of wire-pulling and privileges in which economic justice ceases to have any meaning.[88]

There were remarkable similarities in the arguments put forward and the concerns raised by the anti-collectivists in the 1930s and 1940s. Hayek, however, recognised that the intellectual assault on planning needed a focus if it was to have any influence in the post-war political debate. The remaining liberals in a collectivist world, he pointed out, were intellectually isolated within their own countries. Hayek therefore saw the need for an international society for 'liberals', which would become the focal point of international efforts to repel the intellectual claims of collectivism and to encourage the 'rebirth of liberalism'.

THE MONT PELERIN SOCIETY

The international meeting-ground for anti-collectivists and liberal sympathisers envisioned by Hayek became established in 1947 as The Mont Pelerin Society (MPS), named after its first meeting place. The society was a culmination of the efforts made by liberal intellectuals since the 1930s to keep the small flame of free market economics burning in the wilderness of collectivism. In classical liberalism's darkest hour, the MPS sought, in Max Hartwell's apt military metaphor, to 'save the flag' and 'renew the attack'.[89]

Intellectuals and history

The campaign to revive liberalism was one that centred on the powerful role that ideas played in history. Hayek had long held a belief that the course of history and the development of the national character were largely determined by the life and death of ideas. The main source of change in history, according to Hayek, was to be found in 'the free acceptance or rejection of ideas of the governing groups of the time'.[90] It was ideas rather than interests that held sway over the course of events. Indeed, Hayek maintained that '[w]hat to the contemporary observer appears as the battle of conflicting interests has indeed often been decided long before in a clash of ideas confined to narrow circles'.[91] The revival of liberalism, he thus argued, would ultimately be determined by the success of liberal intellectuals in recapturing the ideological ground from the collectivists. In his essay *The Intellectuals and Socialism*, distributed to members of the MPS after its first meeting, Hayek explicitly compared the task of liberal thinkers to that of the socialists in the late nineteenth and early twentieth centuries. The reason why the socialists were so successful, Hayek claimed, was that they 'regularly and successfully acted as if they fully understood the key position of the intellectuals and have directed their main efforts towards gaining the support of the "elite"'. Further, 'it has only been the socialists who have offered anything like an explicit programme of social development, a picture of a future at which they were aiming, and a set of general principles to decisions on particular issues'.[92]

Hayek suggested that liberals could draw valuable lessons from the socialist example, a task that would require 'an intense intellectual effort'. The main lesson that liberals could learn from the socialists, he argued, 'is that it was their courage to be utopian which gained them support of the intellectuals and thereby an influence on public opinion which is daily making possible what only recently seemed utterly remote'.[93] The task of liberal thinkers was, therefore, to construct a 'liberal utopia' based on the principles of free trade and freedom of opportunity, regardless of how small its prospects of early realisation may be, so as to challenge the present socialist one. They had to design a liberal programme to the 'appeal to the imagination', one 'which seems neither a mere defense of things as they are nor a diluted socialism, but a truly liberal radicalism which does not spare the susceptibilities of the mighty (including the trade unions)'.[94] Addressing the MPS, Hayek stressed the extent of the task ahead: 'we must', he stated, 'kindle an interest in . . . the great principles of social organisation of the conditions of individual liberty as we have not known it in our life-time . . . We must raise and train an army of fighters for freedom.'[95] Hayek acknowledged in a later essay that the intellectual endeavour of building a free society would be a slow process. Substantial transformations, he pointed out, needed to take place in order to create the foundations of the free society. The most important change in society would be a psychological one, 'an alteration in the character of the people'; an acceptance of the political ideas of liberalism among the people Hayek considered as crucial in determining its long-term success as a credible ideology. Hayek, however, pointed out that even in those countries with liberal traditions – Britain, the United States, and, to a lesser extent, Germany – socialism had manifested itself so deeply in the minds of the majority that a return to liberalism would 'necessarily be a slow affair, a process which extends not over a few years, but perhaps over one or two generations'.[96] The monumental task facing the liberal intellectuals was therefore to resolve their differences and work together over an unspecified period of time to change the 'climate of ideas' and 'make the philosophical foundations of a free society once more a living intellectual issue'.[97]

The founding of the Mont Pelerin Society

The MPS became the focal point of this task. Founded in 1947 under Hayek's guidance, the MPS represented an attempt to promote liberal values throughout the world. Like Marxists of an earlier time, the neo-liberals at Mont Pelerin constructed their own utopia. Liberal scholars of all nationalities were drawn together by a sense of crisis, to discuss the intellectual revival of liberalism. In many ways, the idea behind the society, of creating an international forum for liberal intellectuals, was drawn from the ill-timed Paris conference in 1938. The former president and historian of the society, Max Hartwell, states that the MPS

> can be best described as a voluntary association of like-minded people who have more than an ordinary attachment to the idea of a free society and a conviction that ideas ultimately determine the way in which the world is seen and the methods by which it is organised.[98]

The society was committed to persuading intellectuals, and hence the masses and their political leaders, to change course. It was part of an ideological movement to regain a belief in the power of liberal ideas and to refute those of socialism. The MPS's intention was not to create a political orthodoxy or to align itself with a particular political party or parties, but to facilitate discussion and an exchange of ideas between like-minded individuals, in the hope of re-establishing the principles of liberal society and those of the market order. In a statement of its aims, the members of the MPS made explicit its principal objective: 'Its object is solely, by facilitating the exchange of views among minds inspired by certain ideals and broad conceptions held in common, to contribute to the preservation and improvement of society.'[99]

The founding meeting of the MPS took place in 1947 and was attended by thirty-eight individuals, almost all of whom were academics and intellectuals. The initial membership of the MPS by no means consisted of just classical liberals; rather, the society involved a diverse range of individuals who were broadly liberal in their views and critical of collectivism. The individuals whom the society brought together for mutual enlightenment included the British delegates Lionel Robbins, John Jewkes and Michael Polanyi; the Austrian émigrés Ludwig von Mises, Karl Popper, Fritz Machlup and, of course, Hayek himself; from The United States, Milton Friedman, Frank Knight, Henry Hazlitt and George Stigler; from Germany, Wilhelm Röpke and Walter Eucken; and, from France, Maurice Allais and

Jacques Rueff.[100] From such a diverse gathering of scholars and intellectuals, there inevitably resulted much intellectual disagreement at the early meetings of the MPS.[101] There was no shared interpretation of the causes of liberalism's decline or of the best means by which to reverse the decline. All participants were, however, united in common agreement as to the dangers which threatened the foundations of civilised society: they saw danger in increasing public intervention in economy and society, not least in the welfare state; in the power and influence of trade unions and business monopolies; and in the continuing threat and reality of inflation.

Again without any specific agreement, the members set out their fundamental principles of a free society in a statement of the MPS's aims on 8 April 1947, drafted by Lionel Robbins from the London School of Economics. Hartwell comments that this statement 'is especially interesting as a forthright statement of the concerns of liberals at that particular point in time'.[102] In it, the emphasis was on the intellectual errors which had led to the destruction of free society. Among the most dangerous of these intellectual errors were 'views of history which deny all absolute moral standards' and 'theories which question the desirability of the rule of law'.[103] The future direction of a free society, Hayek claimed in an opening address to the MPS, would have to be based on 'general principles of a liberal order'. However, these principles, warned Hayek, could only be realised by both 'purging traditional liberal theory of certain accidental accretions which have become attached to it in the course of time, and facing up to some real problems which an oversimplified liberalism has shirked'.[104] The remaining part of the MPS statement of aims was devoted to this very cause. The statement declared that liberals around the world must, as part of 'what is essentially an ideological movement' and through intellectual argument, reassert the values of liberalism: they must analyse 'the nature of the present crisis so as to bring home to others its essential moral and economic origins'; redefine the functions of the state 'so as to distinguish more clearly between totalitarianism and the liberal order'; re-establish and develop the rule of law 'in such manner that individuals and groups are not in a position to encroach upon the freedom of others and private rights are not allowed to become a basis for predatory power'; establish minimum standards 'by means not inimical to the initiative and functioning of the market'; develop methods for 'combating the misuse of history for the furtherance of creeds hostile to liberty'; and, finally, create 'an international order conducive to the safeguarding of peace and liberty, and permitting the establishment of harmonious international economic relations'.[105]

This statement of aims, whilst not being overly specific, makes extremely clear the scale of the crisis facing liberalism and the course of action needed to redress the ideological unbalance in the world. It is apparent from the statement that the fundamental aim of the MPS was not merely to revive liberalism as a credible creed, but also to reinvent it as a coherent philosophy for the twentieth century. Hayek put it bluntly:

> The old liberal who adheres to a traditional creed *merely* out of tradition is not of much use for our purpose. What we need are people who have faced the arguments from the other side, who have struggled with them and fought themselves through to a position from which they can both critically meet the objection against it and justify their views.[106]

Mont Pelerin liberalism

The significance of the MPS, in terms of its actual achievements, and its contribution to the history of modern liberalism, are difficult to place. Certainly the society, through its collaborative efforts, helped to initiate the rebirth of liberalism in the dark post-war years. It carried forward the 'neo-liberal' cause from the Paris conference of 1938, and kept alight the lamp of classical liberalism at a time when collectivism threatened to extinguish it. Indeed, Robert Higgs states that '[i]ts influence was probably most significant during the dark age between its founding and the mid-1970s, when classical liberal ideas came close to being suffocated by the dominance of collectivism among Western intellectuals'.[107] Hayek was in no doubt as to the significance of the society. He observed later that the first conference and the founding

> constituted the rebirth of the liberal movement in Europe. Americans have done me the honour of considering the publication of *The Road to Serfdom* as the decisive date, but it is my conviction that the really serious endeavour among intellectuals to bring about the rehabilitation of the idea of personal freedom especially in the economic realm dates from the founding of the Mont Pelerin Society.[108]

The MPS's influence was in the realm of ideas. Its meetings dealt with abstract ideas rather than practical policy alternatives to collectivism. Hartwell notes that it was not the original intention of the society to be politically active. He writes: 'It never had either the organisation or the resources to be a successful lobby or interest group, and, being international, it never had a national focus.' Rather, the society evolved into a 'special kind of club, an intellectual club with an ideological bias'.[109] Its sole purpose was to meet, so as to discuss and debate the preservation of a free society. The MPS was, however, more than just a simple debating club; its meeting brought together some of the most prominent liberal intellectuals in the world, and it is herein that its influence lies. Hartwell explains that the MPS exerted an influence beyond its members, 'because many of those individual members were themselves important' – such as Ludwig Erhard from Germany, and later, in the 1960s and 1970s, Enoch Powell, Keith Joseph and Geoffrey Howe from Britain – 'and were influenced in their decision-making on public issues by society decisions'. Thus, in some loose sense, the ideas and concerns expressed by the MPS participants can be said to have had some form of impact on the attitudes of politicians and of the public at large and, by implication, on policy decisions, although the line of causation is often impossible to draw.[110]

The MPS's place in the history of liberalism is equally difficult to discern. Unlike political parties, pressure groups and think-tanks, the MPS has remained an obscure and somewhat secretive organisation, in which members engage in serious discussions on capitalism and on the interventionist state. Certainly during the first twenty years of its existence the society, through its important intellectual contacts, established a variant of liberalism – 'Mont Pelerin liberalism', as Hartwell terms it – as a counter-ideology to collectivism. Hartwell sets out the central tenets of 'Mont Pelerin liberalism'. Basic to this strand and to 'its worldly realism', he writes, 'is respect for the individual and concern about threats to individual autonomy. To achieve and protect this liberty, Mont Pelerins emphasised the need for two institutional safeguards: the limited state and the free economy'.[111] This stream of thought, expressed through think-tanks and political parties in specific national contexts, inevitably became part of the corpus of neo-liberal ideology.

Conclusion

This chapter has explored the intellectual origins of neo-liberalism in the twentieth century: the ideological context in which it has evolved and the intellectuals who have helped to establish it as part of mainstream liberal thought. It has examined the enthusiasm for various forms of collectivism during the first half of the twentieth century such as central planning, protectionism, and Keynesianism, which neo-liberals rallied against. The chapter has identified the late 1930s and 1940s as the crucial period in which neo-liberal ideas originated – a period when socialist interventionist views were ascendant and those of liberalism were virtually extinct throughout the Western world. Neo-liberals like Hayek, Milton Friedman and Lionel Robins successfully set up a false dichotomy in their thought between collectivism and liberalism, which later became the cornerstone of neo-liberal ideology. The chapter has demonstrated that the rise of neo-liberalism was not simply a revival of classical liberal ideas on free trade and the minimal state; rather, neo-liberalism originated as a counter-movement, in reaction to the various forms of collectivism that it saw sweeping throughout the Western world. These various formulations of collectivism not only formed the context in which neo-liberalism arose, but also provided one of its key distinguishing arguments: that all forms of collectivism, even milder rationalist liberal forms, lead to dictatorship and economic catastrophe.

The efforts made by neo-liberals to revive liberalism as an intellectual force during this period culminated in the meetings of the Mont Pelerin Society in 1947. These meetings of liberally minded academics generated and disseminated a wide range of liberal ideas through a vast network of international members. Whilst Mont Pelerians made it explicit that it was not their intention to create a new political orthodoxy, the society's network became an important source of ideas and inspiration in the construction of neo-liberal policy programmes in Germany, Britain and the United States in the years that followed.

Notes

1. See F. A. Hayek, 'History and politics', in F. A. Hayek (ed.), *Capitalism and the Historians* (Chicago: University of Chicago Press, 1954), pp. 3–29.
2. Here Hayek is referring to Nazi Germany. He admits that is impossible to trace in any great detail the way historians have produced the ideas that rule Germany today, but states with some certainty that 'even some of the most repulsive features of Nazi ideology trace back to German historians whom Hitler has probably never read but whose ideas have dominated the atmosphere in which he grew up'. See his essay, 'The historians and the future of Europe', in F. A. Hayek, *Studies in Philosophy, Politics and the History of Ideas* (London: Routledge and Kegan Paul, 1967), p. 138.
3. Quoted in Richard Cockett, *Thinking the Unthinkable: Think-Tanks and the Economic Counter-Revolution, 1931–1983* (London: HarperCollins, 1994), p. 103.
4. A. V. Dicey, *Lectures on the Relation Between Law and Public Opinion in England during the Nineteenth Century* (London: Macmillan, 1905).
5. For a discussion of the relationship between the old and new in Keynes's economic thought, see Robert Skidelsky, 'The reception of the Keynesian revolution', in Milo Keynes (ed.), *Essays on John Maynard Keynes* (Cambridge: Cambridge University Press, 1975), pp. 89–107.

6. Peter Clarke, *The Keynesian Revolution in the Making, 1924–1936* (Oxford: Clarendon Press, 1988), pp. 244–5.
7. J. M. Keynes, 'A drastic remedy: Reply to the critics', *Nation*, 7 June 1924, p. 228, quoted in Peter Clarke, 'The politics of Keynesian economics, 1924–1931', in M. Bentley and J. Stevenson (eds), *High and Low Politics in Modern Britain* (Oxford: Clarendon Press, 1983), p. 175.
8. J. M. Keynes, 'The end of *laissez-faire*', in his *Essays in Persuasion* (London: Rupert Hart Davis, 1952), p. 294.
9. Ibid., p. 319.
10. J. M. Keynes, *The General Theory of Unemployment, Interest and Money* (London: Macmillan, 1936).
11. Robert Skidelsky, 'The political meaning of the Keynesian revolution', in Robert Skidelsky (ed.), *The End of the Keynesian Era: Essays on the Disintegration of the Keynesian Political Economy* (London: Macmillan, 1977), p. 35.
12. F. A. Hayek, *A Tiger by the Tail* (London: IEA, 1972), pp. 103–4.
13. Keynes, 'The end of *Laissez-Faire*', p. 316.
14. Quoted in D. E. Modderidge, *Keynes* (London: Macmillan, 1993), pp. 42–3.
15. R. Lekachman, *The Age of Keynes* (New York: McGraw Hill, 1975), p. 303.
16. J. M. Keynes, 'The economic transition in England', quoted in Peter Clarke, *The Keynesian Revolution in the Making 1924–1936* (Oxford: Clarendon Press, 1988), p. 80.
17. Daniel Bell, 'The prospects of American capitalism: On Keynes, Schumpeter and Galbraith', in his *The End of Ideology: On the Exhaustion of Political Ideas in the 1950s* (New York: Free Press, 1960), p. 74.
18. Joseph A. Schumpeter, *Capitalism, Socialism and Democracy* (London: Allen and Unwin, 1943), p. 76.
19. Joseph A. Schumpeter, 'The instability of capitalism', *Economic Journal*, 38 (September 1928), p. 385.
20. Schumpeter, *Capitalism, Socialism and Democracy*, p. 159.
21. Ibid., p. 84.
22. Bell, 'The prospects of American capitalism', p. 75.
23. Karl Polanyi, *The Great Transformation* (Boston, MA: Beacon Press, 1944), p. 140.
24. Ibid., p. 29.
25. Mark Blyth, *Great Transformations: Economic Ideas and Institutional Change in the Twentieth Century* (Cambridge: Cambridge University Press, 2002), p. 5.
26. Polanyi, *The Great Transformation*, p. 150.
27. W. H. Greenleaf, *The British Political Tradition, Vol. I: The Rise of Collectivism* (London: Methuen, 1983), pp. 26–7.
28. A. V. Dicey, *Lectures on the Relation between Law and Public Opinion*.
29. Rodney Barker, *Political Ideas in Modern Britain* (London: Methuen, 1978), pp. 7–10.
30. Michael Freeden, *Liberalism Divided: A Study in British Political Thought, 1914–1939* (Oxford: Clarendon Press, 1986), p. 357.
31. See Cockett, *Thinking the Unthinkable*, p. 15.
32. Daniel Ritschel, *The Politics of Planning: The Debate on Economic Planning in Britain in the 1930s* (Oxford: Oxford University Press, 1997).
33. Ibid., pp. 232–3.
34. Barbara Wootton, *Plan or No Plan* (London: Victor Gollancz, 1934) and Herbert Morrison, *Can Planning be Democratic?* (London: Routledge, 1944).

35. Ritschel, *The Politics of Planning*, p. 150.
36. Quoted in J. Harris, *William Beveridge: A Biography* (Oxford: Oxford University Press, 1977), pp. 432–3.
37. Greenleaf, *The Rise of Collectivism*, p. 75.
38. Robert Skidelsky, *The End of the Keynesian Era: Essays on the Disintegration of Keynesian Political Economy* (London: Methuen, 1977), ch. 10.
39. Alan Brinkley, 'The two world wars and American liberalism', in his *Liberalism and its Discontents* (Cambridge, MA: Harvard University Press, 1998), pp. 79–80.
40. See Arthur S. Link, 'What happened to the progressive movement in the 1920s?', *American Historical Review*, July 1959 (4), pp. 833–51.
41. See Stephen Showronek, *Building a New American State: The Expansion of National Administrative Capacities, 1877–1920* (Cambridge: Cambridge University Press, 1982).
42. Alan Brinkley, 'Historians and the interwar years', in his *Liberalism and its Discontents*, p. 121.
43. David Plotke, *Building a Democratic Political Order: Reshaping American Liberalism in the 1930s and 1940s* (Cambridge: Cambridge University Press, 1996), ch. 4.
44. Alan Brinkley, 'The late New Deal and the idea of the state', in his *Liberalism and its Discontents*, pp. 44–5.
45. John W. Jeffries, 'The 'new' New Deal: FDR and American liberalism, 1937–1945', *Political Science Quarterly*, Vol. 105, No. 2 (1990), p. 397.
46. Edwin Amenta and Theda Skocpol, 'Redefining the New Deal: World War II and the development of social provision in the United States', in Margaret Weir, Ann Shola Orloff and Theda Skocpol (eds), *The Politics of Social Policy in the United States* (Princeton: Princeton University Press, 1988), pp. 81–122.
47. See Kim Mcquaid, *Uneasy Partners: Big Business in American Politics, 1945–1990* (New York: Johns Hopkins University Press, 1994).
48. Brinkley, 'Historians and the interwar years', p. 129.
49. K. N. Beck, 'What was liberalism in the 1950s?', *Political Science Quarterly*, Vol. 102, No. 2 (1987), pp. 233–58.
50. Brinkley, 'The two World Wars and American liberalism', p. 92.
51. P. Schmitter, 'Still the century of corporatism', in P. Schmitter and G. Lehmbruch (eds), *Trends Towards Corporatist Intermediation* (London: Sage, 1979), p. 67.
52. Werner Abelshauser, 'The first post-liberal nation: Stages in the development of modern corporatism in Germany', *European History Quarterly*, Vol. 14 (1984), pp. 285–318.
53. Gustav Stolper, *The German Economy: 1870 to the Present* (London: Weidenfeld and Nicolson, 1967) pp. 34–51.
54. Hans Rosenberg, 'Political and social consequences of the Great Depression of 1873–1896 in central Europe', *Economic History Review* (1943), p. 312.
55. Abelshauser, 'The first post-liberal nation', p. 311.
56. Richard Bessel, *Germany After the First World War* (Oxford: Clarendon Press, 1993), pp. 54–5.
57. L. E. Jones, *German Liberalism and the Dissolution of the Weimar Party System, 1918–33* (Chapel Hill: The University of North Carolina Press, 1988), p. 258.
58. Abelshauser, 'The first post-liberal nation', p. 301.
59. Karl Hardach, *The Political Economy of Germany in the Twentieth Century* (Berkeley: University of California Press, 1976), pp. 71–2.

60. Stolper, *The German Economy*, p. 157.
61. This is the argument later developed by Hayek in his *Road to Serfdom* (London: Routledge, 1944). Hayek declared that the antithesis of totalitarianism was not democracy but *laissez-faire* liberalism.
62. F. A. Hayek, 'The nature and history of the problem', in F. A. Hayek (ed.), *Collectivist Economic Planning: Critical Studies on the Impossibilities of Socialism* (London: Routledge, 1935), pp. 1–40.
63. Ludwig von Mises, *Socialism: An Economic and Sociological Analysis* (London: Bradford and Dickens, 1936), pp. 31–2.
64. Hayek, 'The nature and history of the problem', p. 1.
65. Walter Lippmann, *The Good Society* (London: Allen and Unwin, 1937), pp. 3–4.
66. Ibid., p. 9.
67. Max Hartwell, *A History of the Mont Pelerin Society* (Indianapolis: Liberty Fund, 1995), p. 20.
68. Cockett, *Thinking the Unthinkable*, p. 56.
69. Quoted in Cockett, *Thinking the Unthinkable*, p. 12.
70. A. J. Nicholls, *Freedom with Responsibility: The Social Market Economy 1918–1963* (Oxford: Oxford University Press, 1994), pp. 96–7.
71. Ibid., p. 49.
72. D. Abel, *Ernest Benn: Counsel for Liberty* (London: Ernest Benn, 1960), p. 110, quoted in Julia Stapleton, 'Resisting the centre at the extremes: English liberalism in the political thought of inter-war Britain', *British Journal of Politics and International Relations*, 1: 3, 1999, p. 287.
73. George H. Nash, *The Conservative Intellectual Movement in America since 1945* (Wilmington, Delaware, Intercollegiate Studies Institute, 1996), pp. 5–6.
74. Hayek, *The Road to Serfdom*, p. 31.
75. Ibid., p. 63.
76. Quoted in Cockett, *Thinking the Unthinkable*, p. 88.
77. George Orwell, 'Review: *The Road to Serfdom* by F. A. Hayek', in S. Orwell and I. Angus (eds), *George Orwell: The Collected Essays, Journalism and Letters of Orwell, Vol. III, 1943–1945* (London: Secker and Warburg, 1968), p. 118.
78. Herman Finer, *The Road to Reaction* (London: Dennis Doleson, 1946), p. 1.
79. Ibid., p. 24.
80. Ibid., p. 8.
81. Jeremy Shearmur, *Hayek and After: Hayekian Liberalism as a Research Programme* (London: Routledge, 1996), pp. 191–2.
82. Cockett, *Thinking the Unthinkable*, p. 82.
83. Quoted in Cockett, p. 82.
84. Cockett, *Thinking the Unthinkable*, p. 83.
85. Jeremy Shearmur, *The Politics of Karl Popper* (London: Routledge, 1988), pp. 102–4.
86. John Jewkes, *Ordeal by Planning* (London: Macmillan, 1948), p. vii.
87. Ibid., p. viii.
88. Ibid., p. 9.
89. Hartwell, *History of the Mont Pelerin Society*, p. 17.
90. Hayek, 'The historians and the future of Europe', p. 147.
91. F. A. Hayek, 'The intellectuals and socialism', in his *Studies in Philosophy, Politics and Economics* (London: Routledge, 1967), p. 179.
92. Ibid., p. 183.

93. Ibid., p. 194.
94. Ibid., p. 194.
95. Hayek's paper on 'The prospect of freedom', Mont Pelerin Society Archires, quoted in Cockett, *Thinking the Unthinkable*, p. 104.
96. F. A. Hayek, 'The road to serfdom *after* twelve years', in his *Studies in Philosophy, Politics and Economics*, p. 224.
97. Hayek, 'Intellectuals and socialism', p. 194.
98. Hartwell, *History of the Mont Pelerin Society*, p. 24.
99. Quoted in Robert Higgs, 'Fifty years of the Mont Pelerin Society', *Independent Review*, 1: 4 (1997), p. 624.
100. Hartwell, *History of the Mont Pelerin Society*, pp. 45–6.
101. Indeed, Cockett cites the infamous occasion at a later MPS meeting where, 'in a session chaired by Friedman, Mises became so enraged by what he heard that he stormed out, shouting "You're all a bunch of socialists!"'. Cockett acknowledges: 'Tempers coud, and did, become frayed with such combative and opinionated intellectuals as von Mises and his like competing for attention'. See his *Thinking the Unthinkable*, p. 114.
102. Hartwell, *History of the Mont Pelerin Society*, p. 40.
103. The Mont Pelerin Society Statement of Aims reprinted in Hartwell, pp. 41–2.
104. F. A. Hayek, 'Opening address of the Mont Pelerin Society', 1 April 1947, reprinted in his *Studies in Philosophy, Politics and Economics*, p. 149.
105. Mont Pelerin Society Statement of Aims, reprinted in Hartwell, pp. 41–2.
106. Hayek, 'Opening address to a conference at Mont Pelerin', p. 151.
107. Higgs, 'Fifty years of the Mont Pelerin Society', p. 625.
108. Quoted in Alan Ebenstein, *Friedrich Hayek: A Biography* (New York: St Martin's Press, 2001), p. 146.
109. Hartwell, *History of Mont Pelerin Society*, p. 192.
110. Ibid., p. 193.
111. Ibid., p. 222.

Chapter 4

Reinventing the liberal agenda

Introduction: Ideas and action

Political figures and think-tanks in Germany, Britain and the United States carried forward the process of liberal reinvention started at Mont Pelerin in the post-war years. The revival of liberalism in intellectual life through the Mont Pelerin Society was accompanied by its slow revival in political life in these three countries. In these national contexts, serious attempts were made by liberal politicians to overcome the 'interventionist chaos of the world today'[1] and to recapture the ideological ground through the creation of a preliminary political agenda. The intellectual interest in liberalism evident at Mont Pelerin became part of a wider liberal counter-movement in Germany, Britain and the United States after 1950, which went beyond the bounds of anything ever envisioned by the society: liberal ideas were disseminated in think-tanks and made accessible to a wider audience; these ideas captured the minds of eminent political figures and thus had a direct bearing on policy discussions; and, ultimately, they created a discourse which shaped the parameters of political debate in the second half of the twentieth century. It was against this background that the term 'neo-liberal' started to be more widely deployed, so as to define a particular shade of opinion within the liberal camp. A conscious attempt was made to articulate and publicise a 'new' strand of liberal ideology in Germany, Britain and the United States in the post-war world. Although this strand of liberalism was not always referred to, in name, as 'neo-liberalism' by those who advocated it, it is termed neo-liberalism in this chapter, to prevent confusion and to distinguish it from the ideas and policies of prevailing liberal creeds.

This chapter explores early neo-liberal movements in national contexts and identifies the networks of intellectuals, politicians and think-tanks that made the restoration of a liberalised market economy a reality in the twentieth century. Its focus is on the mental climate in which political activity occurred. The purpose of the chapter is not to present a simple historical interpretation of the period, but to provide a detailed analysis of the richness of the political movements which came out of Germany, Britain and the United States after 1950 and to assess their significance for transforming and reformulating the nature of liberal ideology in the twentieth century.

The chapter examines, one by one, the growth of early neo-liberal movements in Germany, Britain, and the United States. For Germany, it discusses the nature of 'ordo-liberalism' and chronicles the rise of the Social Market Economy in the 1950s. For Britain, it identifies the 1960s and 1970s as a period in which neo-liberalism became associated with a grassroots opposition movement within the Conservative Party and with the rise of the New Right. Finally, it assesses the impact of neo-conservatism on American political life in the 1970s. The chapter highlights the different policy priorities of neo-liberalism in these three countries: in Germany, neo-liberalism prioritised an anti-monopoly policy for large cartels; in Britain, the focus was on trade unions and monopolies of labour, whilst in the United States emphasis was placed on welfare and on the size of government. The chapter argues that, while neo-liberal movements in these three countries may have disagreed on many issues, they were united in their contempt for the collectivist left and in the support for the free market and competition. Indeed the original ideas of neo-liberalism were not based on some party's political manifesto, but on philosophical views about the proper working of an economic system and on the analysis of economic systems, past and present. This situation points out that there was, therefore, a significant transfer of ideas between the countries. A vast network developed comprising intellectuals, economists, journalists, and politicians – not just in individual countries, but also between countries dedicated to the reinvention of the liberal agenda.

Germany: The social market economy

Ordo-liberalism and economic order

Neo-liberalism in Germany has its origins in the Freiburg School of liberal economists. Like its neighbouring Austrian School, the Freiburg School, being concerned with the effects of state intervention, monopolies and trade union power on prices, wages and employment, defended the liberal tradition against nationalist and Marxist heresies. The ordo-liberals, Walter Eucken, Wilhelm Röpke, Alexander Rüstow and Franz Böhm, in a series of articles and statements published between the 1920s and 1940s, championed a return to the liberal values of an earlier age. They saw the cause of dictatorship in Germany in the betrayal of liberal values – both political and economic. Germany, they claimed, would have to look back to the liberal traditions of her past – in particular, to the humane principles of the eighteenth-century Enlightenment – in order to discover her future course.[2] The views expressed in these articles were of central significance for setting out the core ideas of German neo-liberalism or ordo-liberalism, and they formed the prehistory of the Social Market Economy.[3] Henry M. Oliver points out that, whilst the 'ordo-group' of German liberals 'may not have agreed completely among themselves when they described their own policies as when they attacked planning, *laissez-faire*, and middle ways, on the whole, agreements and repetition was impressive'.[4] The essence of German neo-liberalism can be located within a particular definition of freedom and relations of power encapsulated in the relationship between the state and the economy. In an article published in 1923, Röpke protested against a definition of German liberalism which identified the state as a night-watchman, a definition, exemplified by Herbert Spencer's notorious tract *Man and Society*. The ordo-liberals not only rejected state intervention and the concentration of economic power in monopolies, trusts and cartels, but also remained hostile to the underlying principles of *laissez-faire* associated with classical liberalism. Manchester liberalism, they claimed, could not provide the answers to Germany's economic problems. Röpke urged the liberals to 'work for the idea of the state and against the lack of freedom in which private economic monopolies – supported by a government leading a shadow existence – keep the economy captive'.[5] In a later statement in 1932, Rüstow called for a 'strong and independent state' which must be 'vigorous . . . independent . . . neutral . . . powerful not by coercion and imperative control, but rather by its authority and leadership'.[6]

German ordo-liberals emphatically addressed the problem of public and private power: totalitarian regimes, they claimed, concentrated power in the hands of a central state, and *laissez-faire* capitalism tended towards private concentrations of power which eventually resulted in political power. Edward Megay, therefore, contends that the neo-liberal project was 'a continuous search for a balancing point between the two'.[7] Rejecting social power and its effects, ordo-liberals argued that individual freedom could only be secured in a *Rechtsstaat* which protected the rights of citizens against the arbitrary use of power by its own executive and private individuals. A. J. Nicholls states that this entailed working out a legislative framework to regulate economic activity, rather than leaving the market to function by itself. Clear rules firmly and fairly set out by an 'enlightened state' would not entail a return to a centrally directed economy, but would provide the necessary framework for the operation of market society.[8]

In 1936, the Freiburg academics Böhm, Eucken and Hans Grossmann-Doerth published a four-volume set of essays entitled *The Economic Order*, which collectively became known as 'The Ordo Manifesto'.[9] The manifesto set out the theoretical basis for the policy ideas of ordo-liberalism adopted by the so-called 'Freiburg Imperative' later, in 1940. According to the manifesto, ordo-liberalism rested on a number of 'constituent principles: perfect (free) competition, primacy of price stability, open markets, private property, freedom to enter into contracts, liability, regularity and predictability of economic policy – and 'regulative principles' – monopoly controls, social equalisation, correction of external effects, correction of anomalous supply restrictions. A new economic order based on these principles was captured in the Freiburg Imperative in 1940. Eucken, Rüstow, Röpke and other like-minded liberals in exile made it clear that the creation of a new 'liberal' economic order after the war would not be achieved by a 'workable market economy alone'; additional organisation was needed. Eucken argued that the new modern economy would have to create an order which is both 'economically efficient' and 'humanly acceptable'. The former would be achieved through the operations of open, competitive markets, the latter through a commitment to the principles of Christianity and to the concept of a 'community of the people'.[10]

Ordo-liberalism's position in relation to the development of neo-liberal ideology is a contentious issue. Some academics, for instance John Gray, see German ordo-liberalism as separate from mainstream economic liberalism and therefore from neo-liberal ideology in general.[11] This interpretation is, however, based on a fundamental misreading of the core tenets of German liberal thought in the 1940s. Ordo-liberals upheld a particular conception of the state, which was not inconsistent with the views of F. A. Hayek and other prominent neo-liberal thinkers of the time. It was not paradoxical that the German ordo-liberals were highly critical of state intervention, but at the same time allocated a substantial role to the state in the preservation of individual liberty. Rüstow distinguished between the weak state and the strong state: the former, he claimed, represented a state without a will of its own, in which interests dominate the management of the economy and which leads to incoherent interventions in the economic process; the latter, a state in which government performs those functions which only it can perform, in view of specific social goals and values. In a programmatic declaration characteristically entitled 'Free Economy – Strong State', Rüstow thus rejected pluralist interpretations of the state and saw the state as a central source of authority, but one that must not interfere in certain areas of economic life; for this is not the sign of a strong state, but 'a sign of lamentable weakness'.[12] It was this combination of features in the state, conceived to be strong but minimal, in order to prevent social excesses and a competitive market system, that formed the basis of the Social Market Economy in post-war Germany and later influenced the ideas behind the New Right in Britain in the 1970s.

Economic organisation in the Federal Republic of Germany

In the Federal Republic of Germany, a powerful social dimension accompanied ordo-liberalism's defence of competition, sound money and the free market. During the three years after the Second World War, Alfred Müller-Armack developed his concept of the Social Market Economy, in an attempt to overcome the antithesis of social progress and free enterprise. The Social Market Economy represented an attempt to define the relationship between commerce and society politically, under the conditions of modern industrial society. There was an implicit moral aspect to this economic system. It aimed to link market freedom and efficiency with a compensatory social system, whilst retaining the maximum degree of individual freedom. As Müller-Armack stated: 'The aim must be to establish a market economy tempered by social safeguards which are consistent with free market principles.'[13] The German ordo-liberals made it explicit that the idea of a Social Market Economy did not entail planning any rational socialistic order. On the contrary, its very premise was consistent with liberal thinking. Many of the ideas behind the Social Market Economy were put forward as part of a comprehensive liberal reform programme of the economy, and two of its principal architects, Eucken and Erhard, were members of the Mont Pelerin Society.[14] Erhard had learned from the experience of Nazism that a 'neo-liberal programme for a free, humane and efficient economic order' would entail 'neither central planning, nor *laissez-faire*, nor short-sighted interventionism'. Instead, he envisioned a 'third way' between the two: a liberal free market economy modified by those measures which could be taken in conformity with market principles.[15]

Other neo-liberals such as Hayek empathised with the need to create a revised liberal system in Germany, but were wary of the implications of the use of the word 'social' to describe such a system. Although Hayek was closely associated with the ordo-liberals, he complained that

> the constitution of the Federal Republic of Germany, instead of adhering to the clear and traditional concept of the *Rechtsstaat*, used the new and ambiguous phrase 'a social *Rechtsstaat*'. I doubt very much whether anyone could really explain what the addition of this adjectival frill is supposed to denote.[16]

For Hayek, the depiction of the market system as 'social' implied the imposition of collective purposes on individual transactions. To emphasise his reservations, however, is to overlook the common ground between his ideas and those of the ordo-liberals: both Hayek and the ordo-liberals started with the same, common and basic, value-judgement (individual liberty), focused on similar subject matters (like competition and social order) and, in principle, arrived at similar policy solutions (such as limited government). Despite their differences, both Hayek and the ordo-liberals shared an uneasiness towards the dominant mainstream economic modelling and proposed 'neo-liberal' alternatives.[17]

Features of the Social Market Economy found their way into German public policy after 1948. In response to the political and economic crisis in the German Federal Republic in 1947 and 1948, in May 1948 Müller-Armack outlined the conditions for the creation of the Social Market Economy, the need for currency reform and for the reduction of the money supply to below 10 percent of its current level being prominent among the initial conditions. Keith Tribe observes that

> he also listed ten social measures which were to be associated with the social market, beginning with the creation of a new participatory enterprise organisation, proceeding through a publicly regulated competition order and the pursuit of anti-monopoly policy in order to forestall possible misuse of power in the economy, provision for the extension of social insurance, and concluding with the need for the securing of individual wages through free wage agreements.[18]

A. J. Nicholls singles out the Currency Reform of June 1948, pioneered by Müller-Armack, as the policy measure responsible for the success of

German economic recovery. The Currency Reform, he claims, marked a return to an ordered relationship between purchasing power, demand, prices and the supply of goods, through a radical reduction of the money supply. For ordo-liberals, the Currency Reform marked a turning point in the future direction of German economy: it restored the price mechanism and 'therefore marked the inception of a new economic programme, a programme which continued in the 1950s with legislation on cartels and monopolies, and participatory democracy in enterprises'.[19]

The Social Market Economy in the 1940s and 1950s also pursued 'social' policy objectives. The ordo-liberals highlighted the primacy of market economics as the basis for social justice. The delivery of social benefits, they claimed, need not itself conflict with the precepts of the Social Market Economy. Jeremy Leaman thus observes that the 'social' in Social Market Economy 'did not mean primarily a policy which would involve a wealth-transferring state apparatus, but rather a policy of competition which would indirectly allow for the formation of private social security funds'.[20] In line with classical liberal thinking, the ordo-liberals argued that extensive state welfare services would lead to a decline in the liberal incentives of individual responsibility and independence. Müller-Armack and Röpke, however, constructed a particular social model, which took a much broader view of the social process than their neo-classical contemporaries. The ordo-liberal school emphasised the importance of competitive markets as a means of efficiently delivering social goods and services as much as of preserving individual freedom from the dangers of coercive devices such as licensing and certification, but recognised that spontaneous individual action could not produce a humane society – some form of intervention would be necessary to make markets work for the good of society. The ordo-liberals' model of the social process began from what they saw as a 'moral position', from which the rules on intervention could be derived. That position was concerned with the specific principles – the moral precepts – that guided systematised intervention in the market process. 'Social balance' could be achieved through the coordination of different spheres of society represented by the market, the state and social groups.[21] The German social policy model in the late 1940s and 1950s was, therefore, very different from that of the Keynesian model in Britain. Specific social policies were pursued – for example, pension policy and the delivery of health care – where decision-making and implementation were carried out not directly by the state, as in Britain, but by citizens' groups or occupational groups. The consequence of such a system in the delivery of policy was that politico-economic pressure groups, such as trade unions, monopolised the decision-making process to the exclusion of other, less powerful or well-organised, groups. Therefore, as Jack Wiseman observes, the system in the end contradicted its liberal incentive – 'the protection of personal freedom of decision'.[22]

There was a significant overlap in the social market system between the ordo-liberals' commitment to social policy and to perfect competition, embodied in the concept of 'state-protected competition'. Nicholls points out that, in his post-war lectures on perfect competition, 'Eucken made it clear that his main answer to social problems lay in the support for competition, which would so increase the nation's wealth that it would render other forms of social welfare superfluous'.[23] In its present state, however, the ring of the competitive market was hindered by monopolies and unfair trading practices. At the heart of the ordo school's rejection of *laissez-faire* was its view that markets were capable of spontaneously producing monopolies and cartels which posed as much threat to individual freedom as direct state control. The prohibition of cartels was, therefore, the *sine qua non* of serious reform. The state that Eucken, Rüstow and Erhard argued for would have to play a 'protective' role in the preservation of competition, enforcing rules which prevented unscrupulous companies from manipulating the market. In February 1947, Erhard established a decartelisation committee which 'demanded laws to regulate cartels, but not to ban them altogether'. It did, however, pronounce in favour of 'a fundamental set of principles for the German economy based on achievement and the principles of competition'.[24] The most effective way of dealing with cartels, the committee concluded, was to 'remove their legal status'. As Nicholls points out, 'since cartel treaties would then be unenforceable at law, the cartel system would disintegrate'.[25] This policy of 'ordered competition' was consistent with neo-liberalism's commitment to the rule of law and to personal freedom.

Obstacles to the free market

In the late-1950s and 1960s, the German Social Market Economy faced a number of obstacles to the realisation of its liberal programme. The first area of concern was the potential conflict between Germany's economic recovery and its membership in the European Community. In the late 1950s, the ordo-liberals became wary of the pace at which European integration was proceeding and of Germany's involvement in the Common

Market. While Germany's participation in the EEC had many advantages from a neo-liberal point of view, the ordo-liberals and their academic supporters in the Mont Pelerin Society viewed the restricted nature of the Common Market as a grave disadvantage to Germany's economic development. They favoured the largest free trade area that was possible. Nicholls comments: 'They wanted the economic integration of the Western world as a whole, including Britain and the USA, and they wanted this to be achieved by lowering tariffs, establishing convertible currencies, and breaking down other commercial barriers.'[26] Röpke and Erhard made well known their objections to the terms of the European Community at the Messina conference in 1956. German interests, they argued, would not necessarily be secured by forging ahead with the creation of a European economic union. In direct opposition to the Federal Chancellor, Konrad Adenauer, Erhard maintained that '[e]rrors and sins against the economy are not made good by proclaiming them to be European'.[27] He argued that Germany could only achieve her political objectives by collaborating with both Britain and the United States.

Neo-liberals' uneasiness over the future direction of the EEC continued into the 1960s. They argued that the proper way to integrate Europe was not through 'supranational interventionism', but rather through all the participating countries' adoption of free trade policies and freely convertible currencies. Thus they attacked the proposals of the European Commission in 1962 for the long-term planning of the economic development of the European Community. Erhard argued that economic planning for the long term never worked in practice – 'it only led to a dangerous dependence on planning bureaucracies which were incapable of appreciating the human factor in the economy'. What was needed, he maintained, was a 'common understanding' of the ways in which free competition could be realised throughout the community, rather than central direction from Brussels.[28] The ordo-liberals also rallied against what they saw as other illiberal aspects of the EC, including President De Gaulle's veto of British membership of the EC 1963, and the Common Agricultural Policy which, according to Röpke, had developed into 'the most grotesque system of price-fixing, subsidies, and artificial purchasing arrangements that had ever been created in a modern industrial economy'.[29]

The German ordo-liberals also faced obstacles to the realisation of their free-market programme within the Federal Republic. In the 1960s there was a general shift in the definition of the Social Market Economy within the West German establishment. Norman Barry notes that, as the German system developed, it was the 'social' element that began to predominate over the 'market', and throughout the 1960s the country began to resemble a Scandinavian welfare state, to which its original liberal theorists had originally been vehemently opposed.[30]

The original intention of the German neo-liberals was not to create an egalitarian system of redistribution and free provision for all, but to develop an efficient and successful market economy with a social dimension – a limited safety net for the very poor – through which all individuals would benefit from an increase in the gross national product of the country through competition. The hostility of policy-makers to this 'liberal' model in the 1960s and after was reflected in a number of social measures pioneered by the Social Democrats and the labour and Roman Catholic 'social' wing of the Christian Democratic Union: substantial increases in unemployment pay and sick leave, the extension of the Bismarkian state-pension scheme and the establishment of a system of universal and life-long public education. These measures were blatantly incompatible with original neo-liberal principles.[31] Voices were subsequently raised in doubt as to whether ordo-liberalism could survive in the face of such increased state participation and bureaucratic direction. The social democrats and Christian democrats argued that Germany still possessed a Social Market Economy – an economy coordinated by competition, but private benefits would no longer equal common utility.[32]

BRITAIN: RETRIEVING LIBERAL INDIVIDUALISM

Against the consensus

In contrast with Germany, liberal economic thought in British political life in the 1950s went into eclipse. Britain had not experienced the collapse into totalitarianism that Germany had, and hence there was no urgency to sustain a unified liberal movement during and after the war, as there was in Germany. Three separate publications dominated anti-collectivist thought in Britain in the immediate post-war years: Hayek's *Road to Serfdom*, John Jewkes's *Ordeal by Planning* and Michael Oakeshott's essay 'The political economy of freedom'. As the previous chapter has demonstrated, these publications directed their criticisms of planned economies at the post-war labour government's attempt to create a new form of society. In particular, Oakeshott's important essay, 'The political economy of freedom', published in 1949, identified the tendencies in modern British politics that where undermining the traditional liberal order. In his essay, Oakeshott presented an account of the corrosion, through rationalist error, of the traditional understanding of conservative government and of its offspring, modern collectivism. The role of government, he maintained, was not to direct private individuals and impose beliefs upon them; rather it was, simply, to rule. Ruling, for Oakeshott, implied a limited role of making and administering laws, and overseeing political life without directly participating in it. Oakeshott urged British conservatives to regain their belief in the tradition of a free society and the rule of law, which had dominated British politics for much of the eighteenth and nineteenth centuries.[33]

The majority in the British Conservative Party in the immediate post-war years, however, failed to acknowledge the liberal–conservative thinking represented by Hayek, Jewkes and Oakeshott, and sustained a belief in 'Butskellism'. As Barry comments, '[t]he Conservative Party, under the influence of R. A. Butler, seemed anxious to shed as much of its association with *laissez-faire* as possible, and to act merely as a moderating force against the growth of interventionism'.[34] The policy agenda of the conservative government of 1951 did not stick rigidly to Labour's consensus programme – emphasis was laid on reductions in taxation and on property ownership, many of the regulations imposed on private enterprises were ended, and there was a reduction in public expenditure in proportion to gross national product.[35] This was, however, a long way from the neo-liberal policy agenda being pursued in the Federal Republic of Germany. In comparison with Germany, all British political parties remained remarkably anti-market in various degrees. Indeed, some post-war conservative leaders, most notably Harold Macmillan and, to some extent, Anthony Eden, were critical of the *laissez-faire* policies of classical liberalism and sought to move the party towards a revised form of conservatism. The aim was not to supplant capitalism, but rather to use the state in a positive way, so as to provide a 'planned capitalism', as Macmillan put it in his *Middle Way* published in the 1938, within which private enterprise could flourish.[36] It was during the Macmillan government (1957–63) that the foundations of the British corporatist state were laid. While Germany had abandoned its corporatist past, Britain by the 1960s had started to embrace a 'corporatist mentality' in favour of close relations between organised labour, powerful interest groups, big business and government, and in 1961 the National Economic Development Council was initiated.[37]

There were, however, at the grassroots level of the party, voices dissenting from Macmillan's vision of a new capitalism. There was a back-bench neo-liberal critique of the government's control of the economy, in particular its relations with industry. Enoch Powell sustained, perhaps, the most powerful opposition to state aid in industry. He stated:

> Consistent vigilance is necessary if we are not to slip from one industry to another, into a position where it is the government that takes the vital decisions on development and investment, thereby lifting these decisions entirely out of the plane of the free economy.[38]

Similarly, Nigel Birch and Peter Thorneycroft, both of whom, along with Powell, resigned from the Treasury over public expenditure in 1958, argued that governmental intervention in the economy deprived individuals of the power to make decisions for themselves. Two prominent Conservative Party groups shared these concerns: the One Nation Group, a group of post-war conservatives meeting to formulate policy suggestions, and the Bow Group, a gathering of younger party members largely from the Cambridge University Conservative Association. Neither of these groups was purely neo-liberal in orientation, but they did display, from their formation in 1950 and 1951 respectively, a willingness to stand against the Conservative Party's 'compromise' with socialism and to argue in favour of a revised conservatism that respected the free economy. The One Nation Group was a heterodox group of MPs which included among its members Enoch Powell, Edward Heath, Angus Maude, Robert Carr and Keith Joseph, who maintained that private enterprise and voluntary services were essential for prosperity.[39] The Bow Group pursued a similar line of reasoning and was at one with the One Nation Group in its attempts to create an 'Intelligent Conservatism'.[40] Among its early members were Geoffrey Howe and Russell Lewis, both of whom had been influenced in their political opinions by the works of prominent members of the Mont Pelerin Society – Hayek, Karl Popper and Lionel Robbins. Influenced by Erhard's economic reform programme in West Germany, the main focus of the Bow Group's policy ideas was on the modernisation of the economy with regard to promoting free trade, containing government expenditure and increasing industrial productivity.

Another non-party organisation, the Institute of Economic Affairs (IEA), shadowed the thinking of many of the members of the One Nation and Bow Groups. The IEA was founded by Antony Fisher in 1955 as a think-tank for free market philosophy. The Directors of the IEA, Ralph Harris and Arthur Seldon, were united with discontented Conservative Party members in their opposition to the prevailing fashion in collectivist thought. They opposed not just the ideological consensus within the main political parties in Britain, but also what they saw as a 'collectivist bias' in the economics departments of British universities, and what was a widespread recognition of collectivist ideas of vocal economists such as Andrew Shonfield and Michael Shanks.[41] Harris and Seldon argued that the Keynesian consensus was based on macro-economic distortions, and they launched they their own attack on the Macmillan government. In 1959, the IEA produced a set of essays entitled *Not Unanimous*, in which it criticised the Radcliffe Report on the credit and money system in a quasi-monetarist fashion, and endorsed general liberal propensities towards individual freedom. The IEA, Harris claimed, would have to follow 'the path of radical reaction' in order to preserve a free society.[42] Indeed, Maurice Cowling comments that '[i]n the 1960s the IEA was radical in the way in which *Mill and Liberalism* was radical: it wanted to blow up the consensus . . . the collectivist consensus about economic policy'.[43] In the early 1960s, however, the IEA's influence was marginal; it was not until the late 1960s and 1970s that the IEA came to exert a considerable influence over the formation of New Right ideology.

Ideological renewal

There was a conscious change of ideological direction in the Conservative Party after the 1964 election defeat. A neo-liberal ideological current that had been germinating at the grassroots level of the party during the Macmillan years came to the fore during the early 1960s, and influenced the remaking of conservative economic policy under Edward Heath. Indeed, Brendan Evans and Andrew Taylor observe that '[n]eo-liberal ideas were dominant in policy areas – taxation, public spending, and union reform – which were central to Heath's recasting of conservative doctrine after 1965'.[44] In particular, Heath's commitment to a programme of economic modernisation gave the Bow Group and the One Nation Group an opportunity to put their ideas into practice. What was known as 'competition policy' was outlined in the document *Putting Britain Right Ahead*. It included proposals for the modernisation of the economy that were consistent with neo-liberal thinking – the reform of industrial relations, the reshaping of social services to ensure that resources only go to those mostly in need, increased investment in industry and a rigorous check on public expenditure levels.[45] The ideological challenge by the Right of the Conservative Party in 1960s, however, 'lacked real unity'. While neo-liberals at the grassroots level of the party may have long campaigned for lower taxes, less intervention and trade union reform, Andrew Gamble argues that there was no single theme 'to orchestrate all the dissent forces in the party'; there were 'no well-defined economic interests'.[46] Nor was there widespread support at the leadership level of the party for neo-liberal ideas. The leadership of the party, concerned with maintaining political support, resisted the Right's challenge to the consensus. However, as Gamble contends, 'the electoral perspective they [Heath and his supporters] espoused underwent substantial change as a result of the constant ideological pressure from the Right', reflected in Heath's proposals for competition policy.[47]

The resurrection of an interest in micro-economics among rank-and-file members of the Conservative Party was influenced by the economic arguments of the IEA. The IEA had little confidence in Heath's economic conversion after 1964 and put forward its own case for a critical examination of the consensus. The two most important areas to be addressed, as far as the IEA was concerned, were trade unions and monetary stability – the two areas Hayek had originally stressed as important for the preservation of a market society during the opening address at Mont Pelerin in 1947. During the mid-1960s and after, these issues were pushed to the forefront of the IEA's policy concerns. The IEA argued that powerful trade unions were detrimental not only to the functioning of the market economy by lowering industrial productivity and thus preventing competition in world markets, but also to their members' interests, because they hindered the mobility of labour. Hayek's persuasive critique of trade union power, in his *Tiger by the Tail*, published through the IEA, argued that a return to market economics was possible only if the labour market was made more flexible by curbing the monopoly position held by privileged trade unions in Britain. For Hayek, it was not so much mismanaged monetary policy that was responsible for defects in the market system, as it was union strength. The 'chief obstacle to the functioning of the price mechanism', he wrote, 'is trade union power'.[48] Here Hayek was at variance with the views of Milton Friedman and other exponents of monetary economics. Friedman delivered his Wincott lecture 'Counter-revolution in monetary stability' to the IEA in 1970 against a background of rising inflation. In the paper, Friedman argued that

> A steady rate of monetary growth at a moderate level can provide a framework under which a country can have little inflation and much growth. It will not produce perfect stability . . . but it can make an important contribution to a stable economic society.[49]

Friedman's contribution to the debate was significant for neo-liberalism in Britain, as it represented a different strand of the ideology imported from the United States that would have a fundamental impact on policy measures in the early 1980s.

The neo-liberal critics

There was a definite upsurge in neo-liberal ideas in Britain after 1965. This movement away from the 'socialism' of the consensus is reflected in the economic opinions of several influential Conservative Party members. Enoch Powell was, perhaps, the most ardent critic of economic norms and conservative policy leading up to the 1966 general election. During the 1960s, Powell became an apostle of free market conservatism, and he 'drew on the IEA for intellectual sustenance and support'.[50] Powell made the case for a policy of complete de-nationalisation, campaigned for a drastic reduction in the level of income tax and the size of the state sector, highlighted the evils of syndicalism and rejected out of hand most forms of economic interventionism. The state must, of course, argued Powell, have certain responsibilities. He saw the state as having two general modes of operation: 'government by specific prescription' and 'government by the maintenance of a spontaneous or automatic system of decision'. In areas such as defense and the maintenance of law and order, Powell argued that the state should act with intention; in economic matters, Powell adopted a Hayekian argument on the inadequate supply of information held by the state and made the case for the market mechanism as the only viable alternative to socialism. The market, P. Douglas and Powell claimed, promoted economic efficiency, acted as a means of distributing power by de-centralising decision-making and ensured the freedom of individuals.[51]

It is the last of these beneficial outcomes of competitive markets that was to become the motivating force behind Powell's faith in the capitalist system. In his *Saving in a Free Society*, published by the IEA in 1960, he used the terms 'free economy' and 'free society' interchangeably. He stated clearly that capitalism had on its side 'the powerful emotive idea of freedom'.[52] The capitalist system, he maintained, was the most effective system for pursuing the public interest, and the overriding theme throughout his speeches became the contempt shown by the state for individual freedom. The Conservative Party, which had sometimes in its history pursued authority, declared Powell, must challenge the socialist state and become the champion of liberty. Powell's right-wing economic views made him somewhat of a 'maverick' in the Conservative Party in the 1960s and gained him the support of a small group of enthusiastic MPs, as well as of small businessmen and shopkeepers in his native West Midlands.[53] The Conservative Party leadership, however, especially Heath, turned their backs on what became known as 'Powellism'. Cockett points out that '"Powellism" became a dirty word among the Conservative Party leadership, and his brand of economic liberalism was irredeemably besmirched'.[54]

The election defeat of 1964 and the growing economic crisis during the 1960s made other conservative politicians become disillusioned with the party and seek guidance. The most notable of these was Keith Joseph, who came to prominence in the late 1960s. John Ranelagh states that Joseph 'saw himself as picking up the baton that Powell had dropped'.[55] Like Powell and other neo-liberals in the Conservative Party, Joseph was critical not just of the increases in state control following the war, but, more fundamentally, of 'the belief in the efficiency, indeed the omnicompetence of state intervention'.[56] Joseph rallied against the ideas underpinning the social democratic consensus, and proposed that the Right should adopt an alternative and distinctive economic model. Joseph favoured the 'free economy – strong state' model of economic organisation pioneered by the ordo-liberals in Germany after 1945, with its prioritisation of liberty over democracy, law over bureaucracy and the market over planning.[57] In 1975, the free market think-tank, the Centre for Policy Studies (CPS) created by Joseph himself, made its first publication: Joseph's *Why Britain Needs a Social Market Economy*. In the pamphlet Joseph explained how he had founded the CPS, 'to survey the scope for replacing increasingly interventionist government by social market policies'.[58] For Joseph, the meaning of the term 'social market' was the same as it was for Müller-Armack and Erhard in West Germany:

> A socially responsible market economy is perfectly compatible with the promotion of a more compassionate society . . . Industry alone creates wealth which pays for social welfare . . . Government intervention is justified *only* where it is designed to limit market distortions such as abuse of monopoly power or restrictive practices.[59]

During the late 1960s Joseph developed many of the ideas later set out in his CPS publications. Together with Powell and Geoffrey Howe, he formed an alliance with the IEA, re-educating himself in market economics. In the run-up to the 1970 general election, Joseph presented his ideas to the party leader Edward Heath. He shared Heath's 'modernising' vision and made the case for a social market economy in Britain. Thus Heath's election victory in 1970 raised hopes among neo-liberal conservatives that the new government's policy priorities would radically break those of the Buskellite middle way. However, within eighteen months the Heath government had rejected free-market policies, awarding substantial handouts to 'lame duck' firms and industries, taking the bulk of Rolls Royce into public ownership, and boosting consumer demand in response to rising unemployment, in a neo-Keynesian manner.

The IEA was first to publish a book criticising the government's performance. Its *Government and the Market Economy* by Samuel Brittan, published in 1971, put forward the case for alternative approaches to policy, arguing for strict monetary disciplines to counter the inflationary consequences of the 'Barber boom', the privatisation of state industries, and the development of private alternatives to the state provision of pensions, health and education. Brittan declared that the IEA 'provided an alternative focus which has become a sort of an anti-establishment'.[60] The IEA launched another attack in 1975. Its *British Economic Policy: Two Views*, by Ralph Harris and Brendon Sewill, attacked the inflationary legacy of the Heath government. Harris and Sewill pleaded with 'British politicians in government and oppositions to preserve (Milton) Friedman's golden rule of moderate, steady monetary expansion' as a means of controlling inflation and of providing a framework for steady economic growth.[61]

After the 1974 election defeat, Joseph, Howe and Margaret Thatcher became part of the 'anti-establishment' movement described by Brittan. The CPS, under the directorship of Alfred Sherman, became the focal point of their efforts to convert the Conservative Party to the ideology of neo-liberalism. Cockett points out that, unlike the IEA, which, like Mont Pelerin, was purely a forum for ideas, the CPS was 'self-consciously a political institute designed to articulate in political terms what the IEA had been thinking'.[62] The CPS sought to find political solutions to the problems encountered by the Heath government during its 'supposedly "free-market"' phase in 1970–1. As Cockett explains, Joseph and Thatcher saw no problems with the ideas of the administration, it was 'the political application' of the ideas 'to the real economy that had not been thought through'. Thus the CPS cannot be labelled a 'think-tank' in the strict sense – the thinking had already been done; the task of the CPS was to 'change peoples' minds'.[63] Indeed, Joseph and Thatcher saw the CPS purely as a means of changing the 'climate of opinion' both in inside and outside of the Conservative Party in favour what the Fabians had first identified as the ideas of the 'New Right'. The role of the Conservative Party would be to draw on the CPS 'to show the weakness of socialism' and 'reverse the trend'; 'it should be moving ahead and moulding opinion to prepare it for more radical measures'.[64]

In 1974, Joseph embarked on a number of well-publicised speeches in which he contrasted the free-market economic model with Soviet central planning. Andrew Denham and Mark Garnett point out that 'he tended to speak as if the British and continental compromise of a "mixed economy" were no longer an option'.[65] In his famous Preston Speech, Joseph pioneered his 'new conservatism'. In the speech, Joseph repudiated the post-war commitment to full employment and the welfare state, and argued that monetary control and the free-market economy were essential preconditions to Britain's economic recovery. He spelt out the relation between the money supply, inflation and unemployment, arguing that 'spending by the government and the subsidised employment of labour divorced from its economic function might temporarily relieve "symptoms" but could not eliminate the "cause" of Britain's illness'.[66] The message was stark: Britain was 'over-governed, over-spent, over-taxed, over-borrowed and over-manned'. Monetarism, Joseph however explained, was not enough. Britain at the same time needed to abandon its 'socialist anti-enterprise climate', the 'indifference, ignorance and distaste on the part of politicians, civil servants and communicators for the processes of wealth creation and entrepreneurship'.[67] By 'taxation, inflation, the remorseless flood of regulations and legislation', and by 'constant and arbitrary interventions', governments since the war, he claimed, had 'destroyed the rewards that once made risk-taking worthwhile'. Without entrepreneurship and wealth creation, Joseph argued that the welfare state could not be sustained. He thus made the case for an 'enterprise culture' driven by the incentive for profit.[68]

Joseph's brand of conservatism opened up the economic liberalism versus state intervention debate in the Conservative Party that paved the way for the 'Thatcherite Revolution' after 1975. His critique of the Heathite commitment to post-war conservatism led to a wider recognition that, with the decline of the post-war economic boom, economic policies based on consensus politics were no longer effective in overcoming Britain's economic problems. Joseph pioneered an alternative conservative ideology, based on the beneficial outcomes of the free market, the principle of sound money supply and a reduction in state intervention, which offered a 'new direction' for the party following the election of Thatcher as leader in 1975. While there may have been nothing particularly original about Joseph's conservatism, he managed to popularise ideas within his own party that were deemed 'politically impossible' and to construct a policy framework for the future in favour of neo-liberalism.

THE UNITED STATES: CONSERVATIVE CAPITALISM

The Great Society and its discontents

After the Second World War, the federal government played a central role in boosting the American economy and in solving social and economic ills. Economic prosperity reaffirmed the liberals' belief in the ability of a compensatory state to boost capitalism and mitigate social inequalities. Liberal activists such as Arthur Schlesinger and John Kenneth Galbraith pioneered their vision of 'qualitative liberalism'. They made an eloquent case for increased public services and a redistribution of wealth. In his *The Affluent Society*, Galbraith contended that, unless the government actively directed a larger and larger share of America's economic prosperity, society would literally choke on its own affluence.[69] Remedying this contrast between private wealth and public poverty became the incentive behind the Great Society programme pursued by liberal policy-makers in the late 1950s and 1960s. The Great Society programme was a logical product of post-war liberal orthodoxy. Although the programme never proposed the kind of sweeping reforms Galbraith envisioned, it was founded on the belief that the war on poverty could be won if government intervened to expand social security, provide health services to the poor and elderly and pour federal funds into education and housing. The creation of an 'equal opportunity welfare state' under Lyndon B. Johnson's administration of 1964 was the 'most far-reaching domestic reform programme since the New Deal'. It was not Johnson's intention to eliminate poverty directly through government measures, but to encourage incentives for the poor to lift themselves into the social and economic mainstream. The Great Society, Johnson proclaimed, would enable individuals to move beyond the 'progressive freedom' encapsulated in Roosevelt's New Deal, and to pursue other forms of freedom – 'freedom to learn', 'freedom to grow', 'freedom to hope', 'freedom to live as people want to live'.[70]

Traditional American liberals, however, did not share the vocabulary of the progressive liberals associated with the late New Deal and Great Society. The idea of a socially conscious interventionist state, they claimed, overrode the most fundamental form of human freedom, economic freedom: de-centralised political power, limited government and a free-market economy. Therefore American intellectuals supportive of the anti-statist tradition of nineteenth-century liberalism increasingly turned away from the term 'liberal', preferring the term 'conservative' or 'neo-conservative' (taken in a liberal individualist sense) or, in extreme cases, 'libertarian', to describe their belief systems.[71] Yet the adoption of these labels does not necessarily equate with a pure neo-liberal ideological stance. Certainly, there are close affinities between neo-liberalism and many of the central tenets of neo-conservatism for example, but this crossover does not automatically make all neo-conservatives neo-liberals. Rather, it is argued that, whilst American conservatism is a much broader movement than neo-liberalism, there are important currents of that ideology that align it with neo-liberalism. Some neo-liberal intellectuals were, however, critical of the use of the term 'conservative' to describe what they perceived as essentially a 'liberal' movement. For instance, Hayek in 1956 exclaimed, 'I am still puzzled' that American conservatives have allowed 'the left' to control the definition of liberty, 'this almost indispensable term'.[72] Whilst traditional American liberals may have adopted the conservative label, ideologically their political programme was rooted in the central tenets of classical liberalism. As Alan Brinkley proclaims: 'To be an American conservative, it is necessary to reassert liberalism.'[73]

It was not until the immediate years after the Second World War, when it moved towards the shoreline of the Right, that conservatism gained some recognition as a major intellectual and political force. Indeed, George Nash points out that, until at least 1945,

> no articulate, co-ordinated, self-consciously conservative intellectual force existed in America. There were, at most, scattered voices of protest, profoundly pessimistic about the future of their country. Not until the post-war era did large numbers of conservatives manage to articulate a serious and important critique of liberal culture.[74]

What has been referred to as a 'counter-establishment'[75] movement, composed of rebellious insurgents, rose up to confront the 'end of ideology' thesis heralded by liberal intellectuals.[76] This movement stood in opposition to many of the basic premises of modernity, which were centred on the modern welfare state that had prevailed in American society since the New Deal in the 1930s. For some conservative intellectuals, there was no such thing as 'the end of ideology'. On the contrary, the dominance of liberal ideology in the post-war years was being challenged by what the right-wing columnist Patrick Buchanan labelled a 'conservative counter-reformation', preparing to transform its vision of a conservative society into the ruling orthodoxy.[77]

In the United States, the spread of neo-liberal ideas in the post-war years was largely a result of campaigns carried out by organisations and think-tanks and of the publications of dedicated conservative journals. In the 1950s, American conservatism became associated with the beliefs of the John Birch Society, which was dedicated to restoring and preserving individual freedom under the Constitution. Although its activities were primarily orientated towards an anti-communist campaign, the society also leaned towards neo-liberalism in its political agenda. It was one of the first organisations to launch a sustained attack on the central economic features of the late New Deal state – government intervention, high taxes and unbalanced budgets. This form of economic organisation, it argued, went hand-in-hand with communist rule and, in effect, would lead to the gradual death of capitalism and of the economic power to resist. The John Birch Society opened numerous right-wing bookstores and worked with schools, churches and local communities to roll back the liberal gains that, in its eyes, threatened the nation. Lisa McGirr attributes a central role to the society in the development of post-war conservatism: 'No organisation', she writes, 'was more important in channelling grassroots fears of liberalism than the John Birch Society, whose resources and inspiration were crucial to right-wing mobilization.'[78]

A number of important journals and magazines, suspicious of federal control, attempted to formulate a cohesive set of conservative ideas and policies. One of the most influential conservative journals to come out in the 1950s was the *National Review*, founded by William F. Buckley's in 1955. Its first issue summed up the basic mien of American conservatism: 'It stands athwart history, yelling Stop, at a time no one is inclined to do so, or to have much patience with those who so urge it.'[79] Buckley and his fellow editors at the *National Review* became representatives of the new, fusionist American right: they stood for the free market, aggressive anti-communism, as well as traditional conservative Christian values. The journal, and more specifically Buckley himself, published some of the most radical polemics against the Left in the late 1950s and early 1960s, and became one of the most important sources of ideas for conservative intellectual revival in the decades that followed. Similar journals appeared in the forthcoming years. Russell Kirk followed Buckley's *National Review* in 1957 with the more scholarly journal *Modern Age*. The intention of the journal was to 'forthrightly oppose political collectivism, social decadence, and effeminacy'.[80] Similarly, Irving Kristol's *The Public Interest*, founded in 1965, took a neo-conservative approach to policy issues. It was Buckley's journal, however, that provided American conservatives of all political persuasions with a political goal and a vision worth fighting for, at a time when they needed it most.[81]

While Buckley may have successfully reconciled the various strands of conservative thought, for other members of the new American Right there was only one ideology with which to distinguish their ideas from those associated with the Great Society – neo-liberalism. At the heart of the new American right was a hostility towards the modern liberal state which was shared by all conservatives, but for neo-liberals or 'conservative libertarians' the basis for this opposition was clear: only the market was capable of embodying individual freedom through competition. As in Britain, the leading advocate of neo-liberal ideas in the immediate post-war years, in the United States too, was Hayek. Blumenthal comments that 'Hayek's American appeal lay mostly in his advocacy of what appeared to be the old-fashioned native virtues of hard work and individualism', which made his *Road to Serfdom* a popular success when it was first published in America.[82] Another member of the Austrian School, Ludwig von Mises, was also vitally important in the revival of classical liberal ideas in the United States. Mises emigrated to America in 1940 and published his rendering of free-market doctrine, *Human Action – A Treatise in Economics*, in 1949; it struck a responsive note amongst conservative intellectuals. The views of the Austrian School reinforced the traditional liberal principles, from American history, of minimal government and of the free exercise of property rights. Both Hayek and Mises were critical of the Great Society programme on economic grounds. They saw private ownership as an absolute, and thus the liberal state's redistribution of property through taxation as a form of socialism. Political freedom, they claimed, was impossible without economic freedom: a free market and a free society were corollaries.

A number of American economists, especially at the Chicago School, were sympathetic to the 'liberal' ideas of Hayek and Mises. One economist, in particular – Milton Friedman – became associated with neo-liberalism in the United States. Like Hayek, Friedman never regarded himself as a conservative. 'I'm not a conservative', he averred, 'I'm a liberal in the traditional sense.'[83] Where Friedman and the Chicago School's neo-liberalism went further than Hayek and Mises was in their application of an ultra-free-market ideological stance to practical policy. Friedman's writings adopted a classical free-market position through a specific means, money. During the

1950s, he constructed a vast critique of monetary policy and its effect on the Great Depression. In his *A Monetary History of America: 1867–1960*, Friedman argued that the massive cut in the money supply engineered by the Federal Reserve between 1929 and 1933 produced a deflation which was the immediate cause of the Depression.[84] In his *Capitalism and Freedom* he recommended a liberal economic approach to monetary policy. In order to avoid the dangers of inflation and deflation, Friedman claimed that it was necessary to limit the money supply by a fixed rule, as determined by increases in production. In his theory of monetary policy, Friedman explicitly rejected the Keynesian 'trade-off' between inflation and employment. Following the monetarist approach of Irving Fisher, a Yale economics professor, Friedman pioneered the idea that, by regulating the money supply, the Federal Reserve could stifle inflation, reduce unemployment, liberate markets and produce prosperity.[85] Although other free-market economists before Friedman had developed monetary theory, Cockett points out that 'it was Friedman who had done the empirical work linking the history of inflation to the money supply in America, and who became the monetarists' most energetic and enthusiastic spokesman'. At the time Friedman was writing, inflation was the most serious economic problem facing Western nations, so 'his arguments were peculiarly relevant to the circumstances of the era'.[86] He was, as Blumenthal put it, 'a one man think-tank'.[87]

Freidman and other sympathisers of the new American right were active members of a number of free-market think-tanks, such as the American Enterprise Institute (AEI) and later, in the 1970s, the Hoover Institute and Heritage Foundation. The AEI was the first free-market think-tank to emerge during the dark years of conservatism in the 1940s. The AEI, in many ways, paralleled the IEA in Britain. Like Anthony Fisher and the founding of the IEA, the AEI (then the American Enterprise Association) was created by Lewis H. Brown in 1943, an entrepreneur of ideas, who wished to restore free-market economics in the aftermath of the New Deal. His aim was to gather together conservative intellectuals to turn ideology into power. The AEI was designed to be an advisory body for conservative republicans, the way the Brookings Institute had been for liberal democrats. It was, during its early years, a small and obscure foundation, but one at the heart of conservative politics in Washington, which counted among its fellows Friedman, Irving Kristol, Michael Novak, Herbert Stein and Ben Wattenberg.[88] It was not until 1964, during the Goldwater presidential campaign, that the AEI had its first real opportunity to stand up and be acknowledged as a leading exponent of neo-liberal ideas.[89]

Goldwater and the turn to the Right

The presidential campaign in 1964 of Senator Barry Goldwater, the republican presidential candidate and arch-conservative, marked a milestone in the resurgence of American conservatism. For the first time the ideas of the new American Right were given a political platform. The nomination of Goldwater as a presidential candidate not only signalled a move towards the Right in American political life, but also a substantial shift in Republican Party ideology, away from an era of Eisenhower liberal republicanism towards a new age of radical conservatism. In his *Conscience of a Conservative*, published in 1960, Goldwater expressed an 'extreme' conservative view that shared many similarities with that of neo-liberalism. The book, which sold over three million copies, represented, for Goldwater and his followers, a 'new testament', which 'contained the core beliefs of our political faith'.[90] Reiterating many of the central arguments of Hayek's *Road to Serfdom*, Goldwater contended that the 'Leviathan' of federal government had destroyed individual autonomy by enforcing 'confiscatory' income tax on private individuals and by encouraging reliance on state assistance, and thus served as the thin end of the wedge for socialism. He dismissed the claims made by the democrats that conservatism was a defunct ideology and insisted that conservative principles were fundamental 'spiritual' truths. As he exclaimed: 'Conservatism, we are told, is out-of-date. The charge is preposterous . . . The laws of God and of nature have no dateline.'[91] A network of 'Goldwaterites' set the tone for the uncompromising ideological direction of the presidential campaign. Among Goldwater's intellectual army was Milton Friedman, acting as his economic adviser. Friedman, backed by other free-market economists such as George Stigler, championed the idea of a negative income-tax plan, which proposed to replace government 'handouts' with a compensatory basic allowance for the poor.[92] William Baroody, director of the AEI, was in charge of policy suggestions. Baroody had planned Goldwater's presidential bid and during the campaign acted as his senior political advisor. Under Baroody's urging, the AEI assumed control of policy issues and speechwriting.[93] William F. Buckley advised Goldwater through the pages of the *National Review*, and the journal's publisher, William Rusher, organised a conservative network of young republicans known as 'The Syndicate' to campaign on his behalf. Finally, Ronald Reagan made a 'dramatic entrance' into Republican Party politics in 1964, with a 'rousing' television speech in support of Goldwater's presidential candidacy.[94]

The themes of the Goldwater presidential campaign were twofold – one neo-liberal, an attack upon 'Big Government', and one neo-conservative, a militant attitude towards communism. The neo-liberal theme of the campaign was accompanied by a radical policy agenda. Goldwater's agenda championed the expansion of free enterprise and competition, and a drastic reduction in federal control. One area of policy, in particular, was a source of contention between the parties: welfare. Goldwater had long held an unmitigating hostility towards the welfare state. With regard to welfare reform, he explained in his *Conscience of a Conservative*: 'My aim is not to pass new laws, but to repeal them.'[95] During the campaign, Goldwater proposed radical changes to the way the welfare system worked. He advocated the repeal of the Social Security system and its 'drastic tax'.[96] Goldwater called for the substitution of private charity for Social Security, and for the abolition of graduated income tax. The ideological significance of the Goldwater campaign, as Lee Edwards observes, was that, 'for the first time in thirty years, a presidential candidate was challenging the basic assumptions of the welfare state'.[97]

Lyndon B. Johnson's subsequent landslide victory in the presidential elections represented, for many in the Republican Party, a monumental defeat for Goldwater's brand of radical conservatism. As McGirr comments, 'conservatives in 1964 were left with few illusions about the attractiveness of their politics to most of the nation's voters'.[98] However, in other ways, the Goldwater campaign had many other, more positive, implications for the future of American conservatism, and more specifically for neo-liberal ideas. The nomination of Goldwater as the Republican Party candidate represented a substantial ideological victory for the grassroots conservatives in the party and gave them a strong base from which to mobilise support in favour of their policies. These conservative politicians, along with prominent businessmen and national intellectuals, formed a 'brain trust' to 'promote and present the conservative view after the defeat and plan for the future'. The conservative organisation, the John Birch Society, expanded its membership following Goldwater's defeat, as discontented activists joined 'out of frustration from the Goldwater loss'.[99] The most significant outcome of Goldwater's campaign, however, was the rise to national prominence of a largely unknown political activist, Ronald Reagan, after his highly successful televised speech, 'A time for choosing', in support of Goldwater. Only two years after the presidential election, Reagan had picked up Goldwater's mantle and from it constructed his own variant of conservative ideology.

The rise of populist conservatism

After the 1964 debacle, the grassroots supporters of conservatism in the Republican Party became aware of the need to gain wider support for their cause than Goldwater had been able to do. In 1966 a campaign was initiated by Reagan, to win over the democratic voters and other constituencies that had so eluded Goldwater. In his efforts to create a populist conservatism, Reagan appealed to a broad spectrum of political and social groups. Taking advantage of the splits in the Democratic Party, Reagan reached out to rank-and-file democrats and attempted to convert them to conservative republicanism 'as the American way of life'.[100] By the late 1960s, the conservative Right had made important, political gains both in the Republican Party and in the nation. In 1968, however, it was a centrist republican, Richard Nixon, rather than Reagan, who had become the party's presidential nominee and won the election. Unlike Reagan, Nixon was not concerned with creating a new populist brand of conservative ideology, but committed to the resurrection of traditional republicanism. A lot of conservatives were thus distrustful of Nixon's political objectives.[101] Social and regulatory policies pursued by the Nixon administration confirmed their anxieties. Neo-liberals in the Republican Party were critical of Nixon administration's 'regulatory revolution', which, according to Herbert Stein, one of Nixon's economic advisors, 'probably imposed more new regulation on the economy than in any other presidency since the New Deal'.[102]

Nixon's approach to economic policy, in particular his policy response to the problem of inflation, was an even bigger source of consternation for republican neo-liberals. Steven Hayward recalls how, on inauguration day in January 1969, Nixon 'tacitly endorsed the Keynesian premise with the only sentence in his inaugural address that mentioned the economy: 'We have learned at last to manage a modern economy to assure its continued growth.'[103] Nixon further alienated the free marketeers in the Republican Party with his 'New Economic Policy' programme in 1972, which, according to the *Washington Post*, showed 'an activist flexing of government muscles not seen since the early Roosevelt experiments'.[104] The programme embraced the compensatory state, which neo-liberals had been rallying against since the original New Deal, by imposing price and wage controls in an effort to reduce inflationary pressure. Friedman was one of the few dissenting voices, writing in *Newsweek* that Nixon 'has a tiger by the tail. Reluctant as he was to grasp it, he will find it hard to let go.'[105] Nixon's resignation in 1974 following the Watergate affair gave the conservative Right an opportunity to reclaim ideological ground in the Republican Party. The attendant demise of traditional republicanism was a crucial turning point in conservative fortunes in American political history. It was at this political interval that the threads of what was to become known as 'Reaganism' began to organise and rally. As in Britain, it was in the mid-1970s that the United States saw the rise of an organised, coherent and credible neo-liberal alternative to the liberal establishment. This 'neo-liberal' epoch in American politics was an outgrowth of post-war conservatism, personified by Goldwater and the counter-establishment movement.[106]

In the mid-1970s, all the forces that would eventually drive American politics to the Right in the 1980s were in place. At the core of the neo-liberal movement was Reagan and his vision of a united and accessible conservatism. Reagan's political vision went beyond the confines of the Republican Party, to embrace the values of the American liberal tradition. At the heart of 'Reaganism', Blumenthal writes, was a '"mythology" taken from Reagan's life', based on the accomplishments that 'self-made' individuals could achieve through the free market. He points out that, according to Reaganism, 'America exists as a New World' in which 'the chosen people (Americans) have the gift to draw upon the primal power of creation itself'.[107] Central to this 'grand mythology' were the ideas of Hayek. Like Hayek's market order, the New World is dynamic where risks are taken in the pursuit of profit and gain. Only in this world is the individual truly free: it equates competition with liberty, and individualism with prosperity. By contrast, 'big government' not only restrains progress by intervening in free competition, but also weakens the moral fibre of the individual by inhibiting personal achievement.

The conservative think-tank, the Heritage Foundation set up in Washington in 1973, was designed to do for the American Right what the CPS had done for the British New Right.[108] It played an important role in packaging Regan's ideas and in presenting them to a wider audience, publishing hundreds of essays every year, each one dealing with specific policy issues ranging from trade negotiations to gun-control legislation. Similarly, the Hoover Institute, founded in 1919, took on a more overtly political role in the 1970s, making Reagan an honorary fellow in 1974. Martin Anderson, a Hoover Institute scholar, became Reagan's first chief of domestic policy. In 1979 Anderson, through Hoover, drafted the policy memo – the '"supply-side" plan' – concentrating on controlling federal spending and on liberating economic growth. The memo outlined the main objectives of Reagan's economic reform programme: a reduction in federal spending; reform of government regulation; a stable monetary policy; and economic stability.[109]

After mounting an unsuccessful challenge for the White House in 1976, Reagan embarked on a victorious presidential campaign in 1980. For inspiration, Reagan looked to the American past, its tradition of conservative capitalism and the notion of 'American exceptionalism'. Indeed, Lou Canon wrote that, by making the subtext of the election campaign the reversal of America's economic decline, 'Reagan spoke to the future with the accents of the past'.[110] Reagan, along with free-market conservatives in Britain, viewed the state and public expenditure as the major obstacle to economic growth. As Thatcher had in Britain, Reagan argued that the restoration of the marketplace would be the nation's saviour from too much government interference. He adopted monetarist policies as means of curbing inflation and advocated aspects of the newly enunciated supply-side economic theories to argue for cuts in taxation as the key to economic growth. In line with neo-liberal thinking, he argued in favour of drastic reductions in public expenditure in order to free resources for the private sector by way of an incentive, both to productivity and to investment. In 1980 Reagan successfully defeated the liberal establishment and shaped the electorate around a new set of neo-liberal policy issues.

Conclusion

Early neo-liberalism in Germany, Britain and the United States did not constitute a single unified movement, but rather a heterogeneous one. Although there were obvious differences in the context and presentation of the ideology in these three countries, early neo-liberal movements were united in their aspirations through their connections to the Mont Pelerin Society. They can be seen as separate strands of a larger ideological counter-movement to the modern interventionist state, encapsulated in the objectives set out at Mont Pelerin in 1947. This chapter has identified neo-liberalism as a nationally based ideology. While Mont Pelerin may have been an international forum for neo-liberal ideas, their transfer to the world of practical politics was nationally based. The chapter has highlighted the different national policy priorities of neo-liberals in Germany, Britain and the United States, which reflected what each national movement saw as the greatest threat to the realisation of its liberal programme. In Germany, this threat was embodied by large cartels and other monopolies of capital; in

Britain, it was to be found in the strength of trade unions and labour; and in the United States it was contained within the Great Society programme and the growth of the state. Each of these separate national concerns was reflected in the different policy programmes pursued by neo-liberals in these three countries.

There was, however, a significant transfer of ideas between Germany and Britain, and between Britain and the United States, and in this sense there was an international dimension to the ideology. The rise of neo-liberalism in these three countries was essentially a product of their national liberal traditions, rather than an overlap of ideas between countries. In Germany, neo-liberals returned to the free economy and embraced the 'social *Rechtsstaat*', Britain looked back to its tradition of classical liberalism from the nineteenth century, while in the United States the tradition of conservative capitalism was resurrected to counter the liberal establishment. Mont Pelerin may have set the intellectual agenda, but the transformation of the political agenda – the change from a policy agenda determined by the desirability of intervention to one determined by the desirability of the market economy – was set at the national level.

Notes

1. F. A. Hayek, 'The nature and history of the problem', in his Collectivist Economic Planning (Routledge: London, 1935), p. 24.
2. A. J. Nicholls, 'The other Germany – The neo-liberals', in R. J. Bullen, H. Pogge von Strandmann and A. Polansky (eds), *Ideas into Politics: Aspects of European History, 1880–1950* (London: Croom Held, 1984), pp. 164–5.
3. Norman Barry, 'Political and economic thought of German neo-liberals', in A. Peacock and H. Willgeradot (eds), *German Neo-Liberals and the Social Market Economy* (London: Macmillan, 1989), p. 106.
4. Henry M. Oliver, 'German neo-liberalism', *The Quarterly Journal of Economics*, 74: 1 (1960), p. 117.
5. Wilhelm Röpke, 'Wirtschaftlicher Liberalismus und Staatsgedanke', *Hamburger Fremdenblatt*, Nov. 13, 1923, quoted in Edward E. Megay, 'Anti-pluralist liberalism: The German neo-liberals, *Political Science Quarterly*, 85: 3 (1970), p. 425.
6. Alexander Rüstow, *Schriften des Vereins für Sozialpolitik*, 187 (1932), p. 68, quoted in Megay, 'Anti-pluralist liberalism', p. 426.
7. Megay, 'Anti-pluralist liberalism', p. 442.
8. Nicholls, 'The other Germany', p. 169.
9. Heinz Rieter and Matthias Schmolz, 'The ideas of German ordo-liberalism 1938–45: Pointing the way to a new economic order', *The European Journal of the History of Economic Thought*, 1: 1 (1993), p. 96.
10. Walter Eucken, *Die Grundlagen der Nationalökonomie* (Jena: Gustav Fischer, 1940), quoted in Oliver, 'German neo-liberalism', p. 119.

11. See John Gray, *The Moral Foundations of Market Institutions* (London: IEA, 1992).
12. Quoted in Carl J. Friedrich, 'The political thought of neo-liberalism', *The American Political Science Review*, 49: 2 (1955), p. 512.
13. A. Müller-Armack, 'The principles of the Social Market Economy', *The German Economic Review*, 3: 2 (1965), p. 91.
14. Max Hartwell, *A History of the Mont Pelerin Society* (Indianapolis: Liberty Fund, 1995), pp. 214–15.
15. V. Berghahn, 'Ideas into politics: The case of Ludwig Erhard', in Bullen et al., *Ideas into Politics* (above, n. 2), p. 179.
16. F. A. Hayek, 'What is "Social"? – What does it mean?', in his *Studies in Philosophy, Politics and Economics* (London: Routledge, 1967), p. 238.
17. See Manfred E. Streit and Michael Wohlgemuth, 'The market economy and the state: Hayekian and ordo-liberal conceptions, in Peter Koslowski (ed.), *The Theory of Capitalism in the German Economic Tradition: Historicism, Ordo-Liberalism and Critical Theory* (Berlin: Springer-Verlag, 2000), pp. 224–71.
18. Keith Tribe, 'Genealogy of the Social Market Economy', in his *Strategies of Economic Order: German Economic Discourse, 1750–1950* (Cambridge: Cambridge University Press, 1995), p. 236.
19. A. J. Nicholls, *Freedom with Responsibility: The Social Market Economy 1918–1963* (Oxford: Oxford University Press, 1994), pp. 193–4.
20. Jeremy Leaman, *The Political Economy of West Germany, 1945–1985* (Basingstoke: Macmillan, 1988), p. 52.
21. Jack Wiseman, 'Social policy and the Social Market Economy', in Peacock and Willgerogt, *German Neo-Liberals and the Social Market Economy*, pp. 172–3.
22. Ibid., p. 170.
23. Nicholls, *Freedom with Responsibility*, p. 325.
24. Ibid., pp. 325–6.
25. Ibid., p. 338.
26. Ibid., p. 343.
27. Quoted in Nicholls, *Freedom with Responsibility*, p. 345.
28. Nicholls, *Freedom with Responsibility*, p. 348.
29. Ibid., p. 349.
30. Barry, 'Political and economic thought of German neo-liberals', p. 119.
31. Konrad Zweig, *The Origins of the German Social Market Economy: The Leading Ideas and their Intellectual Roots* (London: ASI, 1980), pp. 32–3.
32. Nicholls, *Freedom with Responsibility*, p. 396.
33. Michael Oakeshott, 'The political economy of freedom', in his *Rationalism in Politics and Other Essays* (London: Methuen, 1962), pp. 37–58.
34. Norman Barry, *The New Right* (London: Croom Helm, 1987), p. 111.
35. T. F. Lindsay and M. Harrington, *The Conservative Party 1918–1970* (London: Macmillan, 1974), p. 173.
36. Kenneth Hoover and Raymond Plant, *Conservative Capitalism in Britain and the United States* (London: Routledge, 1989), pp. 138–9.
37. Nigel Harris in his *Competition and the Corporate Society: British Conservatives, The State and Industry, 1945–1964* (London: Methuen, 1972).
38. Quoted in Harris, *Competition and the Corporate Society*, p. 245.

39. Richard Cockett, *Thinking the Unthinkable: Think-Tanks and the Economic Counter-Revolution, 1931–1983* (London: HarperCollins, 1994), p. 163.
40. J. D. Hoffman, *The Conservative Party in Opposition, 1945–51* (London: Macgibbon and Kee, 1964), p. 210.
41. Gerald Frost, *Antony Fisher: Champion of Liberty* (London: Profile Books, 2002), p. 72.
42. Arthur Seldon, *Not Unanimous: A Rival Verdict to the Radcliffe Report on the Workings of the Monetary System* (London: IEA, 1960), p. 18.
43. Maurice Cowling, 'Sources of the New Right', in his *Mill and Liberalism* (Cambridge: Cambridge University Press, 1990), p. 31.
44. Brendan Evans and Andrew Taylor, *From Salisbury to Major: Continuity and Change in Conservative Politics* (Manchester: Manchester University Press, 1996), p. 134.
45. Andrew Gamble, *The Conservative Nation* (London: Routledge and Kegan Paul, 1974), pp. 92–3.
46. Ibid., p. 92.
47. Ibid.
48. F. A. Hayek's *A Tiger by the Tail* (London: IEA, 1972), p. 39.
49. Milton Friedman, *The Counter-Revolution in Monetary Theory* (London: IEA, 1970), p. 25.
50. Cockett, *Thinking the Unthinkable*, p. 167.
51. P. Douglas and J. E. Powell, *How Big Should Government Be?* (London: Macmillan, 1968), p. 48.
52. J. E. Powell, *Saving in a Free Society* (London: IEA, 1960), p. 32.
53. Simon Heffer, *Like the Roman: The Life of Enoch Powell* (London: Weidenfeld and Nicolson, 1998), p. 358–9.
54. Cockett, *Thinking the Unthinkable*, p. 167.
55. John Ranelagh, *Thatcher's People* (London: HarperCollins, 1991), p. 138.
56. Keith Joseph, *Stranded on the Middle Ground* (London, Centre for Policy Studies, 1976), p. 28.
57. Andrew Gamble, 'The free economy and the strong state: The rise of the social Market Economy', *Socialist Register* (1979), p. 6.
58. Keith Joseph, *Why Britain Needs a Social Market Economy* (London: Centre for Policy Studies, 1975), p. 2.
59. Ibid., p. 3.
60. Samuel Brittan, *Government and the Market Economy* (London: IEA, 1971), p. 13.
61. Ralph Harris and Brendon Sewill, *British Economic Policy 1970–74: Two Views* (London: IEA, 1975), p. 26.
62. Cockett, *Thinking the Unthinkable*, p. 237.
63. Ibid., p. 237.
64. Sir Keith says Centre will challenge ideas', *The Times*, 19 January 1975.
65. Andrew Denham and Mark Garnett, 'From guru to godfather: Keith Joseph, "New" Labour and the British conservative tradition', *The Political Quarterly*, 72: 1 (2001), p. 101.
66. Keith Joseph, *Monetarism is Not Enough* (London: Centre for Policy Studies, 1976), p. 19.
67. Ibid., p. 11.
68. Ibid., p. 12.
69. John Kenneth Galbraith, *The Affluent Society* (Boston, MA: Houghton-Mifflin, 1958).

70. Eric Foner, *The Story of American Freedom* (London: Picador, 1999), pp. 285–6.
71. Gillian Peele, *Revival and Reaction: The Right in Contemporary America* (Oxford: Clarendon Press, 1984), pp. 19–50.
72. Quoted in Foner, *The Story of American Freedom*, p. 308.
73. Alan Brinkley, 'The problem of American conservatism', in his *Liberalism and its Discontents* (Cambridge, MA: Harvard University Press, 1998), p. 287.
74. George Nash, *The Conservative Intellectual Movement in America since 1945* (Washington: Intercollegiate Institute, 1996), pp. 17–18.
75. Sidney Blumenthal, *The Rise of the Counter-Establishment: From Conservative Ideology to Political Power* (New York: Times Books, 1986).
76. Daniel Bell, *The End of Ideology* (New York: Free Press, 1962).
77. Blumenthal, *The Rise of the Counter-Establishment*, pp. 5–6.
78. Lisa McGirr, *Suburban Warriors: The Origins of the New American Right* (Princeton: Princeton University Press, 2001), pp. 76–7.
79. *National Review*, 19 November 1955, p. 5, quoted in John B. Judis, *William F. Buckley, Jr.: Patron Saint of the Conservatives* (New York: Simon and Schuster, 1988), p. 23.
80. Quoted in McGirr, *Suburban Warriors*, p. 63.
81. Blumenthal, *The Rise of the Counter-Establishment*, pp. 216–17.
82. Ibid., p. 17.
83. Quoted in Blumenthal, *The Rise of the Counter-Establishment*, p. 89.
84. M. Friedman and A. Schwartz, *A Monetary History of America, 1867–1960* (Princeton: Princeton University Press, 1963).
85. Milton Friedman, *Capitalism and Freedom* (Chicago: University of Chicago Press, 1962).
86. Cockett, *Thinking the Unthinkable*, pp. 151–2.
87. Blumenthal, *The Rise of the Counter-Establishment*, p. 88.
88. Ibid., p. 108.
89. David Ricci, *The Transformation of American Politics: The New Washington and the Rise of Think-Tanks* (New Haven: Yale University Press, 1993), pp. 213–14.
90. Quoted in Robert Alan Goldberg, *Barry Goldwater* (New Haven: Yale University Press, 1995), p. 139.
91. Barry Goldwater, *The Conscience of a Conservative* (Shepardsville: Victor, 1960), p. 46, quoted in M. Isserman and M. Kazin, *America Divided: The Civil War of the 1960s* (Oxford: Oxford University Press, 2000), p. 214.
92. Goldberg, *Barry Goldwater*, p. 249.
93. Blumenthal, *The Rise of the Counter-Establishment*, pp. 108–9.
94. Ibid., p. 61.
95. Quoted in Isserman and Kazin, *America Divided*, p. 205.
96. Goldberg, *Barry Goldwater*, p. 289.
97. Lee Edwards, *Goldwater: The Man Who Made a Revolution* (Washington, DC: Regnery, 1995), p. 314.
98. McGirr, *Suburban Warriors*, p. 143.
99. Ibid., p. 145.
100. Ibid., p. 201.
101. J. M. Schoenwald, *A Time for Choosing: The Rise of Modern American Conservatism* (New York: Oxford University Press, 2001), pp. 11–12.
102. Quoted in Steven F. Hayward, *The Age of Reagan: The Fall of the Old Liberal Order, 1964–1980* (Roseville, CA: Prima Publishing, 2001), p. 257.

103. Ibid., p. 258.
104. Ibid., p. 263.
105. Ibid., p. 293.
106. John Gerring, 'The neo-liberal epoch (1928–1992)', in his *Party Ideologies in America, 1828–1996* (Cambridge: Cambridge University Press, 1998), pp. 125–58.
107. Blumenthal, *The Rise of the Counter-Establishment*, p. 253.
108. Cockett, *Thinking the Unthinkable*, p. 181.
109. David Graham and Peter Clarke, *The New Enlightenment: The Rebirth of Liberalism* (London: Macmillan, 1986), p. 27.
110. Quoted in Hayward, *The Age of Reagan*, p. 609.

Part II: Political Concepts

Chapter 5

The market: Against the state

Introduction: Market values and Western civilisation

Markets and the market order are central to neo-liberal thinking. Markets for neo-liberals and the rules of exchange are sacrosanct to the functioning of the economy and, by implication, to the existence of capitalism; they exist as the only alternative to some form of rational organisation of economic life. They are part of a natural, 'spontaneous' order of 'civilised' values and mutual cooperation, which sustain capitalism and freedom in Western societies. As Keith Joseph proclaimed: 'Markets are a state of nature which has spontaneously evolved, and to disregard their rules is as pointless as attempting to ignore the laws of gravity.'[1]

In the last quarter of the twentieth century, neo-liberal free-market ideas were ascendant in national and international political economy. The 1970s and 1980s witnessed a radical move away from the Keynesian demand management of the post-war era, and free markets came to be seen as the ultimate instrument of economic efficiency in modern capitalist economies. Free trade found a new audience and restraints on global investment were slowly unbuckled. This neo-liberal policy paradigm makes the claim that the market economy is the superior economic system because it inextricably connects liberty and efficiency and enables free exchange and trade, which maximises the welfare of all parties by enabling each to specialise in their areas of competitive advantage. By implication, in neo-liberal orthodoxy the state is seen as inefficient and corrupt, damaging the performance of the national economy by taking on functions which are beyond its appropriate and proper role of offsetting market distortions.

In this chapter, the concept of the market and its adjacent concepts such as evolution, spontaneous order, limited knowledge, individualism and entrepreneurship in neo-liberal ideology are examined. A succinct account of the ideas of the classical and neo-classical liberal economists is presented, and the relevance of these ideas to modern market processes is explored. The obstacles confronting modern market economies – monopolies of both labour and capital, regulation, and imperfect competition – are considered. The chapter goes on to analyse the so-called dynamism and vigour of the free market, aptly demonstrated by the continuing dominance of Western capitalist states and international financial institutions such as the World Bank and IMF. The centrality of the market to neo-liberal ideology is presented in terms of its unqualified opposition to state-led or state-mediated economic strategies. This chapter points out that there may be several neo-liberal interpretations of the market and of its role in the economic process. However, regardless of these differences in interpretation, two themes emerge: the importance of guiding policy by a clear and credible set of rules determined by the market order, and the importance of keeping in check monopolistic, regulatory and bureaucratic forces which hamper the spontaneous order of the market and economic growth. These two themes are at the core of the neo-liberal ideology espoused by Ludwig von Mises, F. A. Hayek and others.

The chapter argues that neo-liberalism is not an exclusive theory of the market order propelled by an insight into the proper functioning of the free market: it is a complex movement of economic, social and moral objectives. Its own objective is the intellectual coordination of the life force of the market, of the state and of society. It reaches beyond the supply and demand theories of classical liberal economics (Say's Law), and represents values and beliefs that have their origins in the cultural and intellectual traditions of Western civilisation. Neo-liberals' main contention is that free market processes, not the apparatus of the modern state, are at the core of Western civilisation and progress. The chapter concludes by pointing out that the neo-liberal market order must be seen as an integral part of a Foucaultian social discourse. In neo-liberalismm, this discourse is centred on a particular conception of the individuals and their rights. The market order, however, is part of a wider, constructed, social order, which situates both the individual and the state at its core.

Classical liberal political economy

The classical economists

The basic premise for the market economy was outlined by Bernard Mandeville in 1714. Mandeville's poem, *The Fable of the Bees*, first laid out the rationale for the competitive market. Mandeville proposed that private vices are public benefits, and that 'every species of virtue is at bottom some form of gross selfishness, more or less modified'. Private vices such as luxury and pride and the pursuit of individual self-interest, he claimed, were beneficial in producing public benefits such as employment, trade and general affluence.[2] Adam Smith applied Mandeville's logic to the internal workings of the market economy in his *Wealth of Nations* in 1776. Smith's work was based on the rationalist and individualist beliefs of the eighteenth-century Enlightenment. In his *Wealth of Nations*, Smith defined markets as the uncoordinated voluntary transactions between buyers, which resulted in mutually beneficial outcomes. The central argument of the book was that wealth is created through a process of market competition. In the economic sphere, he claimed, the pursuit of individual self-interest and wealth in commerce resulted in collective prosperity for society, which could not be as effective as if planned by an external agent. Market transactions, Smith famously argued, were not overseen by a bureaucratic authority, but rather, as D. D. Raphael points out, led by an 'invisible hand'. This hand is guided by the Stoic idea of a 'natural harmony' which comes into being automatically, through the interplay between individual interests and the system of exchange.[3] At the heart of Smith's understanding of the market economy is the vital, if limited, role played by government. The functions of the state in a market economy, according to Smith, go beyond the traditional protective duties of the night-watchman state. Smith assigned the state three important duties: the administration of justice, the provision of defence, and the maintenance of certain public goods aimed specifically at improving welfare. These duties, Smith maintained, facilitate the operation of market exchanges and provide a moral code which is consistent with the free-market virtues of 'natural liberty' and 'natural equality'.[4]

It was in *The Wealth of Nations*, as Desmond King points out, that 'the market acquired modern intellectual significance'.[5] Indeed, the significance of Smith's work is that it challenged the governmentalisation of the national politico-economic system and presented the market economy as a credible alternative system in the organisation of economic and political life. He was the first to attempt to develop an understanding of the internal workings of markets, which still constitutes the basis for much economic theorising on markets today. As Charles E. Lindblom noted, 'We may no longer live in a Smithian world of atomistic competition, but the market remains one of the few institutions capable of organising the co-operation of millions of people. We owe his *Wealth of Nations*, written over 200 years ago, much of our understanding of what markets can and cannot do.'⁶

Smith's ideas were significantly refined and elaborated by subsequent economists. David Ricardo's classical micro-economic model of the market economy, formalised in modern economic theory as the 'perfect competition' model, emphasised the role and activities of individual markets in the production and consumption of individual goods and services. In his *On the Principles of Political Economy and Taxation*, published in 1817, Ricardo claimed that equilibrium is maintained through the price system, which balances the supply and demand for goods. Ricardo's theory of comparative advantage provided a rationale for ending the government's regulation of markets by arguing that the advantages of specialisation and trade outweighed the constraints of social considerations. Markets, he maintained, regulate themselves through a process of 'market clearing', whereby the price mechanism adjusts itself naturally to accommodate changes in consumer demand. Like Smith before him, Ricardo claimed that the freely operating market system, through processes of specialisation in production and market clearing, generates economic growth and welfare.⁷

John Stuart Mill's *Principles of Political Economy* approached the market economy and the distribution of wealth from a utilitarian standpoint. In his work, Mill attempted to detach himself from the statist utilitarianism associated with Jeremy Bentham. Like Smith and Ricardo, Mill pioneered the market economy as the best means of producing wealth and of safeguarding individual liberty. Participation in the free market system, Mill argued, gives individuals a degree of 'self-rule' with which they can meet their values, ideals and desires. The free and voluntary relationships of the market economy, he wrote, enables individuals to pursue a life course of their own, choosing free from arbitrary interventions by the state. However, unlike the other classical economists and neo-liberal theorists, Mill did not view production and distribution as an inseparable part of a single economic system. While he saw the production of wealth as having the 'character of physical truths', he viewed its distribution as 'a matter of human institutions solely'. Mill contended that, although the state should not interfere in the production of capital and labour, it was within the moral capacity of the government to intervene in the distribution of wealth where substantial inequalities of income existed. Mill envisioned a 'social state' in which 'humane' laws and customs governing distribution in a market society were determined by democratic means.[8] Consequently, neo-liberal economists such as Hayek argued that Mill's ideas presupposed a 'false distinction' between production and distribution, and that led him to advocate a particular conception of social justice, one notably associated with equality of opportunity.[9]

The neo-classical economists

The concept of the market went through a major transition in the late nineteenth and early twentieth centuries. The classical economists' conception of the market, embodied in their 'sociology of the economy' perspective, was superseded by the 'marginalist revolution' led by the neo-classical economists. Three neo-classical schools of thought dominated economic theorising on markets – the Marshallian school in Britain, the Megerian school in Austria and the emerging Walrasian school on the continent. These schools led the marginalist revolution that had begun to dominate mainstream economic thought by the late nineteenth century. Marginalist techniques effectively bypassed the problem of value and offered superior quantitative methods to either the classical or the historicist system of thought in Germany.[10]

In Britain, the foremost architects of the Marshalllian mainstream approach to economics were Alfred Marshall and Lionel Robbins. Marshall approached the market from a scientific standpoint, claiming that economics was 'a branch of biology broadly interpreted'.[11] He was influenced by the ideas of Herbert Spencer in his evolutionary interpretation of market relations. Marshall's speciality was in micro-economics – the study of individual markets and industries. In his *Principles of Economics*, he emphasised how the price and output of a good are determined by supply and demand. These two forces, he famously argued, are like scissor blades that intersect at equilibrium. Marshall went on to explain how markets adjusted to changes in supply and demand over time. He argued that, like developments in the natural world, changes in economy are determined by an evolutionary process in which technology, market institutions and individual preferences evolve alongside individual behaviour.[12] The Marshallian approach in British economic thought was greatly influenced by the Austrian School, founded by Carl Menger. Indeed, Robbins, who later emerged as a leading liberal economist at the London School of Economics, attended the Vienna seminars in the 1920s. Menger presented a universalist view on the nature and scope of economic activity. His ideas at the turn of the century represented a completely new approach to economics, compared to the ones taught in German-speaking universities at the time; they were non-historical and abstract, like the British approach. Like Marshall, Menger perceived the economy as a biological organism. He put forward a theory of the 'organic' and 'spontaneous' evolution of money from a barter economy. The self-interested individual interactions in the barter economy, Menger argued, led to the spontaneous emergence of monetary units. He claimed that both sides gain from market exchanges when money is introduced, by the reduction of the number of transactions to a minimum. Menger also developed a theory which refuted the classical economists' labour theory of value. In his 'subjective theory of value' Menger claimed that goods acquire value not because of the amount of labour used in their production, but because of their utility in satisfying people's wants. Menger's approach to the market represented a deviation from both classical economics and Marxism, and led to important new insights about the nature of markets and of the capitalist economic system, which were crucial to the intellectual development of Mises and to Hayek's neo-liberal theory of the market order.[13]

The Walrasian approach to the economy developed on the continent in the late nineteenth century saw markets interacting in a system of general equilibrium. The pioneer of the approach, Léon Walras, reached similar conclusions to Menger, but by a different method. Walras's contribution to neo-classical economic theory was his explanation of the functioning of the market system as a whole in terms of the atomistic and individual components of the system. The market system, he claimed, consisted of individual markets tightly embedded in a single, whole economy. Walras's 'general equilibrium theory' stressed the 'natural' equilibriating tendencies of the system. In his theory, Walras argued that markets undergo a constant interactive adjustment process in which supply and demand determine price. He attempted to show how the market could move towards equilibrium as a result of individual interactions and price flexibility, even if the process was periodically interrupted by entrepreneurial activity.[14]

The Austrian paradigm

The classical and neo-classical economists identified the nature of the market economy, described its evolution and attempted to discover the inner laws that explained its operation. One school of thought, however, stands at the forefront of neo-liberal theorising on markets – the Austrian School. The core arguments of its two leading advocates, Mises and Hayek, are used to elucidate the neo-liberal case for the economic superiority of the free market at every level of society, from the individual to the global economy which simply represents the aggregate of individual units. The work of Hayek, in particular, can be seen as part of a wider intellectual project to guide society back to the civilised order of nineteenth-century liberalism and to move beyond what he termed the 'excesses' of classical liberalism, providing a more favourable environment for the operation of markets. Hayek's theorising on markets follows four main themes: spontaneous order, epistemic considerations, economic efficiency, and the limited state.

Spontaneous order and the limits of human reason

The notion of spontaneous order plays a pivotal role in neo-liberalism's conceptualisation of the market. Indeed, adjacent to the core concept of market are the concepts of spontaneous order and evolution. The Austrian School's theory of spontaneous order follows the anti-rationalist tradition in social thought. It adopts a position originally formulated by David Hume, that pure and unaided human reason is incapable of determining a priori those moral and legal norms which the existence of social order is dependent upon. This position rejects the claims made on behalf of reason by the Enlightenment philosophers to the effect that rules could be constructed which are universally appropriate for order and continuity. The theory of spontaneous order is concerned with 'natural processes' which are not the product of reason or human intention. The classical example in neo-liberal ideology is the free-market economy. What Hayek termed the 'market order' is not a product of conscious design, but a spontaneous growth, an evolved order: 'it is a specific outcome of evolution itself'.[15]

Hayek argued that the spontaneous order of the market is the outcome of 'self-coordination'. It is produced by individuals pursuing their own ends, but having no intention of individually or collectively producing such an order. In the free-market economy, the coordination of the aims and purposes of countless actors, who cannot know the aims and purposes of more than a handful of their fellow citizens, is achieved by the price mechanism. A change in the price of a commodity is simply a signal which feeds back information into the system, enabling participants to produce that spontaneous coordination which appears to be the result of an omniscient mind. Hayek contrasted the market order with an organisation which is the result of cooperation and coordination by a central authority. Crucially, a spontaneous order, for Hayek, 'is the result of human action, but not human design'.[16] Hayek therefore conceived of what he termed the Great Society as an evolved order or 'cosmos', rather than a consciously designed organisation or 'taxis'. For Hayek, the orderliness of the Great Society is due to the growth and evolution of institutions, practices and rules 'which had first been adopted for other reasons, or even purely accidentally, and were preserved because they enabled the group which had engendered them to prevail over less well-endowed rivals'.[17] It has developed from a process of trial-and-error, which 'requires the efforts and accumulated hard-earned experience of many generations'.[18] The notion of the spontaneous order of the Great Society is one which sits at the heart of neo-liberalism, appealing to both conservatives and liberals alike. G. C. Roche contends that spontaneous order 'appeals to conservatives' moral concern for a functioning social fabric without imposing a planned order'; and for liberals 'it enshrines personal liberty as the *sine qua non* of its operation'.[19]

The most important spontaneous order for neo-liberals is the market order. Hayek defined the market order as a 'catallaxy' rather than an economy. His concept of catallaxy is the modern counterpart to Smith's 'invisible hand'. A catallaxy is a collection of interacting economies, all operating within a framework of abstract rules. Unlike an economy, a catallaxy has no specific unitary hierarchy of ends; it has evolved without any conscious design, from the voluntary transactions of individuals. By referring to the market order in this way, Hayek did not base the market on the old naïve assumptions of perfect competition and general equilibrium associated with the classical economists. Rather, he perceived the market as an evolving discovery mechanism, complete with uncertainty and shocks. Norman Barry points out that Hayek talked of a 'dynamic equilibrium concept, which, although fictitious, describes the hypothetical movement of the economic process through time, and is consistent with space'.[20]

The market as an epistemic device

Adjacent to the core concept of the market is also the concept of limited knowledge. What makes the spontaneous market order superior over a planned economic order, for Hayek, is its 'use of knowledge in society'; the way knowledge is acquired and transmitted through social interaction. In Hayek's account, markets have a coordinating role to play, imposing order on these social interactions, allowing individuals to use their knowledge in pursuit of their own objectives. Hayek interprets the intractability of central direction in the catallaxy in terms of information and knowledge. Such an ordering of human cooperation, Hayek claimed, exceeds the limits of knowledge and perception. Knowledge of individual preferences and of production factors in mass society is tacit and dispersed, and therefore no single agent could ever know what members' preferences are and how they rank them. Thus Hayek defined the economic problem confronting society as that of the 'utilisation of knowledge which is not given to anyone in totality'.[21] More specifically, the problem for Hayek is

> how to extend the span of utilisation of resources beyond the span of the control of any one mind, and how to dispense with the need of conscious control and provide inducements which will make individuals do desirable things without anyone having to tell them what to do.[22]

For Hayek, this is a problem of 'rational economic organisation' – both a problem of coordinating the actions of innumerable agents without the possibility of any adequate centralised knowledge of their needs and resources, and, more importantly, a problem of generating new knowledge in society.

Hayek argued that only the market order based on private property over the means of production can solve this problem. The market acts as what John Gray terms an 'epistemic machine' – 'an institutional device for the transmission of fragmented knowledge in a form which makes it generally accessible and usable'.[23] Hilary Wainwright states that the market in Hayek's view is an 'engine of self-education'.[24] It performs a central role in generating information, through the unregulated price mechanism, as to how economic agents ignorant of each other may best attain their equally unknown purposes. Individual fields of vision may be limited, but Hayek maintained that in the market these fields overlap so that through many intermediaries the relevant information can be communicated to all participants. The competitive market may not be a perfect system, but it is one which is superior to a planned economy through its coordination of individual activities, enabling dispersed information to be exploited.[25]

Market efficiency

It is this coordination that makes market society the most advantageous economic system for Hayek. The economic agents in Hayek's market order are autonomous individuals. His ideal is a market society composed of self-employed entrepreneurs and commercial agents. The competition between these individual agents in the market is akin to a 'game' in which luck and misfortune are distributed more or less evenly, thereby giving everyone a fair chance of earning a particular income. Indeed, Hayek contended that the market order is beneficial because it 'increases' and even makes 'as great as possible the prospects and chance of everyone selected at random'.[26] He argued that a planned economy is undesirable because it denies chance any role.

Income distribution in the market order is related to luck. The level of distribution, Hayek argued, should not be a matter of political will, but an impersonal self-ordering process which goes beyond any single agent's responsibility. Thus he did not see market outcomes in terms of the old Protestant work ethics: a reward for virtue. For Hayek, there is no such thing as a 'just reward'. Income in a market society is not relative to merit. The rewards an individual receives are related to the market's valuation – 'the value as perceived by consumers of the goods and services produced' and 'these values which services will have to their fellows will often have no relation to their individual merits and needs'.[27] Production and distribution, Hayek asserted, are interdependent – the market can maximise its productive capacity only if the distribution of income is not interfered with. The spontaneous economic order of the market maximises average individual income by increasing everybody's chances as much as possible. Economic success is attributed to the driving forces of market competition and the harnessing of individual initiative. Like Darwinian natural selection, competition in the market order acts to eliminate negative inefficiency by selecting out winners by their profit achievement and eliminating inefficient loss-makers. This makes market society, for neo-liberals, the most productive and efficient economic order.

Limited government

Hayek's idea of a market system of cooperation, establishing and maintaining itself without any interference from a central authority, should not be misinterpreted. It is important to stress that his views are not at the more extreme end of the *laissez-faire* continuum. Like the German ordo-liberals, Hayek had no faith in a system of pure *laissez-faire*. He saw government intervention as a necessary means of maintaining institutions favourable to individualism and market exchange. The fundamental point is to draw up the proper boundaries of the state, where intervention is restricted to non-coercive activities.

Hayek's conception of a limited state stems from his vision of the Great Society. In the Great Society individuals exist prior to, and separate from, society. It is a society that is free and open, therefore respects the individual within the protected spheres of private enterprise and private ownership of the means of production. Hayek was diametrically opposed to the collectivist vision of society, in which government attempts to treat the Great Society as part of its organisation. He argued that such a development 'necessarily leads to a gradual transformation of the spontaneous order of a free society into a totalitarian system conducted in the service of some coalition of interests'.[28] Hayek identified the proper functions of the liberal state as non-interventionist; as being restricted to the individualist minimum sanctioned in the *Constitution of Liberty*, whereby government becomes 'the guarantor, rather than the invader of individual liberty'.[29] Hayek, however, recognising the state as an important feature of real markets, allocated it a catalogue of important tasks in maintaining, correcting and supplementing market deficiencies.

The principle that determines the legitimacy of government activity, Hayek argued, is the rule of law. Embracing a *Rechtsstaat* conception of a liberal legal order, he claimed that how well the market will function is determined by the character of government activity, not by its volume; the rule of law is concerned not with the level of state, but with the methods by which intervention is brought about. This emerges from his distinctive epistemological position concerning the limits of human reason, where law is contrasted with legislation. The former belongs to a spontaneous order, where the 'abstract', 'goal-dependent' and 'agent-dependent' character of law protects negative liberty. The latter is associated with an artificially created social order, in which commands are directed to the achievement of specific ends, such as positive liberty and social justice.[30] In *The Constitution of Liberty*, Hayek set out his ideal rule of law state, in which political arrangements do not interfere with the spontaneous coordination of the market order, but serve to reinforce uncreated social rules of conduct. In Hayek's market order, politics acts as a means of coordination, so that individuals may pursue their ends independently from the body politic. The roles of the state are limited to non-coercive activities 'compatible with a functioning market'.³¹ The state, Hayek argued, has a duty to 'facilitate the acquisition of reliable knowledge about facts of general significance', provide certain regulations within the rules of just conduct such as health and safety regulations, allow for some measure of government intervention in the provision of public goods through proportional taxation, and provide a minimum social safety net for those without marketable skills. Hayek, however, did allow the state one coercive function: enforcing the rules of just conduct so as to prevent coercion by private individuals. He made it explicit that 'a free society demands that government have a monopoly of coercion'.³²

Imperfections of the market order

Hayek may have rejected the neo-classical notion of perfect equilibrium, but other defects sit at the heart of his market order. A number of imperfections appear to cast severe doubt on the omnipotence and exclusivity of market mechanisms in the capitalist system. However, some imperfections to the market order, such as monopoly, some types of bureaucracy and regulation, and other market imperfections are accepted by neo-liberals as inevitable defects and necessary parts of the profit-generating dynamics of the market order. Indeed, for neo-liberals, rather than being obstacles, some market imperfections can be the main source of profit in the market economy and an essential part of its survival.

Monopoly

Monopoly is an obstruction to the market, which appears to undermine the neo-liberal notion of an open and competitive economy. Lindblom identified monopoly as a situation where 'in any one market, where there are only a few buyers or sellers, one person or a collaborating group can restrict production purchases or sales in an arbitrary way'.³³ He argued, however, that monopoly should not in any way be considered an 'impossibility' or a serious 'shortcoming' for competitive markets, but rather as 'one of many defects that markets share with all other forms of social organisation'. Monopolies 'dampen' market competition rather than undermine it.³⁴

Neo-liberals such as Hayek followed Lindbom's interpretation of monopolies of capital. For Hayek, a monopoly in a market does not mean the total absence of competitiveness. Capital monopolies, he claimed, are self-inhibiting rather than self-destructive. In his defence of capital monopolies, Hayek made explicit the distinction between what he terms 'enterprise' monopolies and monopolies of labour. He maintained in his *Law, Legislation and Liberty* that labour and capital monopolies are distinguishable because labour monopolies not only are a greater threat to the smooth functioning of a competitive market, but also pose a greater threat to liberty. He commented that 'enterprise monopoly is the result of better performance, while labour monopoly is due to the coercive suppression of competition'.[35] Hayek did, however, go on to allocate a central role to the state in the prevention of enterprise monopolies which threaten to coerce other particular individual or firms into specific behaviour or to prevent potential competitors from entering the market. Hayek explained that it is usually not the 'existence of the monopolies themselves which is harmful, but the ability of some monopolies to protect and preserve their monopolistic position after the original cause of their superiority has disappeared'.[36] In these circumstances where capital monopolies retain a 'power of discrimination' over prices and competition is restricted in an 'undesirable manner', Hayek argued that it is necessary for such monopolies to be 'curbed by appropriate rules of conduct'. Hayek maintained that, while 'it would not be desirable to make all discrimination illegal, discrimination intended to enforce a certain market conduct should clearly be prohibited'.[37]

Bureaucracy and regulation

A bureaucracy is a hierarchy of authority and system of administration which provides solutions to problems through its specialisation and standardised skills. Neo-liberals are ideologically hostile to this notion of a hierarchical-bureaucratic system, which either authoritatively commands individuals, or seeks to 'educate' them rationally, through unilateral popular persuasion. Hayek contended that this kind of

> great administrative bureaucracy has brought it about that an ever increasing part of the people spend their whole working life as members of large organisations, and are led to think wholly in terms of the requirements of the organisational form of life.[38]

Hayek contrasted these administrative agencies, based on organisational thinking, with regulatory agencies, based on the 'rules of just conduct'. As

Hayek readily acknowledged the imperfections of markets, he recognised that markets require a certain type of bureaucracy in order to exist. Hayek's vision of bureaucracy, however, differs from the traditional model of an administrative agency. For Hayek, the principal role of a bureaucracy or agency is the regulation and universal application of the rules of just conduct, which have evolved with Western civilisation. He was explicit that that these 'rules of just conduct' do not encompass either 'social justice' or the 'public law', which subjects individuals to the commands of authority. The rules of just conduct are abstract 'Lockean' rules which determine the preservation of 'life, liberty and estates'. A regulatory agency confines the scope of an individual's private actions, regulating the 'rules of property, tort and contract'.[39]

Neo-liberals thus acknowledge that markets require supporting regulatory agencies. Rules and regulations which constrain and govern behaviour make market transactions as socially productive as possible by enforcing property rights and penalising non-compliance. Some neo-liberals are, however, careful to guard against compulsory state regulation. Norman Barry, for example, contends that it is possible for all 'regulation to be returned to the market (where it actually began)'.[40] Market failure, he argues, does not necessarily have to entail state involvement to correct errors. Barry points out that 'markets are always to some extent imperfect and it is the continual process of experimentation, guided by prices, that gradually pushes the exchange system to an optimum, albeit temporary and subject to incessant change'. The present system of state regulation, he maintains, is anti-competitive and inefficient: market regulation 'introduces freedom in regulatory regimes delegating authority to de-centralised political units and expanding the opportunities for citizens to move on to one of their choice'.[41]

The necessity for state intervention

A paradox at the heart of neo-liberal market theory is that free markets require the state to operate. As King notes, in a free-market economy the state must be present in the political sphere, to maintain a legitimate judicial system, address market imperfections and 'underwrite those vital public goods which the market fails to produce'. King, however, observes that the legitimate roles and responsibilities granted to the state are confined to the political sphere; the state is 'perceived as necessary although this is denied in the economic sphere'.[42]

Several accounts of the market economy argue that the role of the state in facilitating markets is far greater than neo-liberals are prepared to admit. Karl Polanyi's classical study of the evolution of the capitalist system in the nineteenth century, *The Great Transformation*, discussed in Chapter 3, provides a vivid account of the vital role of the state in market society. More recently, Geoffrey Hodgson has provided the most compelling account of the association between the market and the state. Hodgson develops a theory of capitalism which 'essentially relies on its impurities hidden beneath the surface'. His 'impurity principle' demonstrates how the market system contains 'impurities' or 'non-dominant structures' which may not be typical of the whole system, but which are nevertheless essential if the system is to operate and reproduce itself through time.[43] Like the market, the political institutions of the state act as a coordinating mechanism through which knowledge can be combined and 'the solidaristic values and co-operative habits essential to capitalist survival can be promoted'.[44] Hodgson contends that over-reliance on spontaneous market forces in society, in the long run, destabilises established social institutions – including social norms and rules flowing from state structures – upon which the health of capitalist economy depends. Hodgson's central point is that the state is the primary countervailing power in successful modern economies channelling and taming the power of markets.[45] Thus Andrew Shonfield has pointed out that a legitimately active state in the economic sphere does not lead to the centrally planned economy that neo-liberals deplore, but rather promotes and facilitates a dynamic and prosperous market order.[46]

Neo-liberals do not envisage 'perfectly functioning markets' and thus accept the necessity of the state for certain activities in the political sphere, to correct market imperfections. They do not, however, go as far as Hodgson or Shonfield and assign it an important role in the economic sphere. Hayek argued that the state has a vital role to play in markets, enforcing the rules and laws, but maintained that in a market economy its responsibilities should not extend beyond this.

NATIONAL MARKET CAPITALISM

The Anglo-Saxon model of capitalism

The primacy of the market in neo-liberal discourse in national capitalist economies is captured in the 'Anglo-Saxon' model of capitalism. The

Anglo-Saxon model of capitalism is a neo-American or what Michel Albert refers to as an 'Atlantic capitalist' economic model.[47] The model is driven by the market incentives of individual success and short-term financial gain. It relies for its success on market coordination of economic agents and seeks to address market failures by providing additional market elements where they are missing. The social institutions of the state exist in order to protect and maintain the market, and redress the minor inefficiencies or injustices it produces. David Coates points out that the central actor in this model is not the state, but the private company, 'which is left free to pursue its own short-term profit motives and to raise its capital in open financial markets'. In such capitalist economies, labour markets are unregulated, leaving workers with 'limited and statutory industrial and social rights'.[48]

The dominance of this generic Anglo-Saxon model of capitalism in specific countries in the post-war period was not simply based on a broad acceptance of markets; rather, it manifested itself for very different reasons in individual national contexts. The extent to which Germany adopted features of this market-led model in the immediate post-war years reflected the need both to reconstruct her economy after the war and to break away radically from the state socialism of her past. German neo-liberals, as H. Abromeit observes, were committed to a social market economy on the basis of 'the belief that industrial modernisation and structural change should be best left to the market'.[49] In Britain, the pursuit of market-led capitalism was based on a desire amongst conservative policy-makers to return Britain to the nineteenth-century classical liberal era of free trade, whilst in the United States the principal line of reasoning behind the acceptance of this model was the defence and preservation of freedom. Both Britain and the United States in the late 1970s and 1980s, however, shared a common understanding of the primacy of competition and individualism and an antipathy towards 'Big Government', which became encapsulated in the enterprise society.

Creating the enterprise society

An important peripheral concept of the market is the notion of an enterprise society, marked by the fundamental distinction that neo-liberals make in national market societies between economics and politics. The former is associated with the self-correcting market, spontaneously transmitted transactions and an enterprise culture, the latter, with an active state, corporatism and a culture of dependency. The impersonal forces of the market, neo-liberals claim, create an enterprise initiative by freeing individuals from the constraints imposed by bureaucratic regulation. The Thatcher and Reagan governments in Britain and the United States in the 1980s fostered a new neo-liberal spirit of enterprise. The encouragement of individual initiative and the free play of market forces were marked by an accompanying change in the culture of society. This enterprise culture and society, which ran through much of British and American economic policy-making in the 1980s, concentrated on the short-run outcomes of decisions made by individual entrepreneurs.[50] Economic progress, neo-liberals gleaned from the writings of Hayek, was dependent on the willingness of individuals to act on their own beliefs and incentives. This willingness required the virtues of courage and self-reliance. Success and failure, which cannot be foreseen, were viewed as part of the natural course of market relations. Competition weeded out inefficient firms and resources were reallocated to the general good of the community as a whole.[51]

The pursuit of an enterprise society in Britain and the United States had important domestic policy implications. The movement towards a free and competitive market economy in these countries necessitated the introduction of policy measures to de-centralise the state. Privatisation became the central plank of this policy agenda. The notion of public ownership of major industries was anathema for neo-liberals. The rationale behind privatisation was to expose state-owned enterprises to the full rigours of competition and to restore the central role of the market in the allocation of resources.[52] In theory, privatisation appeared to be consistent with many neo-liberal principles: it would reduce the size and scope of state control; increase individual freedom through the expansion of consumer choice; decrease the Public Sector Borrowing Requirement; lessen government participation in industrial disputes; make industry more efficient by exposing it to the pressures from shareholders; decrease the influence of interest group pressures in investment decisions; encourage the enterprise society and economic success by increasing share-ownership amongst the population; diminish the power of trade unions; and have a general beneficial effect on the rest of the economy.[53] In Britain, the Thatcher government subjected the public sector to market pressures, privatising many large nationalised industries and state-owned assets such as British Aerospace, British Telecom, British Gas and Rolls Royce, and introducing legislation for the sale of council houses. The Reagan administration pursued a similar line of policy, privatising many essential services like American Telephone and the Telegraph Corporation. However, rather than being broken up into separate units, many large public monopolies were simply replaced with private ones, which contradicted neo-liberal free-market principles.[54]

In Britain and the United States, there was also a desire amongst neo-liberal policy-makers to move towards private systems of provision. Both the Thatcher and the Reagan governments were committed to reducing public spending on social welfare and education. The aim was to replace the welfare culture of dependency with one of private enterprise, conducive to market society. In Britain, attempts were made to reduce the burden posed by the National Health Service on the economy with the restoration of income-tax relief on employer-employee medical insurance schemes.[55] Further, in both Britain and the United States, neo-liberals argued that the benefits of reducing social security and welfare entitlements were threefold: cut-backs would reduce the Public Sector Borrowing Requirement and thereby contribute to the war on inflation; reduce the level of taxation levied on private individuals; and, through reductions in the social assistance available, increase the potential for free markets.[56] Moreover, a massive programme of deregulation was pursued by the Thatcher and Reagan administrations in an attempt to enhance the forces of the market and reduce government intervention in the economy. In the United States, in particular, supply-side economists were committed to ending federal regulations paid for by private citizens. In the economic sphere, restrictions on economic activity were removed by the Reagan administration, for example, in railroad transportation broadcasting and in the oil and natural gas industries. In social and environmental spheres, the responsibilities and powers of the Safety and Health Administration to regulate the workplace and those of the Environmental Protection Agency to ensure environmental control were loosened or eroded by the Reagan administration. Neo-liberals claimed that such deregulatory measures had the positive effect of increasing market forces and consumer participation in markets.[57]

Markets and the global economy

The neo-liberal vision of a global market

Neo-liberal aspirations for the eclipse of state power are nowhere more apparent than in their vision of a global market. This vision can be traced back to Hayek's early writings in the 1930s, in which he explicitly rejected the concept of a national economy, linking it to the rise of aggressive nationalism and collectivism. Reflecting on the experience of the early twentieth century, he proclaimed that 'the existence of many sovereign national states will for ever remain a serious danger to peace'.[58] In his essay 'The principles of a liberal social order', Hayek appeared to envision a form of globalism. The spontaneous order of the market, he predicted, 'will progressively grow beyond the organisations of the nation state and empire, and produce at least the beginning of a world society without and often against political authority'.[59] Here Hayek was looking back to the nineteenth-century tradition of British liberalism. The rules of such a global order, he argued, can be traced back to this period of competing visions of the world; the liberal vision of cosmopolitanism, free trade and peace and the conflicting aristocratic one of imperialism, militarism and domination. Hayek endorsed what was in the nineteenth century a radical and progressive liberal view of Britain and the world. He envisioned a world without borders, in which the authority of national governments is undercut by alternative 'international' systems of rule such as the Gold Standard.[60]

Hayek was more explicit in his vision of Europe. In a letter to *The Spectator* in 1939, he appeared to endorse a European system of mutual cooperation based along the lines of the European Union. Indeed, reflecting on the rise of Nazism in Germany, he was convinced that some sort of 'federation' of democracies in Central Europe 'is the only way of securing lasting peace and economic improvement in that part of the world'.[61] Hayek made it clear that Britain would have to take the lead in such a scheme, to offer security to France and help curtail German hegemony. This 'new order of Europe' based on political and economic cooperation, Hayek maintained, would have to be led by the 'strong', since it would 'require restrictions of national sovereignty that a real rule of law in international affairs implies'.[62] Towards the end of the Second World War in 1944, Hayek wrote that a European Federation could gradually be extended beyond the nations of Western Europe. Such a large regional bloc could achieve a level of cooperation with the British Empire and the United States which 'would not be possible on a world scale'.[63]

Later in 1980, Milton Friedman set out his ideal of a global market economy. Friedman, in his *Free to Choose*, identified Hong Kong as a microcosm of the global economy. Hong Kong, he wrote, is 'limited government in practice'. Its economy has 'no tariffs or other restraints on international trade', 'no government direction of economic activity, no minimum wage laws and no fixing of prices'. 'The residents', he continued, 'are free to buy from whom they want, to sell to whom they want, to invest however they want, to hire whom they want, and to work for whom they want'.[64] Like nineteenth-century Britain, Hong Kong in the late twentieth century, he contended, is an example of the economic success brought about by free trade and limited government policy. Friedman transferred Hong Kong's neo-liberal model of a free and competitive economy to the international arena. He claimed that,

> [i]n a free trade world', as in a free economy in any one country, transactions take place among private entities – individuals, business enterprises, charitable organisations. All the parties to that transaction agree on the terms at which any transaction takes place on. The transaction will not place take place unless all parties believe they will benefit from it. As a result, the interests of the various parties are harmonised. Co-operation, not conflict is the rule.[65]

Thus international free trade, he writes, 'would not only promote our material welfare, it would also foster peace and harmony between nations and spur domestic competition'.[66]

The neo-liberal vision of a global market order raises many problematic issues about enforcing and governing such an order. At the heart of the dilemma is the question of what role, if any, should be played by the states in the global economy. The neo-liberal belief in a global market and the struggle for global competitiveness appears to limit severely the ability of nation–states to choose their own economic destiny. Neo-liberal discourse on the global market is an anti-political one. National governments are no longer autonomous, decision-making bodies; the world which is evolving is one where global solutions will flow to where they are needed, without the intervention of states. They present an image of a global economy in a borderless world, with the free movement of capital and corporations across national borders.[67]

However, even if the neo-liberal vision of a global market separate from state is realised, neo-liberalism's own understanding of such a system still necessitates an important role for the state. The spontaneous order of the global economy envisioned by neo-liberals cannot be obtained by dismantling the modern state. It is impossible to imagine the neo-liberal ideal of an elite of altruistic individuals, capable of policing and sustaining the global economy without assistance from central governments.[68] The global market is dependent on a form of order apart from that provided by the market itself. Like national markets, global markets do not work unaided. In neo-liberal discourse, the state will continue to perform its traditional duties in the global economy, of enforcing law and order and maintaining property rights and a sound currency. Moreover, in modern national economies the state has been restructured to accommodate new functions, institutions and wider participation in global economic governance. The unfolding and contrasting systems of economic governance in the contemporary world means that, far from being undermined, the state will continue to play a central role not just at the national level, but also at the sub-national and regional level, for instance in the European Union, where markets and state agencies exist side-by-side.[69]

International financial institutions

Another major source of contention for neo-liberals is the role played by international financial institutions in the global economy. In contemporary literature, especially that of a Marxist persuasion, a prevalent interpretation of international financial institutions such the World Trade Organization (WTO), the International Monetary Fund (IMF) and the World Bank is a neo-liberal one, of pro-market institutions promoting the further liberalisation of world trade in developed economies, at the exclusion of poorer countries. Indeed, many on the Left see these so-called 'neo-liberal' institutions as the enemy of Third World development.[70] Other opponents view them as an instrument of ideological warfare. For instance, John Gray in his *False Dawn* comments that 'the role of the WTO is to project free markets into the economic life of every society'.[71] To label these institutions as simply 'neo-liberal', however, is to misinterpret what the term 'neo-liberal' stands for. While international financial agencies are clearly influenced by neo-liberal free-market thinking, like all Marxists, the majority of neo-liberals are opposed to their policy actions, but for very different reasons. Most fundamentally, neo-liberals see a schism existing between the rhetoric of institutions like the IMF and the World Bank, and what they actually do in practice. Neo-liberals do not oppose the free-market line advocated by these institutions; what they object to is the actions of the institutions themselves. In their actions they institute the kind of top-down economic planning that is anathema to neo-liberals. In the post-war period, global financial institutions like the WTO, World Bank and the IMF, through the Bretton Woods system, acted as inter-governmental organisations of international economic regulation and stabilisation. Since this period neo-liberals like Brink Lindsey claim that they have changed for the worse. They argue that they have been transformed from temporary global stabilisers and rebuilders into permanent crusaders against global poverty and inequality. The IMF, in particular, has become associated with the imposition of international political authority on developing countries. The IMF's generous bailouts, neo-liberals complain, give the governments of developing countries no incentive for reform and prolongs economic backwardness, leaving countries worse off than before.[72]

It is important to note, however, that neo-liberals like Hayek readily accepted the need for a rule-driven approach to international trade – the hallmark of organisations like the WTO. Indeed, Hayek saw a complex and powerful symbiosis between the rules essential for the effective workings of market economies and the rules which constrain arbitrary state power. What he opposed is the policies of institutions that move beyond their rule-enforcing capacity and seek to intervene directly in global economic forces, creating the kind of market distortions that it is their principal task to prevent.[73]

Conclusion

The market, this chapter has shown, is one of the 'decontested' political concepts, which is situated at the core of neo-liberal ideology. It is an indispensable part of the neo-liberal arch that is essential to its formation of as an ideology; its eradication would lead to the destruction of neo-liberalism as a distinctive ideology. This chapter has tried to show that a particular interpretation of the concept of 'market' – an interpretation of a self-generating, spontaneous and competitive market order stemming from the ideas of the Austrian economists Mises and Hayek – determines the structure of neo-liberal ideology. Neo-liberal thinkers have assigned clear meaning to the market, modernising the concept in response to contextual changes and stringently controlling its usage in contemporary neo-liberal discourse. Like all the concepts at the core of neo-liberalism, this chapter has argued that the market does not exist in isolation, rather it is supported by a number of adjacent concepts such as evolution, spontaneous order and limited knowledge. The neo-liberal notion of an open and competitive market economy, the chapter has observed, draws on the tradition of classical economic liberalism dating back to the original conception of the private, self-regarding individual, advanced by Mandeville and Smith. In the post-war years, the market perfectly embodied the economic individualism pursued by neo-liberals at Mont Pelerin. Free-market relationships, they argued, are a civilising force as they abolish the restraints placed on the freedom of the individual in the economic sphere by collectivism. In the 1970s in Anglo-America, interest in the market was revived and popularised through Conservative Party politics. A number of peripheral concepts or loose policy ideas were fleshed out in response to the rise of the market order, for example the enterprise culture, income-tax relief, privatisation, de-regulation and share-ownership.

One of the most important bases of neo-liberal ideology underpinning the market order is the rule of law. Neo-liberals are radically opposed to the notion of an active state beyond that required to secure property rights, market mechanisms, and entrepreneurial activity. However, this chapter has argued that the pursuit of the market order necessitates an important role for the state, overlooked by neo-liberals. In neo-liberalism's own understanding of the market order, markets cannot exist without politics; national strong state capacities and participatory democracy are essential ingredients for the preservation of a global market society.

Notes

1. Keith Joseph, 'The economics of freedom', pp. 19–20, quoted in Michael Freeden, *Ideologies and Political Theory* (Oxford: Oxford University Press, 1996), p. 395.
2. Bernard Mandeville, *The Fable of the Bees* (Harmondsworth: Penguin, 1970).
3. D. D. Raphael, *Adam Smith* (Oxford: Oxford University Press, 1985), pp. 72–3.
4. Adam Smith, *The Wealth of Nations* (Harmondsworth: Penguin, 1976).
5. Desmond S. King, *The New Right: Politics, Markets and Citizenship* (London: Macmillan, 1987), p. 71.
6. Charles E. Lindblom, *Politics and Markets: The World's Politico-Economic Systems* (New York: Basic Books, 1977), pp. 7–8.
7. David Ricardo, *On the Principles of Political Economy and Taxation* (Harmondsworth: Penguin, 1974).
8. John Stuart Mill, *Principle of Political Economy*, Vol. 1 (London: Hodge, 1987), p. 243.
9. See John Gray, *Hayek on Liberty* (London: Routledge, 1988), pp. 102–3.
10. P. Deane, *The Evolution of Economic Ideas* (Cambridge: Cambridge University Press, 1978), pp. 93–115.
11. Quoted in Geoffrey Hodgson, *Economics and Evolution: Bringing Life Back into Economics* (Cambridge: Polity, 1993), p. 28.
12. Alfred Marshall, *Principles of Economics* (London: Macmillan, 1987).
13. Carl Menger, 'On the origin of money', *Economic Journal* (June 1892), pp. 239–55.
14. L. Walras, *Elements of Pure Economics, or The Theory of Social Wealth* (New York: Augustus Kelly, 1956).
15. Hodgson, *Economics and Evolution*, p. 176.
16. F. A. Hayek, 'The results of human action but not of human design', in F. A. Hayek, *Studies in Philosophy, Politics and the Economics* (London: Routledge and Kegan Paul, 1976), pp. 96–105.
17. F. A. Hayek, *The Constitution of Liberty* (London: Routledge, 1960), p. 9.

18. Ibid., p. 5.
19. G. C. Roche, 'The relevance of Friedrich A. Hayek', in F. Machlup (ed.), *Essays on Hayek* (New York: New York University Press, 1976), p. 11.
20. Norman Barry, *Hayek's Social and Economic Philosophy* (London: Macmillan, 1979), p. 41.
21. F. A. Hayek, 'The use of knowledge in society', in his *Individualism and Economic Order* (London: Routledge, 1948), p. 78.
22. Ibid., p. 88.
23. John Gray, 'Hayek on the market economy and the limits of state action', in D. Helm, *The Economic Borders of the State* (Oxford: Oxford University Press, 1989), pp. 130–1.
24. Hilary Wainwright, 'Hayek and the social-engineering state', in her *Arguments for a New Left* (Oxford: Blackwell, 1994), p. 55.
25. Hayek, 'The use of knowledge in society', pp. 86–8.
26. F. A. Hayek, *Law, Legislation and Liberty: The Mirage of Social Justice*, Vol. 2 (London: Routledge, 1976), p. 79.
27. Ibid., p. 72.
28. F. A. Hayek, *The Road to Serfdom* (London: Routledge, 1944), p. 68.
29. Hayek, *The Constitution of Liberty*, p. 140.
30. Richard Bellamy, 'Dethroning politics: Liberalism, constitutionalism and democracy in the thought of F. A. Hayek', *British Journal of Political Science*, 24: 3 (1994), pp. 423–4.
31. Hayek, *The Constitution of Liberty*, p. 222.
32. Ibid., p. 222.
33. Lindblom, *Politics and Markets*, p. 80.
34. Ibid., p. 149.
35. F. A. Hayek, *Law, Legislation and Liberty*, Vol. 3: *The Political Order of a Free People* (Chicago: University of Chicago Press, 1979), p. 80.
36. Ibid., p. 84.
37. Ibid., p. 88.
38. Hayek, *Law, Liberty and Legislation*, Vol. 2, p. 134.
39. F. A. Hayek, *Law, Liberty and Legislation*, Vol. 1: *Rules and Order* (Chicago: University of Chicago Press, 1973), p. 107.
40. Norman Barry, 'Commentary: Markets and regulation', in J. Blundell and C. Robinson (eds), *Regulation Without the State . . . The Debate Continues* (London: IEA, 2000), pp. 31.
41. Ibid., pp. 39–40.
42. King, *The New Right*, p. 86.
43. Geoffrey Hodgson, *Economics and Utopia: Why the Learning Economy is not the End of History* (London: Routledge, 1999), p. 79.
44. Geoffrey Hodgson, *The Democratic Economy* (Harmondsworth: Penguin, 1984), p. 85.
45. Ibid., pp. 86–9.
46. Andrew Shonfield, *Modern Capitalism: The Changing Balance of Public and Private Power* (Oxford: Oxford University Press, 1965).
47. Michel Albert, *Capitalism Against Capitalism* (London: Whurr Publishers, 1994).
48. David Coates, *Models of Capitalism: Growth and Stagnation in the Modern Era* (Cambridge: Polity, 2000), pp. 9–10.
49. H. Abromeit, 'Government–industry Relations in West Germany', in M. Chick (ed.), *Governments, Industries, Markets* (London: Edward Elgar, 1990), p. 61.

50. King, *The New Right*, pp. 78–84.
51. Robert Sugden, 'Naturalness and the spontaneous order of the market', in S. H. Heap and A. Ross (eds), *Understanding the Enterprise Culture* (Edinburgh: Edinburgh University Press, 1992), pp. 161–81.
52. Norman Barry, 'Understanding the market', in M. Loney et al, *The State or the Market: Politics and Welfare in Contemporary Britain* (London: Sage, 1996), p. 236.
53. Kenneth Hoover and Raymond Plant, *Conservative Capitalism in Britain and the United States* (London: Routledge, 1989), pp. 186–7.
54. King, *The New Right*, p. 124.
55. Hoover and Plant, *Conservative Capitalism*, p. 177.
56. Norman Barry, *The New Right* (London: Croom Helm, 1987), pp. 135–6.
57. P. D. Quick, 'Business: Reagan's industrial policy', in J. L. Palmer and I. V. Sawhill (eds), *The Reagan Record* (Cambridge, MA: Ballinger Publishing Co., 1984), pp. 287–308.
58. F. A., Hayek, 'An Anglo-French federation', letter to *The Spectator*, 15 December 1939, in Bruce Caldwell (ed.), *The Collected Works of F. A. Hayek, Vol. 10, Socialism and War: Essays, Documents, Reviews* (Chicago: University of Chicago Press, 1997), p. 163.
59. F. A. Hayek, 'The principles of a liberal social order', in his *Studies in Philosophy, Politics and Economics* (London: Routledge and Kegan Paul, 1967), pp. 163–4.
60. Hayek. *The Constitution of Liberty*, p. 522.
61. Hayek, 'An Anglo-French federation', p. 163.
62. Ibid., p. 164.
63. Hayek, *The Road to Serfdom*, p. 243.
64. Milton Friedman and Rose Friedman, *Free to Choose* (Harmondsworth: Penguin, 1980), pp. 54–5.
65. Ibid., p. 74.
66. Ibid., p. 60.
67. See Kenichi Ohmae, *The End of the Nation State: The Rise of Regional Economies* (London: HarperCollins, 1996).
68. Andrew Gamble, *Politics and Fate* (Cambridge: Polity, 2000), pp. 49–50.
69. See J. Pierre and B. G. Peters (eds), *Governance, Politics and the State* (Basingstoke: Macmillan, 2000).
70. See, for example, Adrian Leftwich, *States of Development: On the Primacy of Politics in Development* (Cambridge: Polity Press, 2000) and Graham Harrison, *The World Bank and Africa: The Construction of Governance States* (London: Routledge, 2004).
71. John Gray, *False Dawn: The Delusions of Global Capitalism* (London: Granta Books, 1998), p. 18.
72. Brink Lindsey, *Against the Dead Hand: The Uncertain Struggle for Global Capitalism* (Washington, DC: Cato Institute, 2002), pp. 78–84.
73. Hayek, *The Constitution of Liberty*, pp. 289–90.

Chapter 6

Welfare: The legitimacy of state provision

Introduction: Welfare and ideology

Like the market in the previous chapter, the concept of welfare forms part of the matrix of key propositions that sit at the core of neo-liberal ideology. Welfare is absolutely essential to neo-liberalism's formation as a distinctive ideology. Yet whilst the concept of welfare may serve as one of the linchpins of neo-liberal discourse, other adjacent concepts connected with welfare – the minimal state, equality of opportunity, personal responsibility, self-reliance, negative rights – reinforce and operationalise it. Analysing these concepts as part of neo-liberalism's wider 'idea environment' would help not only to clarify the meaning of neo-liberal political language, but also, more significantly, to establish common agreement over values and a hierarchy of ends and purposes in society. At the core of this analysis is the intractable question of what constitutes an improvement in well-being and how this level of well-being is most effectively attained. For neo-liberals, this is a question of finding an acceptable rationale for state intervention: an issue bound up with ethics and efficiency. Indeed, neo-liberalism arguments on welfare are constructed within an ideological framework; they inevitably draw on the schism between the state and the market, the public and the private, outlined in the previous chapter. The neo-liberal attitude to the welfare state is a fundamentally hostile one. Unlike the market, welfare or 'welfarism', for neo-liberals, is a pejorative term; one which engulfs other liberal concepts such as individual rights and justice, and perverts their proper meaning. The chapter will, however, point out that, while neo-liberals may be apprehensive about the notion of a welfare state, they are not opposed to the concept of welfare in principle. This distinction rests on their definition of welfare activities that can be regarded as legitimate — types of state provision which are compatible with liberal principles and the rules of just conduct. For neo-liberals, the question of welfare is essentially one about the kind of role the state should play in its provision.

This chapter outlines the neo-liberal approach to welfare and relates it back to its understanding of other liberal concepts such as freedom, individual rights and justice. The concept of welfare, it argues, should not be considered as a peculiarly modern social construct, but rather as one that is historically rooted in the tradition of liberalism. Economists and social philosophers of the old liberal school of thought did not necessarily associate the concept of welfare with the state. A variety of ideals and values in the past and present that have suffused liberal political discourse about welfare have entailed no (or a very limited) conception of state provision.[1] Thus the chapter presents a brief historical discussion of the concept of welfare before its assimilation to the modern state, and it highlights the forms of welfare provision which have influenced neo-liberalism's conceptualisation of welfare, as well as those which it has reacted against. The chapter goes on to analyse the neo-liberal approach to fundamental ideas about welfare such as state provision, equality and social justice, and social rights and needs. Finally, the chapter examines welfare in a market society: the crisis of the welfare state in the 1980s and the policy implications of a neo-liberal welfare regime at the national level. It concludes by arguing that, for neo-liberalism, the concept of welfare is crucial to its ideological identity, as a correct understanding of its meaning is, for neo-liberals, the very symbol of the proper but limited role that the state should play in Western societies.

The rise of the modern welfare state

Welfare before the welfare state

The modern neo-liberal conception of 'welfare' can be traced back to Adam Smith's understanding of public welfare and justice as an outcome of baser motives in market society. Smith understood the concept of welfare as part of the philosophy of economic individualism. His theory of the self-interested individual in competition with others in market society became the common social ethics that underlay the early development of industrial society. If the state was to have a role in the provision of welfare,

Smith argued that it must be restricted to the provision of certain public services which no individual alone could maintain. Fellow classical economist David Ricardo later refined Smith's ideas, arguing that the provision of poor relief was counter-productive. In his *Principles of Political Economy*, he claimed that existing welfare arrangements deriving from the Elizabethan Poor Law were incompatible with the natural liberty of the free-market system, as they marginalised the role of capital in society. In his so-called 'iron law of wages', Ricardo maintained that a rise in Poor Law expenditure or wages would be at the expense of profits on which enterprise, and hence employment, depended.[2]

The classical economists' interpretation of welfare formed the rationale behind the *laissez-faire* policy prescriptions of nineteenth-century British social policy. The provision of welfare, it was argued, should rest on institutions such as the family, the church and charities and, as Samuel Smiles asserted, the principles of 'self-help' and 'mutual aid'. A philosophy of welfare founded on these institutions and ideas was inimical to the suggestion that the state itself should intervene. The gospel of Victorian social philosophy became associated with four principal tenets: work, thrift, respectability and, above all, self-improvement. The state was assigned a purely negative and restrictive role in achieving the superior virtues of Victorianism and the so-called 'progress of the nation'. Asa Briggs, however, observes that the extent to which there was no, or very limited, provision of welfare services by 'organised governmental power' in nineteenth-century Britain should not be overstated. He points to the paradox that Smiles could assert with confidence that the negative role of the state was 'everyday becoming more clearly understood', while The *Times* could record that 'session after session we are amplifying the province of the legislature and asserting its moral prerogatives'.[3] Indeed, it was during the so-called Victorian age of *laissez-faire* that the first hesitant moves towards a state welfare system were made. During the course of the nineteenth century, the creation of central administrative departments and the introduction of legislation that enlarged its practical activities extended the long arm of the state. Although in 1834 attempts were made by the Commissioners of the Poor Law Amendment Act to reform the existing system of poor relief by abolishing the allowance system and replacing it with the harsher 'less eligibility' criterion and 'workhouse test', the general trend in social policy was towards greater intervention. The interventionist social measures adopted by the British state by 1870s included factory legislation limiting working hours and restricting the employment of women and children, nation-wide education legislation financing and supervising schools, a number of public health acts aimed at improving the living conditions of the working class, as well as numerous multifarious services provided by town councils, such as public wash houses, libraries and parks.[4] In line with neo-liberal theorising on welfare, Norman Barry, however, points out that, in nineteenth-century Britain,

> welfare was still a word that was used to describe individual experiences and whatever state aid existed was seen as an adjunct to the market, supplied because of fear of social unrest from an alienated pauper class, or as a consequence of the altruistic motives of other individuals.[5]

Indeed, nineteenth-century Britain, in terms of social policy, was neither an age of pure *laissez-faire* nor one of collectivism, but rather one of Benthamite utilitarianism, which represented a synthesis between the two.[6]

In the United States, the ideas of the classical economists and the *laissez-faire* philosophy received an even more rigid acceptance than in Britain. The Enlightenment reinforced the widely held belief that the poor were personally responsible for their own condition, and the American Revolution only served to exacerbate this view by fostering a belief that poverty could be individually conquered with the right personal incentives and motivation. Indeed, during the nation's worst depression to date in 1821, the New York Society for the Prevention of Pauperism contended: 'No man who is temperate, frugal, and willing to work need suffer or become a pauper for want of employment.'[7] Like in Britain, this philosophy of personal responsibility in American society was accompanied by moves towards the provision of indoor poor relief. State legislatures enacted the County Poorhouse Act in 1824 that set up, out of county tax, funds institutions for all the recipients of public assistance. This limited public aid was accompanied by private charity. Private charitable groups such as the New York Association for Improving the Condition of the Poor (AICP), set up by white middle-class Protestants in 1843, attempted to 'remould' the poor and 'elevate' their moral and physical condition. The group combined limited Christian benevolence with harsh moralism. The Protestant ethics demanded hard work, thrift, observance and temperance: if an individual failed to achieve these it was her own fault, idleness and other bad habits were responsible. In effect, Trattner points out that 'the A.I.C.P was less a charitable agency than an instrument for social control, a means for keeping society orderly, stable and quiet'.[8]

Other state measures followed the provision of indoor relief later in the nineteenth century: special institutions were created to tackle child poverty, legislation was introduced regulating child labour, and in 1872 the American Public Health Association was founded. As in Britain, however, American social measures implemented in the nineteenth century continued to be seen from the perspective of individual (negative) liberty rather than from that of social causation. Barry observes that in Germany the first decisive steps were taken in the direction of state welfare.[9]

The revolution in social reform

It was in Germany that the first state system of social welfare was constructed. While in Britain factory legislation was more advanced by 1900 than in any other industrialised nation, Germany held the record on social security. The German social reform programme under Bismarck represented a landmark in the move towards a comprehensive welfare state. The system of social insurance introduced in Germany in the late nineteenth century can be seen as a 'new social period' in the history of the concept of welfare, characterised by new economic ideas, political views and social programmes. In Germany there was no strong Smithian tradition of classical political economy, as there were in Britain and the United States, which distinguished the economic from the social. The German school of historical economics was critical towards the motives of capitalism and held a belief in social order. 'The state', Bismarck laid down in the preamble to the first bill of 1881, 'is not merely a necessary but a beneficent institution'.[10] His reforms between 1881 and 1889 introduced compulsory social insurance against sickness, accidents, old age and invalidity, defended in terms of the positive improvement of the welfare of the working classes.

Bismarckian social policies marked a decisive turning point in modern social history, and set the precedent for similar social reform programmes elsewhere. In Britain, a supportive observer noted in 1890 that Bismarck had 'discovered where the roots of social evil lie. He has described in words that burn that it is the duty of the state to give heed, above all, to the welfare of the weaker members of the community.'[11] Towards the end of the pre-war period, the British liberal government introduced the Pensions Act in 1909 and its own National Insurance Act in 1911, which applied a scheme of state-sponsored compulsory workers' insurance for the needs of the sick and unemployed. The act was a significant departure from the previous Victorian Poor Law, which was no longer practical in democratic society. It represented a fundamental transformation in the attitude of the government towards poverty. Specific 'social contingencies' were linked to the need for particular social policies, and for the first time free-market capitalism was made compatible with state-sponsored welfare schemes.[12] The experience of the Great Depression of 1929–33 exacerbated this trend in social philosophy in Britain. Barry points out that poverty was no longer associated with moral failing, but rather with 'the apparently uncontrollable and random economic forces to which almost anyone was potentially vulnerable'.[13] The notion of involuntary unemployment was thus accepted, and for the first time the provision of welfare was linked ineluctably to the management of the economy so as to secure full employment.

In the United States, where there had been entrenched resistance to state intervention in welfare provision, new legislation was also passed. With the onset of a long and deep Depression in 1929, the Protestant moral ethics seemed outmoded as an approach to the problems of unemployment and destitution. Indeed, Franklin D. Roosevelt declared that under his New Deal administration 'aid to jobless citizens must be extended by government, not as a matter of charity, but as a matter of social duty'.[14] Thus in the 1930s tentative moves towards the creation of a modern welfare state were made with the introduction of the Social Security Act in 1935. The act established a federal aid programme of cash payments, which provided security for families in times of unemployment, sickness and old age. In addition, dependent children were removed from state institutions and placed in private homes. For the first time in American history, public welfare was viewed as a right and its provision became a permanent item in the federal budget.

War, want and welfare

Between the early and middle periods of the twentieth century there was a radical shift in ideas in favour of state welfare provision, which neo-liberals vehemently opposed. In Britain, the experience of the Second World War created an unprecedented sense of social solidarity among the public, which made it more willing to accept egalitarian policies and collectivist state intervention. The wartime upheavals made society more introspective and self-critical, and the social evils readily accepted in the past appeared more vivid and intolerable. The public mind became more acutely aware of the evils of large-scale unemployment and there was a growing realisation of how inadequate the social services provided by the state were. The possibilities created by Keynesian policy prescriptions produced an overwhelming desire to build a better future.[15]

The most famous document on wartime reconstruction was the 1942 Beveridge Report, which became a blueprint for the British post-war welfare state. The report claimed that social security was only one part of the provision needed to tackle the 'Five Giants' – want, disease, ignorance, squalor and idleness. It proposed that the state should fulfil three principal areas of provision: first, family allowances should be introduced to prevent poverty in large families; secondly, a national health service should be available to all, independently of National Insurance contributions; and thirdly, government should be made responsible for maintaining a high and stable level of employment.[16] In 1945, the Labour Party, determined to avoid the economic and social failures of the inter-war years, dedicated itself to the proposals set out in the Beveridge Report and proposed far-reaching reform measures. Clement Attlee's 1945–51 labour government put forward an immediate proposal to start a housing programme, attempted to maintain full employment through the adoption of Keynesian economic demand management, introduced the Family Allowances Act in 1945 and the National Insurance Act in 1946, and in 1948 founded the National Health Service. The radical nature of the labour government's reform programme signalled an end to the ad hoc and inadequate welfare measures of the past and the birth of a minimum safety net provided by the state.

American post-war society was markedly different from Britain's. The dominance of McCarthyism directed attention and energy away from domestic reform ideas. The anxieties created by the Cold War pushed the issue of defence to the forefront of the policy agenda, and quashed incentives for the reform of social policy. Moreover, unlike in Britain, there was a widespread belief, in American society, in mass prosperity and affluence, despite a series of recessions throughout the 1940s and 1950s. The issue of improving society, it was believed, had already been accomplished.[17] The welfare state that was constructed in post-war American society consequently became what Alan Brinkley has aptly termed a 'compensatory state'.[18] Although liberal politicians coalesced around the New Deal and during the war years published their own Beveridge Report in the form of the 1942 report *Security, Work and Relief Policies*, such welfare programmes were dismissed by Roosevelt at the time as 'grandiose schemes' and never implemented in the post-war years. Limited social reform measures were put forward in the areas of social security and education, but these were of secondary importance to the larger task of maintaining economic growth. It was the responsibility of the state to intervene to compensate for capitalism's flaws through contributory national insurance and welfare schemes. The experience of world war and the onset of the Cold War had changed the liberal vision. Indeed, Brinkley points out that 'liberals who had once admired the collective character of some European governments looked with horror at the totalitarian states America was now fighting and saw in them a warning about what an excessively powerful state could become'.[19]

In Germany, there was also strong opposition to the social reform policies of the post-war world. While in Britain the war had engendered a sense of national solidarity and confidence in state intervention, in Germany the experience of Nazism and its misuse of power provoked opposition to any form of collectivism. It was paradoxical that Germany, the nation that, ever since Bismarck, had been the leader in matters of social policy, should now be the one to oppose most fervently social reform and the creation of a welfare state in the post-war world.[20] Certainly the opposition to social reform was not universal. The social democrat camp was inclined towards the model of the British welfare state, and campaigned for equal opportunities through social reform measures. However, the ruling political forces in the post-war era had neo-liberal leanings which ruled out the creation of a welfare state. The ordo-liberals, the defenders of the Social Market Economy, objected to the idea of a welfare state, preferring instead a social or 'socially responsible' market economy. They rejected Keynesian 'one-sided' policies to create full employment and instead argued that the market-conforming measures should be adopted to avoid the worst slumps. German ordo-liberals did not deny that state help should be provided to those mostly in need, but contended that it should be 'targeted support' rather than 'blanket projects', which were 'unable to discriminate between those who could pay and those who could not'.[21] In line with conventional neo-liberal thought, German ordo-liberals viewed these welfare measures as simply transitional, which would wither away with economic success of free-market competition. Indeed, one leading ordo-liberal, Eucken, argued that the answer to social problems 'lay in the support for competition which would so increase the nation's wealth that it would render welfare superfluous'.[22]

The late 1940s and 1950s, however, represented a brief 'liberal' moment in modern German history. By the end of the Adenauer era, in the early 1960s, the Federal Republic was in reality an advanced welfare state. For corroboration, Hockerts refers to 'the nearly universal coverage of employed persons and the relatively high levels of contributions and pensions'.[23] To explain this development, he points to the increased political weight of voters supportive of state social benefits, the increase in the ratio of elderly people in Germany, specific post-war problems that necessitated increased state intervention, the influence of the governing party, which 'considered active social policies as a precondition for the internal stabilisation of the new liberal-democratic state', and the threat from communism in the East, which gave stabilisation an added dimension.[24]

'THE FATAL CONCEIT': MISTAKEN IDEAS ABOUT WELFARE

Neo-liberalism has constructed its own counter-philosophy of welfare in response to the changes in welfare provision that took place in Western societies in the twentieth century. Neo-liberals' understanding of welfare rests on the important distinction Hayek made between two types of society: the 'spontaneous order' of liberal society, and the constructivism of state-centred society. Neo-liberals associate the former with market processes and the minimal state, the latter with socialism and the welfare state. Central to neo-liberals' conceptualisation of welfare is their interpretation of fundamental concepts associated with welfare such as state provision, social justice, equality, social rights and citizenship, which they view as 'mistaken' ideas or beliefs; together, they would constitute what Hayek termed 'the fatal conceit' of socialism.[25]

State provision

At the heart of neo-liberalism's opposition to contemporary interpretations of welfare is their association with the concept of 'state provision'. In Western societies since the Second World War, the provision of an 'unconditional minimum' for all, neo-liberals argue, has necessitated a move towards the social engineering state. Rather than defining welfare in terms of a new relationship between individuals and society, they argue that post-war ideologues and policy-makers, in particular Keynes and Beveridge, embedded an interventionist conception of welfare in the public mind which is both destructive of national prosperity and damaging to individual liberty.²⁶

The central argument for neo-liberals is that the market rather than the state embodies freedom and welfare. State intervention in the realm of welfare, they contend, is not simply a 'service activity', but rather a coercive threat to individual freedom. Indeed, Hayek famously argued in his *Road to Serfdom* that the welfare state is a threat to freedom as it coerces individuals into a paternalistic and authoritarian system. Unlike the market, he maintained that welfare provided through the state is simply unable to take into account individual preferences, and thus 'the individual would more than ever become a mere means, to be used by the authority in the service of such abstractions as the "social welfare" or the "good of the community"'.²⁷ By following the methods of totalitarian collectivism, the modern welfare state outlined above, for Hayek and other neo-liberals, represents an overarching social vision which is incompatible with a free society.

As well as the general theoretical criticism of state welfare in terms of its restrictions on individual freedom, neo-liberals also oppose state welfare provision on the grounds of its inefficiency and ineffectiveness. These characteristics, they maintain, are inherent in the very nature of state welfare. The scale of the modern welfare state and its basic instruments, such as bureaucracies and agencies, neo-liberals contend, lead to an inefficient and unresponsive system, with no incentive for innovation or competitiveness. High levels of public expenditure to fund welfare are seen as a burden on the productive elements of the economy, and have created a public hostility towards state welfare programmes. Milton and Rose Friedman, for example, were critical of the universal welfare state in post-war Britain. Writing in 1980, they claimed that taxes to fund the provision of welfare in Britain 'have become a major source of resentment', which has 'been multiplied many-fold by the impact of inflation'.²⁸ The Friedmans pointed out that

> [t]he National Health Service, once the prized jewel in the welfare state crown and still widely regarded by much of the British public as one of the greatest achievements of the post-war Labour government, has run into increasing difficulties. It has been plagued by strikes, rising costs, and lengthening waiting list for patients.²⁹

As a result, the neo-liberals observe that the private health sector has been growing rapidly. High levels of taxation demanded by welfare policies, they claim, reduce individual incentives to find alternative forms of welfare, compatible with a competitive market economy, and unnecessarily interfere in the dynamism and growth of national economies.³⁰

Neo-liberals do, however, concede that the market has a number of deficiencies that can only be remedied by the state. Hayek has most clearly defined which welfare activities can be regarded as legitimate for the state. In his *Constitution of Liberty*, he pointed to state activities that are compatible with 'liberal' principles. He argued that, most fundamentally, taxation should not be used by the state as an instrument for redistribution, and government should never be allowed to claim a monopoly. Hayek saw an important role for the state as a 'service agency', 'assisting without harm in the achievement of desirable aims which perhaps could not be achieved otherwise'.³¹ He acknowledged that it should be the responsibility of the state to provide certain public goods and a 'social minimum', which

> appears not only to be a wholly legitimate protection against a risk common to all, but a necessary part of the great society in which the individual no longer has specific claims on the members of the particular small group into which he was born.³²

Hayek stated that government should not move beyond this minimum provision. The welfare state, he contended, if not tightly limited, 'becomes a household state in which a paternalistic power controls most of the income of the community and allocates it to individuals in the forms and quantities which it thinks they need and deserve'.³³ Hayek argued that this type of state infringes upon the right of the individual to choose and reduces incentives for individual action, and, most significantly, represents a dangerous shuffle down the road to egalitarianism and collectivism.

Social justice and equality

Neo-liberals argue that the fundamental conceptual error of social justice has been the most significant motor of welfare state development in the Western world. In the post-war period, Hayek argued that classical conceptions of law and justice have been superseded by the concept of 'social justice'. Legislative measures have been introduced which aim to 'manipulate' outcomes and redress 'unjust' inequalities, thereby treating social groups differently. Hayek's central argument in opposition to this development was that substantive inequalities in the market can never be considered to be unjust because injustice requires that an outcome is intended. Market outcomes are always unintended consequences of individual processes of exchange, and this led Hayek to argue that the notion of social justice is a 'mirage', an illusion premised upon fundamental misunderstandings of the concept of justice. This illusory concept of social justice is damaging to liberty, as it corrupts the legal framework that preserves individual freedom.[34]

For Hayek and other neo-liberals, therefore, there can be no justification for allowing the state to redress substantive inequalities. Neo-liberals, however, are not opposed to the concept of equality, but rather to a particular 'socialist' interpretation of it. As Hayek put it:

> We do not object to equality as such. It merely happens to be the case that a demand for equality is the professed motive of those who desire to impose upon society a preconceived pattern of distribution. It is this which is irreconcilable with freedom.[35]

For neo-liberals, equality is 'formal equality' or equality before the law, which is the only form of equality that is compatible with individual freedom. The Friedmans subscribed to 'equality of opportunity', which dictates that 'no individual should be prevented by arbitrary obstacles from using his capacities to pursue his own objectives'. Equality for the Friedmans was simply a by-product of freedom. They thus concluded that 'equality and liberty are two faces of the same basic value'.[36]

In the twentieth century there was marked neo-liberal opposition to a particular conception of equality – 'equality of outcome'. The notion of equality of outcome, for neo-liberals, suggests that everyone should be able obtain the same standard of living or income through the pursuit of 'big government' at the expense of individual liberty. As highlighted above, this notion of equality first affected government welfare programmes in Britain during the post-war years, and subsequently became an important source of influence behind the growth of the German corporatist welfare state in the 1960s. It is in American society, however, the society with the most 'liberal' and 'residual' welfare regime, that neo-liberal opposition to the concept of equality of outcome has been most marked. In the United States, this particular conception of equality is seen to promote a welfare entitlement ethics that all neo-liberals stand against. Charles Murray, in particular, makes the point that the idea of equality through the welfare state undermines traditional 'liberal' notions of self-esteem and personal autonomy. The welfare state in turn generates 'cycles of deprivation' and an almost permanent underclass. In his *Losing Ground*, Murray surveys American social policy from 1950 to 1980, noting the rise in public expenditure for welfare and the overall increase in unemployment rates for some social groups and in family breakdown. He contends that the Great Society programmes of the 1960s were unsuccessful in diminishing poverty, as they undermined the self-reliance of individuals and opportunities for self-improvement. It is not the value of the welfare benefits themselves that Murray blames for the over-reliance on the system, but the reduction in the eligibility requirements for obtaining them. Indeed, between 1964 and 1967, he writes that American social policy changed from 'the dream of ending the dole to the institution of permanent income transfers that embraced not only recipients of the dole but large new segments of the American population'.[37] The solution to the dilemma of welfare in America, Murray concludes, is not 'a new wave of federally engineered welfare programmes', but 'small government'.[38]

Social rights and citizenship

Neo-liberals argue that in the twentieth century notions of social rights and citizenship have provided, almost unwittingly, the ethical foundations for the modern welfare state. For neo-liberals there are no positive 'rights' to welfare or rights of citizenship that entitle individuals to a specific standard of living or 'well-being' provided by the state. They contend that legitimate welfare rights are negative rights which grant the individual no more than a minimal 'safety-net' necessary for mere survival. Neo-liberals have a very strong but limited conception of citizenship. They reject out of hand T. H. Marshall's concept of 'social citizenship' that gives all individuals social entitlements to the resources of society.[39] Neo-liberals contend that a conception of citizenship should not include a right to wellbeing, least of all to social justice. Citizenship should be enabling rather than providing, it should create opportunities for individuals to enhance their own welfare independently of the state.

In Britain, a series of publications from free-market think-tanks has developed a policy-orientated analysis, based on the neo-liberal conception of citizenship. Influenced by the underclass debate in the United States, the Institute of Economic Affairs in Britain has focused attention on the social and moral consequences of increases in illegitimacy and unemployment. It claims that the rise in welfare dependency is a direct result of the erosion of individual and community responsibility. Indeed, David Green's IEA pamphlet, *Community Without Politics*, argues that the problem of welfare is 'moral in nature'. Green emphasises the themes of 'freedom' and 'responsibility', and proposes that 'the mainspring of a free and democratic society is the individual's sense of personal responsibility', which is characterised by self-control, independence from government and duty towards fellow citizens.[40] It is possible, he argues, to envisage a private, non-political alternative to the welfare state, where government still has an essential role, whilst an unpoliticised community assumes the chief burden. Looking back at the British 'classical liberal heyday' of 1834–1911, Green's ideal of a 'community without politics' is a moral community where social solidarity springs from an obligation to help others in an ethos of mutual respect between the helper and the helped'. This conception of civic association encourages a concept of duty without rights – 'everyone has a duty to help the less fortunate but no one has a right to receive help'.[41] Green proposes wholesale reform of the taxation and benefits system, to reverse the rights-based character of public provision and to encourage a moral, social and legal framework based on the notion of duty. Legal and public policy, he claims, must contribute to a transformation of ethical principles and morals in order to restore the civic arena. Welfare responsibility, he argues, must lie first with the individual or family, secondly with the community as distinct from the state, and thirdly with the government.[42] Similar proposals were advocated by the Adam Smith Institute in 1983, when the Institute's Omega Report proposed a less radical version of Green's scheme. Like Green, the authors of the report proposed that welfare benefits should only go to those most 'in need', with individuals exercising the free choice over how to spend them; the priority should be to encourage incentives to work, however poorly paid; and there should be a private and compulsory insurance system.[43]

Green's ideas clearly have important parallels with those of neo-liberals. In his IEA publication, *Reinventing Civil Society*, for instance, Green draws out the similarity between his ideas and those of Hayek. He states that the most urgent task for welfare reformers is to de-politicise the law-making process, and he proposes a Hayekian separation of powers, putting law above the government. Thus law-making should be confined to a separate, non-political assembly. 'Britain's mistake', Green contends, 'was to have allowed the same assembly that voted taxes also to make laws.' Law-making requires 'a different temper, an impartial spirit, and a degree of wisdom, of which no hot-house political assembly is capable'.[44] Further, Green admits that his views share common ground with those of the German ordo-liberals. As in the German Social Market Economy, in Green's civil society freedom rests not on markets alone, but 'on a well-constructed system of law and morals'. Like the ordo-liberals before him, Green is critical of both *laissez-faire* economics and of the redistributive state, and embraces instead what he refers to as 'civic capitalism' – a form of order that assists the casualties of capitalism but at the same time respects personal idealism.[45]

In the United States, Lawrence Mead makes a similar criticism of the welfare state's emphasis on rights rather than personal responsibilities and obligations. In his *Beyond Entitlement*, Mead's central argument is that the main problem of the modern welfare state in the United States is its permissiveness rather than its size – it conveys a message of rights without obligations of citizenship. Mead points out that in American society the government is simply unable to obligate the recipients of its welfare programmes, even if it is for their own benefit. In debates about citizenship, he argues that the need for self-discipline and competence has been neglected. Mead states that

> the goal must be to create for recipients inside the welfare state the same balance of support and expectation that other Americans face outside it, as they work to support themselves and meet the other demands of society. Work must be treated as a social obligation, akin to paying taxes and obeying the law.[46]

However, unlike Green, Mead argues that what is required is not small government, but a stronger and perhaps even bigger state, to enforce the social obligation to work. He contends that there is no alternative but 'to use compulsion to force the underclass to accept the obligations of citizenship'.[47]

Mead's conservative approach to welfare reform is one that many neo-liberals would sympathise with. Neo-liberal thinkers like the Friedmans, for example, expressed concerns about personal incentives and suggested devising a new system that would produce different incentives, such as a negative income-tax scheme. Under this scheme, if a person's income falls below the level of their personal tax allowance, they receive a payment from the tax authorities equivalent to the difference between their allowance and their actual income.[48] Mead, however, favours a more interventionist government than most neo-liberals would prefer. Neo-liberals would be more wary about constructing a federal welfare scheme along Mead's lines, to avoid the unwanted effects of earlier measures. Most neo-liberals hold the view that the majority of welfare measures should never have been enacted. They contend that, without them, many beneficiaries would have been self-reliant individuals instead of being dependent on the state.

Retrenching the welfare state

Neo-liberals may hold a theoretical ideal of what the concept of welfare should stand for. However, implementing their ideas in the world of policy has proved problematic. The Thatcher and Reagan governments in Britain and America in the 1980s put forward ambitious programmes, which required widespread rethinking about the state's role in welfare and the restructuring of welfare regimes. A concerted effort was made to change the balance of the mixed economy of welfare – to shift the state from its dominant role and to promote the roles of the market and voluntary sector in the provision of welfare.

The disillusion of welfare

As the first part of this chapter pointed out, the welfare state since the Second World War has become an important feature of all capitalist societies, even so-called 'liberal' ones, like the United States. By the mid-1970s, however, the pace of welfare expansion began to falter. The worldwide economic recession of the early 1970s created difficulties in sustaining the pattern of welfare state policies in their post-war form. The oil price rise in 1973 created mass unemployment throughout the Western world, eroding what had been, for the founders of the welfare state, one of its main 'pillars'. The welfare state was subsequently subjected to challenges and critiques that questioned its role.

The West German welfare regime became unsettled in the mid-1970s as a result of external economic pressures. The oil crisis created an urgency to take control of public spending, which led to a steady fall in social spending after 1975, although the German state continued to play a central role welfare, providing a substantial system of rights-based social assistance.[49] The impact of the recession on national ideological and political debates in Germany was marginal compared to the situation in both Britain and the United States. The British economy in the mid-1970s stood in stark contrast to the relatively high rates of capital formation and the substantial economic growth, which characterised the 1950s and 1960s. Britain, by 1975, was experiencing lower rates of economic growth, higher levels of unemployment, and lower rates of investment. As the problems of economic recession persisted and intensified, the pressures on the public provision of welfare provoked widespread rethinking about the state's role in welfare. Britain witnessed the 'weakening of social democracy'[50] and the birth of a sustained ideological campaign carried out by the Right, which placed a heavy burden of blame on the welfare state for causing economic and moral decline.

Neo-liberal politicians in the British Conservative Party such as Margaret Thatcher and Keith Joseph were critical of Keynesian economic management and Beveridge-style policies that were responsible in the post-war years for the growth of government. They were hostile to the growth of government activities in the twentieth century which, in the words of Richard Rose, had 'expanded in scale far beyond the minimalist conception of the Nightwatchman state to become the central institution of the mixed economy of welfare'.[51] Neo-liberals argued that the expansion of government control was an unmitigated disaster. The massive expenditure on welfare programmes, they proclaimed, had overloaded government to the point of inefficiency and ineffectiveness. The blame, Thatcher argued, lay not just with the 'socialist' mentality of Labour Party, but also, more fundamentally, with the philosophy within the Conservative Party. The notion, she argued, that 'state intervention would promote social harmony and solidarity or, in Tory language, "One Nation"', was the 'final illusion' which collapsed in the '"winter of discontent"'. 'Welfare benefits', she went on, 'distributed with little or no consideration of their effects on behaviour, encouraged illegitimacy, facilitated the breakdown of families, and replaced incentives favouring work and self-reliance with perverse encouragement for idleness and cheating.'[52]

As in Britain, in the United States, too, the onset of economic recession in the mid-1970s marked a starting point for neo-liberalism's challenge to the extended welfare state. Neo-liberalism provided an economic rationale for reform, identifying an over-regulatory, over-interventionist and over-taxing federal state as the major cause of America's declining competitiveness. Neo-conservatives with neo-liberal leanings, such as Irving Kristol, were unanimous in the view that the War on Poverty and the Great Society programmes of the 1960s had been a failure. Kristol argued that the 'skyrocketing costs of the welfare state' were way out of line 'with its modest (if indubitable) benefits'. The extended state and the culture of welfare dependency that it fostered, he claimed, were responsible for economic decline and under-investment, as they diverted resources from the productive to the unproductive sectors of the economy.[53] Neo-conservatives proclaimed that these externalities of 'unprincipled' government growth in the field of welfare constituted 'government failure'. The main source of government failure for neo-conservatives, Ramesh

Mishra observes, was 'the naïve collectivist equation of the common good with state action'.[54] All state actors, in the end, neo-liberals argued, pursued their own objectives at the expense of the wider interests of the organisation. Indeed, the Friedmans maintained that the state and its institutions 'operate in precisely the opposite direction from Adam Smith's "invisible hand"'. 'An individual who intends only to serve the public interest by fostering government intervention is led by an invisible hand to promote private interests, which was no part of his intention.'[55]

Those on the Right of the Republican Party adopted the neo-conservative argument of government failure in the 1970s. Reagan was the most aggressive in his opposition to the growth of welfare. In the late 1960s he had expressed his objections to Nixon's plans to federalise welfare completely. Steven Hayward states that Reagan observed that '[i]f there is one area of social policy that should be at the most local level of government possible it is welfare. It should not be nationalised – it should be localised'.[56] The welfare state, Reagan proposed in his 1970 re-election campaign for Governor of California and again in his presidential campaign a decade later, should be retrenched rather than extended and centralised through a massive reduction in social expenditure.

Setting the new agenda

Neo-liberal politicians' disillusion with the welfare state was articulated into a new policy agenda in Anglo-America from the mid-1970s onwards. Issues of public spending, 'excessive' taxation, 'big government' and 'rolling back' the state were at the forefront of the agenda. Attention was focused on ways of both reducing and changing the role of the state in the provision of welfare. This new policy agenda of the New Right overlaps with neo-liberal ideological claims about the disincentives welfare produces and its inherent inefficiency. These neo-liberal arguments had a substantial ideological impact, shifting public perceptions of the welfare state.

In Britain, neo-liberals on the New Right attempted to construct a post-Keynesian welfare state consensus through a curtailment of state activity and the promotion of market forces. Within the British Conservative Party in the late 1970s, an offensive on welfare started to unfold, supporting the 'rolling back' of the modern state. Mishra distinguishes between the offensive's ideological attack on welfare, which entailed creating an anti-welfare 'climate of opinion', and its policy proposals for implementing political change in the realm of welfare provision. The New Right's attack on welfare, he observes, did not involve dismantling the welfare state which would have been electorally unpopular, but rather reforming the welfare system specifically through reductions in public expenditure and taxation.[57] Indeed, cuts in government expenditure on social welfare, health and education, where it had been growing fastest, became one of the main policy priorities of the Thatcher government in the 1980s. Outlining the economic strategy of the government in 1980, Thatcher proclaimed that 'the government is determined not merely to halt the growth of public expenditure but progressively to reduce it'.[58] King states that the ideological basis of this statement was neo-liberal. He maintains that,

> while it was argued rolling back the state would reduce the Public Sector Borrowing Requirement, thereby lowering the money supply and inflation, the government's commitment to cutting public spending also reflected its antipathy, based in liberalism, towards the public sector.[59]

In other areas of expenditure, however, such as defence and law and order, where the ideological motive was different, there was no such commitment to reducing spending. At the heart of the neo-liberal attack on welfare expenditure was a theoretical rationale stemming from liberal economics, to the effect that, by reducing welfare spending, entrepreneurial and competitive drive in the economy would increase and notions of collective welfare would be superseded by an individualist mentality of familial self-reliance and personal responsibility. As Paul Wilding has argued, 'the Conservative governments promoted, if not universally, the view that public services existed simply for those who could not afford anything better or were too irresponsible to do so'.[60]

The Thatcher government put forward specific proposals for the reform of welfare policy areas such as social security, education and health. In 1980 significant legislation was passed, reforming the social security system. In 1980, the Supplementary Benefits Commission was abolished and the Social Security Advisory Committee was set up. The Committee passed social security legislation in 1980, which reduced discretionary payments, made entitlements more clear-cut, and tightened rules to fight the abuse of social security. In June 1985, a white paper entitled *Reform of Social Security* was published, which led to the passing of the 1986 Social Security Act. The paper set out the reasons for reforming the system. It states that the problem was not just with funding the system, the price of which had soared to forty billion pounds a year by 1985, but also with its piecemeal development, which had resulted in 'a multitude of benefits with overlapping purposes and different entitlement conditions'. The paper proposed a new approach, in line with neo-liberal principles, according to which government would offer 'an underlying basis of provision on which we as individuals can build' and 'not discourage self-reliance or stand in the way of individual provision or responsibility'.[61] The paper thus proposed reductions in the level of government support. The major proposal was for the abolition of the State Earnings-Related Pension Scheme, which relied on the public sector. The conservatives argued that the scheme was fragmented and outdated. The government was anxious to encourage the private sector to take off the state as much of the burden for pensions as possible. The paper claimed that occupational pension schemes or personal private schemes rather than state-funded ones would give greater freedom to individuals and encourage personal incentives for self-provision. In the area of education reform, free-market think-tanks during the 1980s, such as the Institute of Economic Affairs and the Centre for Policy Studies, set out plans to widen the parental choice of schools through education voucher schemes, to make significant cut-backs on school expenditure, and to introduce higher education tuition fees so as to free universities from government control.[62] In the realm of health policy, neo-liberal social reformers proposed changes to the most popular component of the British welfare state, the NHS. As in social security and education, Wilding observes that reforms were proposed in health which 'narrowed the role and purpose and functions of the welfare state from the provision of welfare for all to the very different role of providing only for the needs of the poor'.[63] Thus proposals for reform of the NHS focused on the introduction of health vouchers to encourage a 'mixed' system of private and government financed health programmes, as in America. Health reform, neo-liberals like Arthur Seldon argued, should aim to 'diminish the role of political decisions and to enlarge the influence of consumer choice'. Central government should move away from taxation and free services and 'confine itself to ensuring the maintenance of minimum standards and providing subsidies where necessary'.[64]

In the United States in the 1980s, as in Britain, the Reagan administration sought a massive reduction in the welfare state. David Stockman's conception of the 'Reagan revolution' in welfare was that of a reform programme dedicated to the return of American social policy to a pre-New Deal non-interventionist era, when public welfare was curtailed to a minimum. He argued that neo-liberals on the American New Right wanted to 'cut the umbilical cords of dependency that ran from Washington to every nook and cranny of the Nation', to mount a 'frontal assault on the American welfare state', and to achieve a 'substantial retraction of welfare state benefits that people had come to feel "entitled" to receive'.[65] Social hardship, neo-liberals maintained, should be relieved privately through the market, the voluntary sector and the family.

The private sector provision of welfare in American society was promoted in a variety of ways. As in Britain, free market think-tanks made radical proposals for the privatisation of pensions and for medical care services. These included the Family Security Plan developed by the Heritage Foundation in 1982, which proposed to replace social security with an Individual Retirement Account and to allow social security taxes go to the purchase of private pensions. Similar proposals were made for an Individual Health Account. The use of vouchers in the provision of education was also proposed by Friedman, to free the education system from government control and to give parents a greater control over their children's education. Moreover, Reagan set out plans for a universal 'workfare', whereby recipients would have to work in the private sector in exchange for welfare payments.[66]

Underpinning the social reform measures proposed by the Reagan administration was a deep-seated commitment to enact steep cuts in taxes and federal domestic spending. Neo-liberals on the American New Right employed the precepts of the 'Laffer curve' to legitimise substantial tax cuts. The logic of the Laffer curve implies that cutting taxes leads to increased incentives for work for both employees and employers. Neo-liberals argued that taxation blunted initiative by removing the economic incentive from risk-taking and economic effort. An obvious corollary of this argument was the proposition that public spending was not 'wealth-producing'. Thus reductions in taxation under the Reagan administration were accompanied by the imperative to cut social welfare expenditure. Reagan aimed to curb public spending not only by encouraging greater reliance on private organisations in providing sustenance and assistance, but also by extricating the federal government as much as possible from funding and providing social welfare services. Under the concept of the 'new federalism', he advocated shifting the responsibility for social services to state and local governments. George Peterson points out that 'the expectation was that local governments, directly accountable to local voters, would choose to spend less than central government where the voters' will would be filtered through interest groups'.[67]

Rhetoric and reality

The reform of the welfare state was undoubtedly a high priority for the Thatcher and Reagan administrations, yet the direct impact of neo-liberal policy prescriptions on the welfare state in Anglo-America in the 1980s was limited. Continuity in terms of welfare spending was more apparent than change. Paul Pierson comments that in the area of welfare reform 'both the Thatcher and the Reagan governments' accomplishments fell far short of their aspirations, and of what they were able to engineer in a range of other policy domains'.[68]

In Britain, the Thatcher government's failure to 'roll back' the state is reflected in its record of public spending on social welfare. In spite of all the talks about cut-backs in public expenditure, the percentage of gross domestic product (GDP) being spent on social welfare was the same level in 1987–8 as it was 1978–9: 23 per cent. In a number of social policy areas, notably health care, income support and sickness pay, proposals for reform were reluctantly dismissed by the Thatcher government.[69] Le Grand observes that:

> Overall what this shows is that the welfare state, and indeed, welfare itself, is very robust. Over thirteen years from 1974 to 1987, welfare policy successfully weathered an economic hurricane in the mid-1970s, and an ideological blizzard in the 1980s.[70]

A number of reasons has been advanced for the 'robustness' of welfare spending in Britain. One general point is the effect of the bureaucratic and professional inertia within the state, which makes any attempt to reform policy a much longer process than was anticipated by neo-liberal politicians. Specifically in relation to health care, plans for privatising the NHS would have been too costly and unpopular with the electorate. The Thatcher government also failed to curb social security expenditure, despite frequent changes in government definitions of unemployment and in the conditions for the eligibility for benefit. Although the objective was to bring about cuts, a combination of demography and high levels of unemployment during the 1980s led to rising social security spending. The long-term trend towards a growing elderly population and declining participation in private pension schemes in the 1980s brought with it an increased demand for welfare benefits and services. Wilding observes that:

> What went on in the first two Thatcher governments was a process of policy learning. They discovered that what could be achieved by cuts to welfare programmes was little more than candle ends apart from housing. They discovered that the

potential for the increased targeting of benefits on the worse off and of increasing charges on the better off using services was also limited without increasing disincentives to work and provoking a middle class backlash.[71]

The Reagan administration experienced similar problems in retrenching the American welfare state. Pierson states that the United States in the late 1970s, like Britain, 'revealed growing disquiet about taxation and declining levels of support for particular welfare programmes', attitudes which clearly contributed to the New Right's initial electoral success.[72] 'Once retrenchment began, however, a pro-welfare state backlash occurred almost immediately. Visible cutbacks were unpopular, and by the mid-1980s levels of support for public programmes had returned to roughly the levels of the early 1970s'.[73] Thus the Reagan government not only failed to weaken public support for social expenditure, but was also subsequently unsuccessful in producing a policy shift to curtail the flow of revenues on which social welfare programmes relied. Indeed, Theda Skocpol has observed that 'the United States emerged from "the Reagan era" with social security benefits still universally structured, and still comparably generous social programmes for the elderly'.[74] Reagan and his policy advisors may have managed to reduce the rate of growth of means-tested spending, but 'social security enjoyed too much support from middle-class citizens'.[75] Moreover, the democrats successfully portrayed the Reagan administration reform programme as a threat to the elderly, leaving it unwilling to alter the structure of the American pension system.

From the record of the Thatcher/Reagan years, it would be wrong, however, to assume that neo-liberalism had no impact whatsoever on the welfare state, or on the concept of welfare in general. In Anglo-America in the 1980s neo-liberalism successfully reconceptualised welfare, as the German ordo-liberals did in the post-war years. What neo-liberals did was to alter the terms of political debate and introduce a radically new approach to welfare, where the overriding concern was not with providing social services to those in need, but with economic efficiency and eliminating dependency. Certainly welfare expenditure has survived the politics of retrenchment, but, as Wilding argues, 'collective action as the road to social welfare has been effectively and permanently problematised'.[76]

Conclusion

Neo-liberalism, this chapter has shown, has its own distinctive understanding of the core concept of welfare that forms part of the wider corpus of its ideological configuration. Indeed, the whole debate on welfare, for neo-liberalism, is an ideological one which centres on its opposition to the various models that the concept had come to embody in Germany, Britain and the United States in the post-war years. Neo-liberals hold a de-politicised conception of welfare, which substitutes the welfare concepts of state provision, social justice, social equality and positive social rights with its own adjacent ones, such as the value of freedom, equality of opportunity, individual responsibility and negative rights. These adjacent concepts are some of the most fundamental in neo-liberalism's anti-collectivist value system.

Neo-liberalism's conception of welfare, this chapter has shown, draws heavily on the beliefs and principles of classical liberalism, but rejects its Enlightenment assumptions about reason and progress. It looks back to the classical liberal era when the private market, voluntary organisations and the family rather than the state were the big players in welfare. Indeed, M. O'Brien and S. Penna summarise that:

> In neo-liberalism 'welfare' is understood simply as a revitalisation of market relations, a subordination of everyday life to transactions in an unregulated economy, and a revalidation of those institutions – the family, the community, and charity – that are considered as a substitute for what markets cannot provide.[77]

Neo-liberal perspectives on the welfare state negatively claim that the increasing centralisation of responsibility for individual welfare has undermined the moral foundations of civil society, infringed the freedom of the individual and led to economic inefficiency and ineffectiveness. The neo-liberal ideal is a *Rechtsstaat* that acts to protect and structure the market so that it can achieve welfarist goals. Neo-liberals, however, concede that the market may not be able to guarantee a social minimum, and accept that it is the responsibility of government to guarantee a 'safety net' for those individuals unable to provide for themselves.

Neo-liberal ideas gained a new eminence and influence in welfare debates in the late 1970s. Neo-liberalism's policy ideas about welfare formed their criticism of the universal model of welfare capitalism that became a central element in New Right arguments and retrenchment programmes in Anglo-America in the 1980s. In Britain and America neo-liberal politicians followed economic and social policies that departed in significant ways from those entailed by the Keynesian welfare state. Yet, as the chapter has observed, many welfare services, most notably social security, survived the Thatcher/Reagan years with only relatively minor impairments. The significance of the changes to the welfare state brought about by the New Right has been in the realm of ideas. The magnitude of change in terms of policy may have only been minor, but the direction of change in terms of approaches to welfare has been unmistakable. Neo-liberalism has helped to reshape the terrain of welfare debates in the Western world, restructuring the roles and functions of the welfare state, and stressing the need for social policies that are more responsive to individual needs and wants.

Notes

1. Norman Barry, *Welfare* (Buckingham: Open University Press, 1999), p. 5.
2. See D. Fraser, *The Evolution of the British Welfare State: A History of Social Policy since the Industrial Revolution* (London: Macmillan, 1973), pp. 36–7.
3. Asa Briggs, 'The welfare state in historical perspective', in C. Pierson and F. G. Castles (eds), *The Welfare State Reader* (Cambridge: Polity, 2000), pp. 19–20.
4. A. J. Taylor, *Laissez-faire and State Intervention in Nineteenth-century Britain* (Basingstoke: Macmillan, 1972).
5. Barry, *Welfare*, p. 31.
6. Fraser, *The Evolution of the British Welfare State*, p. 105.
7. Quoted in W. I. Trattner, *From Poor Law to Welfare State: A History of Social Welfare in America* (New York: Free Press, 1979), p. 48.
8. Trattner, *From Poor Law to Welfare State*, p. 63.
9. Barry, *Welfare*, pp. 30–1.
10. Quoted in Briggs, 'The welfare state in historical perspective', p. 23.
11. Quoted in E. P. Hennock, 'The origins of British national insurance and the German precedent 1880–1914', in W. J. Mommsen (ed.), *The Emergence of the Welfare State in Britain and Germany 1850–1950* (London: Croom Helm, 1981), p. 87.
12. G. A. Ritter, *Social Welfare in Germany and Britain: Origins and Development* (Leamington Spa: Berg, 1986), pp. 146–8.
13. Barry, *Welfare*, p. 39.
14. Quoted in Trattner, *From Poor Law to Welfare State*, pp. 226–7.
15. See J. Harris, 'Some aspects of social policy in Britain during the Second World War', in W. J. Mommsen (ed.), *Emergence of the Welfare State in Britain and Germany 1850–1950* (London: Croom Helm, 1981), pp. 247–62.
16. N. Timmins, *The Five Giants: A Biography of the Welfare State* (London: Fontana, 1996), p. 21.
17. Trattner, *From Poor Law to Welfare State*, pp. 245–7.
18. Alan Brinkley, 'The late New Deal and the idea of the state', in his *Liberalism and its Discontents* (Cambridge, MA: Harvard University Press, 1998).
19. Ibid., p. 53.
20. See H. G. Hockerts, 'German post-war social policies against the background of the Beveridge Plan', in Mommsen, *Emergence of the Welfare State in Britain and Germany* (above, n. 15), pp. 317–18.
21. A. J. Nicholls, *Freedom with Responsibility: The German Social Market Economy* (Oxford: Oxford University Press, 1994), p. 321.
22. Ibid., p. 322.

23. Hockerts, 'German post-war social policies', p. 322.
24. Ibid., p. 323.
25. F. A. Hayek, *The Fatal Conceit: The Errors of Socialism*, W. W. Bartley (ed.), (London: Routledge, 1988).
26. B. Jordan, *Freedom and the Welfare State* (London: Routledge, 1976), pp. 111–12.
27. F. A. Hayek, *The Road to Serfdom* (London: Routledge, 1944), p. 100.
28. Milton Friedman and Rose Friedman, *Free to Choose* (Harmondsworth: Penguin, 1980), p. 128.
29. Ibid.
30. Vic George and Paul Wilding, *Welfare and Ideology* (Hemel Hempstead: Harvester Wheatsheaf, 1993), pp. 28–31.
31. F. A. Hayek, *The Constitution of Liberty* (London: Routledge, 1960), pp. 257.
32. Ibid., p. 258.
33. Ibid., p. 261.
34. F. A. Hayek, *Law, Legislation and Liberty: The Mirage of Social Justice*, Vol. 2 (Chicago: Chicago University Press, 1976).
35. Hayek, *The Constitution of Liberty*, p. 87.
36. Friedman and Friedman, *Free to Choose*, p. 159.
37. Charles Murray, *Losing Ground: American Social Policy 1950–1980* (New York: Basic Books, 1984), p. 24.
38. Ibid., p. 40.
39. T. H. Marshall, *Citizenship and Social Class* (Cambridge: Cambridge University Press, 1950).
40. David G. Green, *Community Without Politics: A Market Approach to Welfare Reform* (London: IEA, 1996), p. 113.
41. Ibid., p. 34.
42. Ibid., p. 170.
43. Adam Smith Institute, *The Omega Report* (London: ASI, 1983).
44. David G. Green, *Reinventing Civil Society: The Rediscovery of Welfare Without Politics* (London: IEA, 1993), pp. 122–3.
45. Ibid., pp. 137–8.
46. Lawrence M. Mead, *Beyond Entitlement: The Social Obligations of Citizenship* (London: Free Press, 1986), p. 4.
47. Ibid., p. 4.
48. Friedman and Friedman, *Free to Choose*, pp. 150–55.
49. R. Lawson, 'Germany: Maintaining the middle way', in P. Taylor and V. George (eds), *European Social Policy* (Basingstoke: Macmillan, 1996), pp. 56–78.
50. Andrew Gamble, 'The weakening of social democracy', in M. Loney et al., *The Market or the State: Politics and Welfare in Contemporary Britain* (London: Sage, 1996), pp. 257–72.
51. Richard Rose, *Understanding Big Government* (London: Sage, 1984), p. 1.
52. Margaret Thatcher, *The Downing Street Years* (New York: HarperCollins, 1993), p. 8.
53. Irving Kristol, *Two Cheers for Capitalism* (New York: Basic Books, 1978), p. 247.
54. Ramesh Mishra, *The Welfare State in Crisis: Social Thought and Social Change* (Hemel Hempstead: Harvester Wheatsheaf, 1984), p. 34.
55. Friedman and Friedman, *Free to Choose*, p. 24.
56. Steven Hayward, *The Age of Reagan: The Fall of the Old Liberal Order 1964–1980* (Roseville, CA: Prima Publishing, 2001), p. 241.

57. Mishra, *The Welfare State in Crisis*, pp. 42–3.
58. Quoted in D. S. King, *The New Right: Politics, Markets, Citizenship* (Basingstoke: Macmillan, 1987), p. 120.
59. Ibid.
60. Paul Wilding, 'The welfare state and the conservatives', *Political Studies* (1997), 45, p. 723.
61. Quoted in T. Raison, *Tories and the Welfare State: A History of Conservative Social Policy since the Second World War* (Basingstoke: Macmillan, 1990), p. 134.
62. See for example John Gray's discussion of education policy in his *Limited Government: A Positive Agenda* (London: IEA, 1989).
63. Wilding, 'The welfare state and the conservatives', p. 723.
64. Arthur Seldon, *After the NHS* (London: IEA, 1968), pp. 7–11.
65. David A. Stockman, *The Triumph of Politics* (London: Bodley Head, 1986), pp. 11, 9, 95, quoted in King, *The New Right*, p. 148.
66. Mishra, *The Welfare State*, ch. 2.
67. George E. Peterson, 'Federalism and the state', in J. Palmer and I. V. Sawhill (eds), *The Reagan Record* (Washington, DC: The Urban Institute, 1984), pp. 217–18.
68. Paul Pierson, *Dismantling the Welfare State? Reagan, Thatcher and the Politics of Retrenchment* (Cambridge: Cambridge University Press, 1994), p. 7.
69. Pierson, *Dismantling the Welfare State?*, p. 143.
70. Le Grand, 'The welfare state', in J. Hills (ed.), *The State of Welfare: The Welfare State in Britain since 1974* (Oxford: Oxford University Press, 1990), p. 350.
71. Wilding, 'The welfare state and the conservatives', p. 716.
72. Pierson, *Dismantling the Welfare State?*, p. 149.
73. Ibid.
74. Theda Skocpol, *Social Policy in the United States: Future Possibilities in Historical Perspective* (Princeton: Princeton University Press, 1995), p. 304.
75. Ibid., p. 303.
76. Wilding, *The Welfare State and the Conservatives*, p. 725.
77. M. O'Brien and S. Penna, *Theorising Welfare: Enlightenment and Modern Society* (London: Sage, 1998), p. 103.

Chapter 7

The Constitution: Government and the rule of law

Introduction: Government, liberty and democracy

The Constitution is the third concept that is allocated a core position in neo-liberalism's conceptual configuration. Neo-liberals, as the previous chapters have demonstrated, acknowledge the need for government, but are at the same acutely aware of the dangers that government embodies. The Constitution is a fundamental political concept for neo-liberals because it represents a means through which the powers of government and other state officials can be curtailed. Individual liberty, they contend, can only be safeguarded by constitutional constraints and by the supremacy of law – constitutional government is equated with limited government. There is thus a significant ambivalence in neo-liberal ideology towards the state and politics. At the heart of neo-liberalism is a serious doctrine about politics and government. Neo-liberals recognise that, in order to have a functioning market order, it is vital to have a corresponding form of political order. Indeed, they must emphatically engage in politics in order to free society from politics. In neo-liberalism, the principles and operating procedures of a specific form of constitutional order represent the only acceptable means of both limiting the coercive power of government and upholding the rules of the market.

At the heart of neo-liberalism's conception of constitutionalism is its interpretation of the rule of law. In neo-liberal ideology, the powers of government are constrained by the rule of law underpinning the constitution. The rule of law represents the fundamental fixed rules that stand over and above the political community. It prevents government from stultifying individual incentives in their pursuit of individual ends or desires and is therefore essential in neo-liberalism for the preservation of the market order. Neo-liberals starkly contrast their liberal ideal of the rule of law with collectivist economic planning, which 'cannot tie itself down in advance to the general and formal rules which prevent arbitrariness'.[1] The rule of law, neo-liberals argue, unlike the legislation of central government, guarantees not only equality before the law but also individual liberty, by restricting the exercise of government powers to those determined by a permanent framework of formal laws.

An important tension in neo-liberal conceptions of the constitution is that which exists between democracy and liberty. Neo-liberals like F. A. Hayek argue that it is a misleading and unfounded belief that democratic rule can never be arbitrary rule. Democracy, they point out, does not always guarantee individual freedom. It is allegiance to the liberal constitution and its fixed rules of law, rather than majority rule, that can prevent the rise of arbitrary power and dictatorship. Hayek thus acknowledged that it may be necessary to limit the will of the majority rule (or rather the will of the administrators and agents of the majority) in order to uphold the rule of law and the values of democracy. It is only through a liberal constitution that democracy can be effectively preserved, as individual liberty is an essential precondition for democratic rule.[2]

This chapter will outline neo-liberalism's conception of the Constitution. It will briefly examine of constitutional traditions found in Britain, the United States and Germany, as well as the neo-liberal interpretation of these traditions. The chapter will argue that neo-liberals do not endorse all constitutional frameworks, but rather they support the liberal ideal of a rule-of-law state embedded in the German *Rechtsstaat*. One of the most influential neo-liberal advocates and elaborators of a liberal constitutional has been Hayek. The chapter will assess his contribution to the formation of an ideological constitutional model. It will look at his distrust of democracy, his discussion of the primacy of the rule of law, and the intractable relationship he sees as existing between law and legislation. It will outline the concepts adjacent to the constitution, such as private law, legal responsibility, abstract order, 'rules of just conduct' and evolution, in relation to Hayek's liberal programme. The chapter will go on to set out a neo-liberal constitutional model. It will detail James Buchanan's proposals for constitutional reform and Hayek's agenda for the 'constitution of a liberal state' through a discussion neo-liberal peripheral concepts or policy ideas like the separation of powers, independent administrative courts, a 'fiscal constitution', balanced budgets and restrained democratic rule. The chapter will contend that the Constitution is a fundamental concept for neo-liberalism, since one of its principal aims, as a movement in opposition to collectivist planning and arbitrary power, is the preservation of liberal constitutionalism and the rule of law.

Constitutional traditions

Britain: Constitutional heritage and common law

Britain, unlike most other liberal democracies, does not possess a written constitution. The British state, however, has a number of significant constitutional documents ranging from the Magna Carta of 1215 to acts of parliament such as the Habeas Corpus Act of 1679 and the Bill of Rights of 1689, in addition to customary law and conventions about the fundamental role of parliament and its powers in relation to the monarchy and the judiciary. The so-called Common Law tradition of the British Constitution may not be represented in a codified single document, yet it has still strongly institutionalised a large number of constitutional principles, which remain as rigid and as difficult to change as any written constitution.[3]

In eighteenth-century Britain, the Constitution was seen as a 'monarchical Constitution'. Constitutional monarchy involved the combination of monarchical rule with some dispersion of power to other bodies, namely the executive and judiciary. In his *Spirit of Laws*, published in 1748, Montesquieu derived the vitality of the liberal British state from its institutionalisation of the principles of the separation of powers. He stated that, 'if there were no monarch and the executive power were entrusted to a certain number of persons drawn from the legislative body, there would no longer be liberty, because the two powers would be united'.[4] Lane, however, points out that 'it is questionable whether Britain was not in the mid-eighteenth century already practising some kind of parliamentarianism'.[5] She states that the British Constitution's 'distinctive trait of parliamentarianism was already institutionalised more or less clearly in the eighteenth century', with the government and parliament, rather than the monarchy, representing the two main organs of the state.[6]

In the nineteenth century, Britain carried forward this tradition of parliamentary constitutionalism. A. V. Dicey's classic study of the British Constitution, *Introduction to the Study of Law and the Constitution*, published in 1885, claimed that the British Constitution combined two guiding principles: the sovereignty of parliament and the rule of law. The critical question in Dicey's work is establishing the coexistence of these principles: combing legislative supremacy expressed through the power of the state with the constitutional conventions and customs set out by the rule of law.[7] Constitutional theorists such as I. Jennings and M. Loughlin question how the rule of law can be preserved if it is subservient to the wishes of a majority of elected legislators. Ultimately, they claim that state sovereignty and the rule of law cannot be harmonised.[8] For this reason some neo-liberals have reservations about Dicey's conception of the rule of law and his system of dual sovereignty. Hayek, for instance, whilst sharing an assumption with Dicey that the common law should act as a protection against interventionist government, rejected his assumption that only ordinary courts, rather than specialist administrative law courts, are compatible with the rule of law. In his *Constitution of Liberty* Hayek argued that Dicey's assertion that, unlike in Britain, administrative coercion was exempt from judicial review on the continent is 'somewhat misleading'.[9] He wrote that Dicey's 'severe strictures were inapplicable to the principle of the German administrative courts; these had been constituted from the beginning as independent judicial bodies with the purposes of securing that rule of law that Dicey was so anxious to preserve'.[10] Hayek maintained that, in contrast, Dicey's conception of the British rule of law is hard to reconcile with the grant to official government agencies of substantial powers to act for very broad purposes with only limited judicial control. He states that

> the very idea of separate administrative courts – and even the term 'administrative law' – came to be regarded in England (and to a lesser extent the United States) as the denial of the rule of law. Thus by his attempt to vindicate the rule of law as he saw it, Dicey in effect blocked the development of institutions which would have offered the best chance of preserving it.[11]

The settled political order of the nineteenth-century British constitutional tradition was subjected to upheavals and major adjustments in the twentieth century, and consequently moved even further away from neo-liberalism's ideal constitutional arrangements. In the twentieth century, the concept of a 'political Constitution' was introduced 'in which the constitution was conceived as a direct expression of political exchange in a society divided by conflict'.[12] Michael Foley states that, in such a Constitution, 'there can be no divide between constitutional and political questions; they are simply interchangeable with one another'.[13] One of the leading advocates of this constitutional model was Harold Laski. Laski was dismissive of the concerns over the rise of the bureaucratic state before, during and after the Second World War.[14] He proclaimed that the Constitution needed to reflect the purposiveness of government. Foley claims that Laski thought 'it was wholly justifiable for the executive to use whatever political means were available to force through government programmes of social and economic regulation'.[15]

In Britain in the 1980s, Laski's conception of political Constitution was rejected by intellectuals and politicians on the neo-liberal New Right. Neo-liberals proposed radical reforms to the British Constitution, in an attempt to reduce the public sector to a minimum and remove the obstacles confronting free markets. John Burton advocated a radical change in his IEA paper on the balanced budget rule. Outlining the present position of 'fiscal anarchy', Burton recommended that an Economic Bill of Rights should be introduced which both laid down the balanced budget rule and limited government spending to twenty-five percent of GDP.[16] Under the Thatcher government, however, constitutional reform remained one of potential rather than fulfilment and failed to implement any formal constitutional changes. Indeed, in spite of its reform pledges, the Thatcher government pursued policy objectives that led to an unprecedented degree of centralisation, which politicised previously neutral institutions and effectively unbalanced the constitution in favour of the government. Andrew Gamble states that the Thatcher government from the very beginning found it impossible to introduce major constitutional changes in a political system that was itself responsible for the move towards greater state intervention. The problem for Thatcher was that the structural features of a pluralist democracy were incompatible with her ideological objectives.[17]

The United States: A 'liberal' Constitution?

Constitutionalism has occupied a pre-eminent place in the American political tradition. The American Constitution of 1787 is a presidential constitution committed to a republican constitutional state with democratic elements. Milton Friedman proclaims that the American Constitution embodies two broad principles that, in theory, safeguard the freedom of the individual. First, 'the scope of government must be limited – its major functions must be to protect our freedom both from the enemies outside our gates and from our fellow citizens'. Secondly, 'government power must be dispersed – if government is to exercise power, better in the county that the state, better in the state than in Washington'.[18] Ultimately, the framers of the constitution sought to reconcile republican government and social stability by diffusing power, enforcing property rights, and balancing the interests of conflicting social groups. Liberalism was, therefore, at the heart of the Constitution. The culminating purpose, stated in the preamble of the Constitution, was that it was to 'secure the blessings of liberty to ourselves and our posterity'.[19] The intention of the framers of the American Constitution to create a liberal constitution by de-centralising political power is reflected in the American Bill of Rights. The American Bill of Rights set out a number of 'fundamental' and 'inalienable' rights that where not to be infringed by legislative majorities, such as freedom of speech or of the press, and the right to bear arms. These rights, Jefferson proclaimed, would create the foundations for social harmony and good government.[20]

For Hayek, the founding of the American Constitution and the Bill of Rights represented a unique endeavour to bring into being a liberal government and to write the rules under which it should operate. Hayek comments that the intentions of the Federal Convention in 1787 to 'limit the powers of government' and 'curb the arrogation of powers by the state legislatures' were consistent with liberal principles.[21] The American Constitution, he argued, not only divided power between different authorities, thus reducing the power that any one body may exercise, but also at the same time provided adequate safeguards for private rights. Hayek went on to cite Lord Acton's praise for the American Constitution:

> Of all checks on democracy, federalism has been the most efficacious and the most congenial . . . The Federal system limits and restrains sovereign power by dividing it, and by assigning government only certain defined rights. It is the only method of curbing not only the majority but the power of the whole people, and it affords the strongest basis for a second chamber, which has been found essential security for freedom in every genuine democracy.[22]

In the late nineteenth and early twentieth centuries, the intellectual climate of opinion in American society started to change. The commitment to individual responsibility and reliance on the market was replaced with a belief in social responsibility and reliance on the state. This transition in ideology had important ramifications for the American Constitution. The Friedmans observed that 'the Constitution, shaped by a very different climate of opinion, proved at most a source of delay to the growth of government power, not an obstacle'.[23] The progressive era of the 1930s, in particular, revolutionised the constitutional system in American society. The New Deal programme signified coordination rather than the separation of powers, which made American citizens less legalistic and more political in their constitutional outlook. The conception of the Constitution as the people's political law was promoted, which advocated a transfer of responsibility for the constitution from the Supreme Court to the legislature, and thus to the people where it democratically belonged. During this period, Hayek observed that 'the prohibition that "no state shall make or enforce any law which shall abridge the privileges or immunities of citizens of the United States" was reduced to a "practical nullity"'. The Supreme Court, he argued, overstepped its proper judicial functions when it was presented with more and more legislation 'which seemed contrary to the spirit of the Constitution'.[24] Hayek claims that 'the Court built a body of law concerning not only individual liberties but government control of economic life, including the use of police power and of taxation'.[25] The Supreme Court exhibited a new deference to economic regulation by both the states and the economy, affirming federal power to regulate various aspects of economic life such as wages, labour and production. Walter Lippmann summed up the period in his statement on the new constitutional order: '*Laissez-faire* is dead, and the modern state has become responsible for the modern economy and the task of insuring the continuity of the standard of life for its people'.[26]

During the Cold War years, neo-constitutionalists attempted to reclaim the Constitution as a revered symbol of non-totalitarian social organisation. The argued that, through the Constitution, 'the power of the state ought to be checked and controlled according to the forms of law'.[27] The central place of constitutionalism in American Cold War ideology was aptly illustrated in Lippmann's 1955 analysis of the crisis in Western civilisation. Describing the disintegration of political authority in the Western world, Lippmann found the source of the crisis in the decline of the 'public philosophy'. For Lippmann, the public philosophy was the antithesis of collectivism which reflected 'natural law' and the 'tradition of civility' – it represented the idea of 'reciprocal rights and duties under the law' as the essence of constitutionalism.[28] Similarly, public choice economists such as James Buchanan were critical of the federal government which had extended way beyond the intention of the original framers of the American Constitution. In his *Limits of Liberty* published in 1975, Buchanan claimed that the United States was fast approaching a state of 'constitutional anarchy'.[29] Congress, he pointed out, had taken over large sections of the private economy and acted on behalf of a coalition of interest groups rather than on the will of the majority. The Supreme Court, he also observed, instead of acting as a neutral enforcer of fundamental rules, had become a body actively engaged in the construction of laws, responding to the momentary desires of citizens. Buchanan argued that what was needed in American society was a 'protective state' which embodied the institutions of law and set standards of just conduct, rules of contract and property entitlements. This protective or legal state, Buchanan claimed, should act as an 'enforcing institution of society' or 'outside referee', who can only be changed by general agreement.[30] Buchanan saw the 'productive state' existing alongside the protective state, which represented the 'part of government that facilitates public goods exchanges'.[31] In line with a neo-liberal theory of the state, Buchanan declared that the productive state should not interfere in the private economy and should be limited to the production of public goods and services in accordance with basic rules of contract.

Germany: the Rechtsstaat

In Germany, constitutionalism has historically rested on the concept of the *Rechtsstaat* (rule of law state). The German *Rechtsstaat* is a liberal–constitutional doctrine that stresses the supremacy of law. Drawing on a Hegelian conception of the state as a higher form of rationality that transcends the competitive struggle of social life, it represents a body of impartial law, which was administered without regard for personal or group interests. Franz Neumann pointed out that the fundamental principle of the *Rechtsstaat* is the legality of administration, that is, 'the administrative state is bound by its own laws, and . . . every interference by the state must be reducible to such laws'.[32] He stated that 'this implies the supremacy of the law and only of the law, but of a certain type of law, namely of the general laws'.[33] State interference in liberty and property must be controllable and must be permitted only by independent judges.

It is this emphasis on legal constraints that makes the German *Rechtsstaat* the model constitutional state for many neo-liberals. Hayek, in particular, was enthusiastic about the *Rechtsstaat*'s potential for securing freedom within a natural legal order. Indeed the *Rechtsstaat*, he stated in his *Constitution of Liberty*, represents the 'ideal of the liberal movement'.[34] In Germany in the nineteenth century, he claimed that the main constitutional objective for the liberal movement was to solve problems of the political state not through the advent of democracy and republican government as in the United States, but through 'the limitation of government by a constitution, and particularly the limitation of all administrative activity by law enforceable by the courts'.[35] Hayek pointed to the rise of new separate administrative courts in Germany in the 1860s and 1870s, which were completely independent and concerned exclusively with the application of pre-existing rules or administrative law. The creation of these new courts, he commented, represented an attempt finally to 'translate into practice the long-cherished ideal of the *Rechtsstaat*'.[36] Indeed, the new administrative courts were fundamental to the realisation of the rule of law, as, unlike normal judicial courts, which were always concerned with the aims of the government of the day and could therefore never be fully independent, their main function was to provide a body of detailed legal rules for guiding and limiting the actions of the administration, thereby protecting the freedom of the individual. Hayek readily acknowledged that, while the liberal ideal of the *Rechtsstaat*

> may never be perfectly achieved, since legislators as well as those to whom the administration of law is entrusted are fallible men, the essential point is that the discretion left to the executive organs wielding coercive power should be reduced as much as possible'.[37]

Hayek, however, pointed out that the German conception of the *Rechtsstaat* 'proved to be more considerable in theory than in practice'. He observed that, in Germany in the 1870s and 1880s, 'when the system of administrative courts received its final shape in the German states, a new movement towards state socialism and the welfare state began to gather force'.[38] He commented that 'there was, in consequence, little willingness to implement the conception of limited government which the new institutions had been designed to serve by gradually legislating away the discretionary powers still possessed by the administration'. The tendency, Hayek argued, was to exempt from judicial review those 'discretionary powers' that were required for the new tasks of government.[39]

By the Weimar period, the German Constitution was in an extremely fragile state. It was overburdened by the attempt to combine in one document many institutions. Indeed, Neumann states that the Weimar Constitution was based on the political principles of pluralism; that is, the distribution of state power among socially free organisations. The self-consciousness of the labour movement after the First World War, he argued, transformed the German liberal state into a collectivist democratic state. The Weimar Constitution, Neumann pointed out, was based on 'various social contracts between various groups of society'.[40] He contended that these contracts constituted a system of collectivist democracy where 'the state for the fulfilment of its tasks uses private organisations, and gives them a share in political power' representing, in effect, a 'social *Rechtsstaat*'.[41] This pluralistic constitutional system strengthened bureaucracy, changed the structure of the economy and inevitably subordinated private interests to those of larger social groups.

Under National Socialism, the rule of law in Germany was destroyed completely, leaving only a veneer of legal form and process. Germany under the Third Reich, like most fascist regimes, did not set out a compact constitution, but governed by means of emergency powers. Indeed, Carl Schmitt's doctrine of 'national emergency', where the state is threatened by 'enemies within', was utilised by the Nazis to justify whatever intervention was needed to accomplish their ends.[42] This doctrine enabled leading Nazis to rule by decree. They set up nation-wide judicial apparatus that would deal with the enemies of the Reich under legal cover. Both in theory and practice, it would therefore appear that the national socialist state could never be a *Rechtsstaat*. Schmitt, however, claimed that the national socialist state possessed basic elements that constituted a *Rechtsstaat*. For Schmitt, it was possible for the national socialist state to fulfil at one and the same time the commands of the leader and of enacted law. In a sensational article he argued that 'The Leader protects the law' – 'the leader is not only the supreme legislator, not only the supreme executive, he is also the supreme judge'. He contended that, while national socialism may have rejected the postulate of the rule of law, in reality 'law is nothing but the will of the leader'.[43] However, to accept Schmitt's conception of the *Rechtsstaat* and its association with Nazism is to disregard its liberal roots and basic premises. A rule-of-law state that stands exclusively at the service of the leader can never be *Rechtsstaat*. The *Rechtsstaat* is an embodiment of 'formal' justice, individual liberty and limited government – all, principles rejected by the national socialists. Indeed, for Hayek and other neo-liberals, the rule of law in a planned society can never hold. This, Hayek claimed, is not to suggest that the actions of the leader should not be deemed legal. Rather, 'the government's coercive powers will no longer be limited and determined by pre-established rules'.[44]

In the post-war years, the ordo-liberals attempted to restore constitutional order in German society. A functioning market economy, the ordo-liberals maintained, required an appropriate constitution or 'social state of law'. One of the leading architects of Germany's Social Market Economy, Franz Böhm, set out a number of constitutional principles needed for the state to perform its proper functions. First, the state, Böhm argued, should act as a service organisation for the protection and preservation of society. The most important services that it should provide are defense and the domestic administration of law. Secondly, the state should not intervene in the social process – that is the complex and evolving network of relationships that exist between private individuals in society. Thirdly, 'the state should exist for society' – 'its powers are finite in a legal sense', and this should be achieved through 'effective powers of control secured within the state organisation for representatives of society'.[45] The ideal form of political rule for German neo-liberals was, therefore, a version of the *Rechtsstaat*. The state, the ordo-liberals argued, should be a 'legally responsible' state, one that respected the confines of its own authority.[46] In the long term, however, the Constitution of the Federal Republic of Germany proved inadequate in constraining the power of the state and pressure group interests. Despite the emphasis they placed upon creating a Constitution capable curbing the state and preventing the destruction of the market, Norman Barry points out that the ordo-liberals 'failed to devise adequate institutional arrangements to prevent the decline of the Social Market Economy'.[47]

Law and Legislation

Neo-liberalism's strong constitutional attachment to the German *Rechtsstaat* is reflected in the important distinction that it makes between law and legislation. Hayek in his three-volume *Law, Legislation and Liberty* associated the former with a spontaneous liberal order, the latter with a constructed social order. Pivotal to this distinction is Hayek's conception of the rule of law and its relationship to individual liberty and democracy.

Private law and public law

In his *Law, Legislation and Liberty*, Hayek maintained that the legal order of modern states comprises two very different and conflicting sets of rules, *nomos* and *thesis*. Hayek argued that *nomos* represents a spontaneous order underpinned by universal laws and 'rules of just conduct' that have emerged from an evolutionary and adaptive process. He contrasted this form of order with *thesis*, which stands for rational design implemented, through the statute rules made by government – legislation.[48] Hayek set out three important distinctions between law and legislation, or 'private law' and 'public law', that are fundamental for understanding his conception of liberal constitutionalism and of the rule of law. First, Hayek stated that, whereas law in the proper sense of the word is 'discovered' independently of human will, legislation is 'willed' or 'invented' – it is an artificial construction. Legislation consists of commands directed to the achievement of specific ends. Law, in contrast, allows individuals to pursue their own ends. Secondly, Hayek contended that, while a political authority lays down legislation, law emerges from a 'judicial process'. Unlike legislation or 'public law', which is concerned with 'administrative measures', private law, he stated, can only be 'taught' and 'enforced' by impartial judges. Thirdly, Hayek argued that, whilst the constructed order of lawmaking is compatible with economic planning, positive liberty and social justice, law is consistent with only economic freedom, negative rights and 'abstract justice'.[49]

Hayek pointed to the changing concept of law in contemporary society, in particular to the confusion of law with legislation. He argued that the spontaneous order of the Great Society has, since the late nineteenth century, gradually become part of the constructivist rationalism of an organised social order. Legislative bodies, he maintained, that had always existed in some shape or form for the creation of public law,

> gradually accrued the power of changing also the rules of just conduct as the necessity of such changes became recognised. Since those rules of conduct had to be enforced by the organisation of government, it seemed natural that those who determined that organisation should also determine the rules it was to enforce.[50]

This development, Hayek contended, is detrimental for individual liberty, as it 'gives into the hands of men an instrument of great power', capable of producing an even 'greater evil'. He argued that such a development 'necessarily leads to a gradual transformation of the spontaneous order of free society into a totalitarian system conducted in the service of some coalition of interests'.[51]

There is a strong sense of looking back in Hayek's work to the law of early civilisations. He cited the early law of the Medes and Persians 'that changeth not'; law that was conceived as 'unalterably given'. Early 'lawgivers', he pointed out, 'from Ur-Nammu and Hammurabi to Solon, Lykurgus and authors of the Roman Twelve Tables, did not intend to create new law but merely to state what law was and had always been'.[52] Hayek maintained that the law of these early civilisations did not remain static; law continued to develop, and the changes that were permitted could not be a result of the intention or design of the law-maker. It was through the development of customs rather than the direction of rulers in these ancient societies, Hayek observed, that the general rules of just conduct came to be accepted.[53] Indeed, the classical period of Roman law, Hayek showed in his *Constitution of Liberty*, was fundamental for the development of modern liberalism. Roman civil law, like the later English common law, he stated, was almost entirely regarded as a product of 'law-finding' by the jurists; that is, 'law grew up through the gradual articulation of prevailing conceptions of justice rather than by legislation'.[54] In particular, he points to the writings of Cicero. Hayek wrote:

> To him is due the conception of general rules or *leges legum*, which govern legislation, the conception that we obey the law in order to be free, and the conception that the judge ought to be merely the mouth through whom the law speaks.[55]

Hayek argued that no other author demonstrated more clearly that during the classical period of Roman law it was fully understood that there was no conflict between law and freedom; and it was this recognition, Hayek contended, that had a profound influence over the development of Western law.

Liberty and the rule of law

The ideal constitutional order for neo-liberals, which distinguishes law from legislation, is the rule of law. The rule of law constitutes the political essence of neo-liberal ideology. It restricts the coercive powers of government, encourages economically productive behaviour, safeguards and embodies the liberty of the individual, and ensures equality and justice by making every individual accountable to law and by preserving the legal system. As argued above, neo-liberalism's conception of the rule of law draws inspiration from the German *Rechtsstaat* and from the English common law tradition. As in the German *Rechtsstaat*, in neo-liberalism the rule of law is considered to be a comprehensive and systematic legal framework of rules that exist prior to the state. The rule of law subjects government, making it comply with universal 'rules of just conduct' or with *nomos*, rules that oversee the ordinary relations between individuals and are independent of a particular political stance or policy. In Hayek's account, the rule of law requires a separation of powers, which denies the legislature the right to alter law as it sees fit. He explained that, like English common law, the rule of law is not commanded by any one individual, but has evolved from custom and adapted to its changing circumstances; it is an embodiment of tradition. Indeed, in a 1967 article, 'The results of human action but not of human design', Hayek described the spontaneous legal order created through law. He argued:

> Law is not only much older than legislation or even the organised state: the whole authority of the legislator and of the state derives from pre-existing conceptions of justice, and no system of articulated law can be applied except within a framework of generally recognised but often unarticulated rules of justice.[56]

The essence of the rule of law is, therefore, a body of rules which originate not in a legislative body, but in the evolutionary interaction that exists between individuals as they attempt to build upon these rules in response to changing circumstances. In Hayek's understanding, the rule of law does not enable specific groups or interests to attain their ends, but rather, like Smith's 'invisible hand' of the market, it provides a framework that allows all individuals to pursue their own private ends. Hayek maintained that, for the rule of law to function, there must be agreement not on particular ends of action, but on what constitutes 'just conduct' in the pursuit of differing ends.[57]

The rule of law is fundamental for Hayek and other neo-liberals as it represents 'the law of liberty'. In his *Constitution of Liberty*, Hayek argued that law and liberty could not exist apart from one another, and thus maintained that 'law is the basis of freedom'.[58] Liberty for Hayek is the purpose of law, and law is a means for the achievement of freedom as an end. Indeed, in his *Road to Serfdom* he contrasted the liberal *Rechtsstaat* with communist, fascist, socialist and national socialist states. He wrote that 'nothing distinguishes more clearly the conditions in a free country from those in a country under arbitrary government than the observance in the former of the great principles known as the rule of law'.[59] Gottfried Dietze, therefore, points out that Hayek disputed Schmitt's 'Pure Theory of Law' assertion that 'every state, no matter how despotic, is in tune with the rule of law; that even the Third Reich was a *Rechtsstaat*'.[60] Hayek made it explicit that planning in any shape or form leads down the 'road to serfdom', where rule of law and its liberal values are replaced by 'democratic' legislation and administrative regulations.

Liberalism and democratic government

A major challenge facing the rule of law in modern societies, Hayek argued, is the rise of majoritarian democracy. Hayek's distrust of majoritarian democracy or popular sovereignty is based on its identification of law with the will of the sovereign majority. In such a democratic system there is no room for law other than that which is made by the *demos*. Hayek warned against the dangers inherent in this form of democratic rule. The danger of popular sovereignty, he wrote,

> lies not in the belief that whatever power there is should be in the hands of the people, and that their wishes will have to be expressed in majority decisions, but in the belief that this ultimate source of power must be unlimited, that is the idea of sovereignty itself.[61]

Popular sovereignty, Hayek argued, is a product of a false constructivist interpretation of common rules; he maintained that there can be no justification for the unlimited exercise of power that has derived from some purposive will. What Hayek referred to as 'dogmatic' or 'doctrinaire' democrats advocate unrestrained and 'unlimitable' democracy. These democrats argue that, since power is in the hands of the people, no safeguards are needed for limiting that power. As a result, Hayek proclaimed that 'the ideal of democracy, originally intended to prevent all arbitrary power, becomes the justification for a new arbitrary power'.[62] The root of the problem, Hayek argued, is that 'in an unlimited democracy the holders of discretionary powers are forced to use them, whether they wish it or not, to favour particular groups, on whose swing-vote their powers depends'.[63] He pointed out that this applies as much to organisations like trade unions as it does to central government. The end result, Hayek argued, is a 'democratic' system which, rather than serving the interests of the majority, is forced to serve those select interests with the greatest access to political power.

Hayek presented an alternative 'liberal' interpretation of democracy in his work that is compatible with the rule of law – what David Held refers to as 'legal democracy'.[64] Like law, Hayek maintained that democracy has become an 'undiscriminating' term, used by modern states to the point where it ceases to have any proper meaning. Hayek sought to bring democracy back to its authentic roots by limiting its coercive powers and by subjecting it to the rule of law. He stated that, while both the dogmatic democrat and the liberal may agree that wherever coercive rules have to be laid down they should be decided by the majority, where they differ is 'in the scope of state action that is to be guided by democratic decision'.[65] In Hayek's liberal conception of democracy, the majority do not construct law, but they 'discover' it in the internalised general rules of conduct that underpin the spontaneous order of liberal society. Their 'power is limited by commonly held principles and there is no legitimate power beyond them'.[66] There are therefore definite limits to questions that should be decided by the majority. Hayek acknowledged that, while it may be necessary for a majority to come to some form of common agreement on how to perform certain tasks, this does not imply that it also has the legitimate power to make decisions which threaten to undermine the spontaneous order of society. Hayek stated that

> the limits imposed on democracy by the liberal are those within which it can work effectively and within which the majority can truly direct and control the actions of government. So long as democracy constrains the individual only by general rules of its own making, it controls the power of coercion.[67]

He warned that 'to disregard these limits will, in the long run, destroy not only prosperity but democracy itself'.[68]

In neo-liberalism, democracy therefore needs to be constrained by a constitution that can limit the powers of government. The liberal tradition of shared values, Hayek argued, must underlie constitutional limitations. This liberal constitution, he explained, must recognise society as a 'living organism': 'it will have to deal with a self-maintaining whole which is kept going by forces which we cannot replace and which we must therefore use in all we try to achieve'.[69] Changes in liberal society must therefore be made by working with these forces, or rules of just conduct, rather than against them.

'THE CONSTITUTION OF A LIBERAL STATE'

Neo-liberalism's constitutional ideal of government under the law is set out by liberal economists from the Virginia School such as James M. Buchanan and Gordon Tullock and by economists from Austrian School, in particular Hayek. While differing in many important respects, Buchanan and Hayek both put forward radical policy proposals for limiting the scope of government interference that is permitted under the Constitution. The 'ultra-liberal' constitutional state that they advocated as an ideal would curtail oppressive bureaucratic government, preserve the rule of law, provide limited public goods and maintain collective security against external threats. This constitutional ideal is fundamental for neo-liberalism, as it outlines the necessary legal and political structures for a functioning market order.

The 'New Madisonians'

James M. Buchanan and other prominent members of the Virginia School of Economics have drawn a great deal of inspiration from the American Constitution. Buchanan traced the roots of his public choice perspective on constitutional reform back to the ideas displayed in James Madison's *Federalist Papers*, and in this respect, Nick Bosanquet argues, he can be regarded as a 'New Madisonian'.[70] He retained an admiration for a constitution in which voting systems and constitutional rules curb the power of the executive. Buchanan's central claim, however, was that the American Constitution, traditionally seen in terms of the checks and balances between executive, legislature, and judiciary, had in the twentieth century deviated from its founding rules and principles that once constituted part of the American political order.

Constitutional reform proposals advocated by public-choice theorists like Buchanan, Gordon Tullock and Robert Wagner focused on measures which will re-set limits to government interference. In their *Calculus of Consent*, Buchanan and Tullock applied the individualistic calculus of micro-economics to public action, demonstrating that utility-maximising politicians do not necessarily maximise the public interest.[71] Their subsequent efforts to find the appropriate rules to constrain public figures brought the problem of constitutionalism onto the political agenda in the United States. They favoured, in particular, a 'fiscal constitution' which comprises the set of constitutional rules which regulate government decisions on expenditure and finance. Buchanan stated that he wishes to see a 'constitutional requirement that the federal government balance outlays with revenues except in extraordinary times'.[72] To overcome the inherent bias of majority voting in favour of high demand groups, Tullock suggested a greater use of the two-thirds voting rule for all appropriations.[73]

In *The Consequences of Mr Keynes*, Buchanan, Wagner and John Burton considered similar ideas in the British context. In Britain, they pointed out, there is no written fiscal Constitution outlining the rules that provide constitutional checks upon excessive expenditure or excessive resort to deficit finance by the government. The political actors that implemented Keynesian economic policies were simply unable to 'fine tune' the economy under the conditions of a competitive party democracy. Vote-maximising politicians were responsive to the demands of electoral politics rather than to the policy prescriptions of Keynesian economic rationality. These politicians, taking into account the electoral timetable, pursued 'lax' monetary and fiscal policies in order to secure favourable but temporary economic conditions, especially increases in employment. They simply failed to act as the 'public-interest maximising politicians and officials, the far-sighted statesmen and trustees of the future' envisioned by Keynesian presuppositions.[74] Faced with the reality of the politico-bureaucratic process, politicians pushed forward with plans to increase public expenditure programmes and to avoid cuts, without regard for theories of economic policy or for total budget size.[75]

Perceiving a bias in the British fiscal constitution towards excessive government expenditure and deficit finance, Buchanan, Wagner and Burton argued for a balanced-budget rule. Britain's fiscal constitution, they contended, has historically kept in check the manipulations of those in power, but 'contains a potentially fatal deficiency once the balanced budget rule is usurped and replaced by the Keynesian legitimisation of deficit finance'. 'It retains no rule to prevent vote-buying government manipulation of government expenditure and finance by an Executive that has, through the party system, a (working) majority of votes in the House of Commons'.[76] They maintained that the Keynesian revolution has undermined those shackles on government action – the Gold Standard, and balanced budgets – that were understood by the classical economists as necessary tools to contain the tendency of representative government towards deficit finance and uncontrolled growth of government expenditure. Thus they asserted that 'the danger of government manipulation is far stronger now that it was in the nineteenth century'.[77] Buchanan, Wagner and Burton argued for the amendment of the British (and American) fiscal constitution to include the balanced-budget principle, where by no government would be permitted to function by means of a budget deficit. Adopting this principle is the only means through which one could eradicate the government's ability to manipulate the fiscal system and economy for short-term political gain.

Hayek's model constitution

Like in the Virginia School conception of a liberal Constitution, Hayek was concerned with establishing a constitutional framework that is capable of holding the power of the state in check, whilst respecting the general rules that underpin the market order. Hayek argued that traditional constitutional mechanisms for limiting government through the separation of powers have been rendered redundant by the doctrine of parliamentary sovereignty, uniting executive, legislative and to some extent judicial power in the hands of the governing administration.[78] Hayek outlined his own tri-cameral system, comprising a 'Legislative Assembly', a 'Governmental Assembly' and a 'Constitutional Court'. He made it explicit that it was not his intention 'to present a constitutional scheme for present application', but rather to 'discover' how 'the power of legislation, in the sense in which it was understood by those who believed in the separation of powers, can be effectively separated from the powers of government'.[79] His central aim was to present a constitutional model that will secure 'the containment of power and the dethronement of politics' more effectively than traditional liberal constitutions have done.[80]

The first representative body in Hayek's model constitution is what he confusingly termed a 'Legislative Assembly'. This assembly would be charged with the task of upholding and gradually improving the rules of just conduct or 'law'. Its function would be the articulation of moral norms – 'the views about what kind of action is right or wrong' – that underpin the market order. It would enforce the rules of just conduct, revise private (including commercial and criminal) law, define the principles of taxation and state regulations on matters such as health and safety and production or construction. These tasks would be substantial and difficult, as they would involve 'the preservation of an abstract order whose concrete principles were unforeseeable' and the exclusion of 'all provisions intended or known to affect principally particular identifiable individuals or groups'.[81] Hayek, however, made it explicit that the function of the Legislative Assembly would not be to define the functions of government, but 'merely to define the limits of its coercive powers'.[82] Because of the significance of its task, Hayek suggested that membership of the Legislative Assembly should be severely restricted to particular individuals capable of carrying out its responsibilities. Hayek stated in his *Road to Serfdom* that the liberal notion of an assembly of independent and infallible men entrusted with the task of maintaining the rule of law is an 'ideal that can never be perfectly achieved'.[83] He, however, went on to claim in his *Law, Legislation and Liberty* that it would be possible to select specific members of the community to comprise the *nomothetae* or law-givers' of the Legislative Assembly, who could be paid and pensioned sufficiently to be independent of any interest group. Hayek suggested that membership should be limited to those 'mature' members of the community aged between forty-five and sixty, who had not served in the Governmental Assembly or party organisations. These community members would be independently elected by their peers for a 'fairly long period', such as fifteen years, acting as 'neutral lay judges'. This, Hayek argued, would ensure that members tenure as legislatures 'would be neither dependent on party support nor concerned about their personal future'.[84]

The second representative body in Hayek's constitutional scheme, the 'Governmental Assembly', is entrusted with administration and what he referred to as 'legislation'. The Governmental Assembly, Hayek stated, is representative of existing parliamentary bodies. Its central tasks would be very considerable: it would organise the apparatus of government, decide the use of personal resources entrusted to the government and mobilise popular support around policy measures. Hayek, however, made it clear that the Governmental Assembly would be

> bound by the rules of just conduct laid down by the Legislative Assembly, and that, in particular, it could not issue any orders to private citizens which did not follow directly and necessarily from the rules laid down by the latter.[85]

Unlike the Legislative Assembly, which is guided by opinion, Hayek believed that the Governmental Assembly should be based on a competitive party system and should be guided by the will of the majority. Indeed, he maintained that 'for the purpose of government proper it seems desirable that the concrete wishes of the citizens for particular results should find expression or that their particular interests should be represented'.[86] Hayek acknowledged that the idea of entrusting the task of stating the general rules of just conduct to a representative body, distinct from the body that is entrusted with the task of government, is not entirely new. The ancient Athenians who kept the '*nomothetae*' distinct from the governing body, he pointed out, attempted a system based on these lines. In his article 'The Constitution of a liberal state', he commented, however, that in the modern world, especially in light of the development of the American Constitution, 'the separation of powers has never been achieved because from the beginning of the modern development of constitutional government the power of making law and the power of directing government were combined in the same representative assemblies'.[87] The purpose of Hayek's scheme was to achieve a distinct separation of powers within a democratic system by setting up two distinct representative assemblies, charged with altogether different tasks and acting independently of each other.

The third body in Hayek's model constitution is the Constitutional Court. Its membership would include professional judges, former members of the Legislative Assembly and perhaps, Hayek suggested, former members of the Governmental Assembly as well. The Constitutional Court, Hayek argued, would be concerned with the mediation of conflicts between the two main assemblies. It would address 'problems that would arise chiefly in the form of a conflict of competence between the two assemblies, generally through the questioning by one of the validity of the resolution passed by the other'.[88] In periods of emergency, Hayek stated that it may be necessary to grant limited coercive powers, but he makes it clear that these powers should never be possessed by the same agency that has the power to declare a state of emergency. In Hayek's scheme, the Legislative Assembly would be allotted the right to declare a state of emergency and would thus have to confer upon the Governmental Assembly powers that in normal circumstances it would not normally possess. The Legislative Assembly would, however, be free at all times to restrict the powers granted to the Governmental Assembly, and at the end of the emergency revoke its powers.[89]

Constitutionalism and the global order

In his *Law, Legislation and Liberty*, Hayek set out detailed proposals for a model liberal Constitution for nation–states. However, he also saw his model as being appropriate for a federated global system in which the Legislative Assembly and Constitutional Court would be international bodies, and Governmental Assemblies, highly localised 'quasi-commercial corporations competing for citizens'.[90] David Held states that what Hayek advocated is an 'international market order' accompanied by a 'federation of ultra-liberal states where all interaction is conducted between individuals unimpeded by state boundaries'. Such a federation would be bound by a 'higher authority' – a Legislative Assembly – which 'would specify and help guarantee the rules of international trade and commerce'. In line with Hayek's constitutional model, this authority would be above particular group interests, with 'its brief restricted to the possibility of ensuring the rule of law in international terms'.[91] Hayek did not believe that an international Legislative Assembly can be formed on a transnational basis in the short term, but that like-minded nations can begin to form such an assembly, for instance a regional authority.

Hayek's work, therefore, envisions a global neo-liberal constitutional order. Certainly, neo-liberals have reservations about the construction of supranational institutions, in particular a supranational government beyond some pure service agency, embodied, for example, in an organisation like the European Union. What neo-liberals strive for is an international body like Hayek's Legislative Assembly, which is limited to the negative tasks of restraining the actions of national governments that are harmful to the market order and of upholding the international rule of law.

Conclusion

To conclude, the constitution and its accompanying adjacent concepts such as private law, legal responsibility, abstract order, 'rules of just conduct' and evolution are fundamental concepts for neo-liberalism which strike at the heart of liberal debates on the separation of powers, the protection of individual liberty and the primacy of law. As this chapter has shown, the main dilemma for neo-liberals is establishing legal structures that do not interfere with the market order. They reject nearly all constitutional models in Western democracies, in particular the so-called 'liberal' American Constitution, on the grounds that it has not prevented legislators from making greater inroads into liberty in the United States than in many other Western countries. In no democratic country, the neo-liberals contend, has the ultimate power of government ever been under the law; it has always been in the hands of a body free to make whatever laws it wanted in order to achieve its particular ends. Neo-liberalism's central claim is that too much importance is attached to the apparatus of politics, both at the national and at global level. Neo-liberals have thus attempted to construct a constitutional discourse that places strict limitations on politics. Hayek aspired to a constitutional model that entails the 'dethronement of politics', where discretionary authority is replaced by general rules. Buchanan and other public-choice theorists proposed more constructivist legislative measures, which would require government to balance its budget in order to reduce public expenditure and deficit finance. However, as this chapter has shown, neo-liberalism's conception of a 'liberal' Constitution is an intrinsically political one. The constitutional limitations on the capacities of legislatures that it advocates are inherently political, in the sense that, to a greater or lesser degree, they embody different views about desirable forms of social organisation.

Neo-liberalism's core political objective is to overcome the constitutional ignorance of Western democracies by instituting a constitutional framework of rules, conventions or procedures through which the policies of government can be constrained. This framework, neo-liberals argue, is not only desirable, but is also an indispensable condition of a liberal society. The efficiency of a liberal Constitution, they contend, depends on the strict separation of powers, a government under the law and an effective rule of law. They draw their inspiration from the ancient Athenian 'Constitution', the individualist private law of ancient Rome and the German liberal movement of the nineteenth century that found expression in the *Rechtsstaat*. Neo-liberals are, however, acutely aware of the problems of implementing such a constitutional system. They would need to overcome the limitations of the political system and of established democratic institutions and persuade parties to adopt what Buchanan calls a 'constitutional mentality' in respect of economic policy.[92]

Notes

1. F. A. Hayek, *The Road to Serfdom* (London: Routledge, 1944), p. 79.
2. F. A. Hayek, *The Constitution of Liberty* (London: Routledge, 1960), pp. 115–17.
3. R. Brazier, *Constitutional Practice* (Oxford: Clarendon Press, 1994), pp. 45–7.
4. C. Montesquieu, *The Spirit of Laws* (Cambridge: Cambridge University Press, 1989), p. 161.
5. Jan-Erik Lane, *Constitutions and Political Theory* (Manchester: Manchester University Press, 1996), p. 65.
6. Ibid., p. 66.
7. A. V. Dicey, *Introduction to the Study of the Law of the Constitution* (London: Macmillan, 1905).
8. See I. Jennings, *The Law and the Constitution* (London: University of London Press, 1967), and M. Loughlin, *Public Law and Political Theory* (Oxford: Oxford University Press, 1992).
9. Hayek, *The Constitution of Liberty*, p. 203.
10. Ibid., p. 104.
11. Ibid.
12. Michael Foley, *The Politics of the British Constitution* (Manchester: Manchester University Press, 1999), p. 31.
13. Ibid., p. 32.
14. Harold J. Laski, *Reflections on the Constitution: The House of Commons, the Cabinet, the Civil Service* (Manchester: Manchester University Press, 1951).
15. Foley, *The Politics of the British Constitution*, p. 32.
16. John Burton, *Why No Cuts?* (London: IEA, 1985).
17. Andrew Gamble, 'Economic decline and the crisis of legitimacy', in C. Graham and T. Prosser (eds), *Waving the Rules: The Constitution Under Thatcherism* (Milton Keynes: Open University Press, 1988), pp. 31–2.
18. Milton Friedman, *Capitalism and Freedom* (Chicago: University of Chicago Press, 1962), pp. 2–3.
19. Quoted in R. Ketcham, *Framed for Prosperity: The Enduring Philosophy of the Constitution* (Kansas: University of Kansas Press, 1993), p. 38.
20. Eric Foner, *The Story of American Freedom* (Basingstoke: Macmillan, 1988).

21. Hayek, *The Constitution of Liberty*, pp. 180–1.
22. Ibid., p. 184.
23. Milton Friedman and Rose Friedman, *Free to Choose* (Harmondsworth: Penguin, 1980), p. 287.
24. Hayek, *Constitution of Liberty*, p. 188.
25. Ibid., p. 189.
26. Quoted in Ronald Steel, *Walter Lippmann and the American Century* (Boston, MA: Little Brown and Company, 1980), p. 308.
27. A. H. Kelly, *Foundations of Freedom in the American Constitution* (New York: Free Press, 1958), p. 51.
28. Walter Lippmann, *Essays in the Public Philosophy* (London: Hamilton, 1955), pp. 99–101.
29. James M. Buchanan, *The Limits of Liberty: Between Anarchy and Leviathan* (Chicago: University of Chicago Press, 1975), p. 67.
30. Ibid., p. 97.
31. Ibid., p. 98.
32. Franz Neumann, *The Rule of Law: Political Theory and the Legal System in Modern Society* (Leamington Spa: Berg, 1986), p. 181.
33. Ibid., p. 182.
34. Hayek, *The Constitution of Liberty*, p. 198.
35. Ibid., pp. 199–200.
36. Ibid., p. 201.
37. Hayek, *The Road to Serfdom*, p. 76.
38. Hayek, *The Constitution of Liberty*, p. 202.
39. Ibid.
40. Neumann, *The Rule of Law*, p. 270.
41. Ibid., p. 271.
42. J. W. Bendersky, *Carl Schmitt* (Princeton: Princeton University Press, 1983), pp. 227–9.
43. Quoted in Neumann, *The Rule of Law*, p. 296.
44. Hayek in his *The Road to Serfdom*, pp. 85–6.
45. Jan Tumlir, 'Franz Böhm and economic–constitutional analysis', in Alan Peacock and Hans Willgerodt (eds), *German Neo-Liberals and the Social Market Economy* (Basingstoke: Macmillan, 1989), pp. 133–4.
46. Ibid., p. 125.
47. Norman Barry, *The New Right* (London: Croom Helm, 1987), p. 187.
48. F. A. Hayek, *Law, Legislation and Liberty, Vol. I: Rules and Order* (Chicago: University of Chicago Press, 1973), pp. 95–6.
49. Ibid., pp. 124–44.
50. Ibid., p. 90.
51. Ibid., p. 72.
52. Ibid., p. 81.
53. Ibid., p. 83.
54. Hayek, *Constitution of Liberty*, p. 166.
55. Ibid., p. 167.
56. F. A. Hayek, 'The results of human action but not human design', in his *Essays in Philosophy, Politics and Economics* (London: Routledge and Kegan Paul, 1967), p. 102.
57. Hayek, *Law, Legislation and Liberty, Vol.I*, p. 95.

58. Hayek, *The Constitution of Liberty*, p. 148.
59. Hayek, *The Road to Serfdom*, p. 82.
60. Gottfried Dietze, 'Hayek on the rule of law', in F. Machlup (ed.), *Essays on Hayek* (London: Routledge and Kegan Paul, 1977), p. 132.
61. Hayek, *Law, Legislation and Liberty, Vol. III: The Political Order of a Free People* (Chicago: Chicago University Press, 1979), p. 33.
62. Hayek, *The Constitution of Liberty*, p. 107.
63. Hayek, *Law, Legislation and Liberty, Vol. III*, p. 139.
64. David Held, *Democracy and the Global Order: From the Modern State to Cosmopolitan Governance* (Cambridge: Polity, 1996), p. 243.
65. Hayek, *The Constitution of Liberty*, p. 107.
66. Ibid., p. 115.
67. Ibid., p. 116.
68. Ibid.
69. Ibid., p. 70.
70. Nick Bosanquet, *After the New Right* (London: Heinemann, 1983), p. 71.
71. J. M. Buchanan and G. Tullock, *The Calculus of Consent: Logical Foundations of Constitutional Democracy* (Michigan: University of Michigan Press, 1962).
72. J. M. Buchanan and R. E. Wagner, *Democracy in Deficit* (New York: Academic Press, 1977), p. 178.
73. G. Tullock, *The Politics of Bureaucracy* (Washington, DC: Public Affairs Press, 1965), pp. 47–56.
74. M. Buchanan, John Burton and R. E. Wagner, *The Consequences of Mr Keynes* (London: IEA, 1978), pp. 58–9.
75. Ibid., p. 60.
76. Ibid., pp. 73–5.
77. Ibid., p. 82.
78. F. A. Hayek, 'The Constitution of a liberal state', in F. A. Hayek, *New Studies in Philosophy, Politics, Economics and the History of Ideas* (London: Routledge and Kegan Paul, 1978), pp. 98–104.
79. Hayek, *Law, Legislation and Liberty, Vol. III*, p. 107.
80. Ibid., p. 109.
81. Ibid.
82. Ibid., p. 110.
83. Hayek, *The Road to Serfdom*, p. 76.
84. Hayek, *Law, Legislation and Liberty, Vol. III*, pp. 113–14.
85. Ibid., p. 119.
86. Ibid., p. 112.
87. Hayek, 'The Constitution of a liberal state', p. 101.
88. Hayek, *Law, Legislation and Liberty, Vol. III*, p. 121.
89. Ibid., p. 125.
90. Ibid., p. 132.
91. Held, *Democracy and the Global Order*, p. 244.
92. Buchanan, *The Limits of Liberty*, p. 19.

Chapter 8

Property: Individualism and ownership

Introduction: Private property and the market order

The fourth core concept in neo-liberalism's ideological configuration is property. Private property and individual ownership are integral concepts for neo-liberalism, as they are indispensable to the spontaneous order of the market. Property for neo-liberals does not just simply represent inanimate objects or possessions, but, as this chapter will argue, it is also an abstraction defined by custom, conventions and, most integrally, law. Individual ownership and possession is established by the existence of rights and powers that are determined by law. Neo-liberals are committed defenders of private property on the grounds that, unlike social justice, the former is capable of safeguarding individualism. It gives individuals independence and a sense of self-reliance, enabling them to participate freely in the market. Indeed, neo-liberals like F. A. Hayek portray property ownership as the most fundamental of civil liberties and argue that individual freedom can only reign within a free-market system. In Hayek's view, government intervention in economic life necessarily escalates to the point where all aspects of social existence, including private ownership, are brought under state control. In effect, any encroachment upon property contains the seeds of totalitarian oppression.[1] Similarly, Ludwig von Mises contended that private property is absolutely fundamental for the existence of liberalism. 'The programme of liberalism', he maintained, 'if condensed into a single word, would have to read: *property*, that is private ownership of the means of production. All the other demands of liberalism result from this fundamental demand.'[2]

This chapter will outline the centrality of property to neo-liberal ideology. It will briefly explore the evolution of the concept of property in liberal thought in the national contexts of Britain, the United States and Germany, in which the disparities in modern neo-liberal conceptions of property can be found. It will then examine neo-liberalism's defence of private property: the fundamental distinction that it makes between common property and private property; its interpretation of ownership and property rights; and its understanding of property as legal privilege. Property's adjacent concepts such as ownership, possessive individualism, legal privilege, individual initiative and negative justice will be explored. The chapter will go on to reflect upon the character of different forms of property confronting neo-liberals, in particular the rise of the firm and of large corporations, and to assess the solutions that neo-liberals present to such concentrations of property. The chapter will argue that private property was essential for the rise of modern capitalism, and, in turn, for the formation and existence of different forms of neo-liberal ideology. Indeed, neo-liberals see the foundations of modern liberal civilisation as being based upon private ownership. When private property is constrained or hampered in any way by government, they argue that the freedom of the individual is infringed. It is the function of private property to oppose political power and to become the basis of all activities that are free from state interference. Private property guarantees the freedom of all individuals rather than of just a minority. It is only in a market economy based on private ownership of the means of production that the individual can be independent of the arbitrary decisions of public authorities and can effectively participate in the free exchange of goods. Private ownership strengthens individual initiative through free access to markets. In this system, private capital accumulation can take place as well as voluntary savings on the part of individual economic entities.

National conceptions of property

Property as a liberal concept has its origins in Roman law, which protected private ownership rights. Cicero described how the laws of 'free Rome' vigorously asserted the right to private property, and thereby he made them 'as far as possible removed from modern socialism'.[3] It was not until the rise of commercialised society in the seventeenth and eighteenth centuries, however, that property as a liberal concept came into being. The increase of wealth and trade by commerce challenged the sovereign's divine right over property, and liberty and individualism found a mode of expression. In Britain, the United States and Germany, property as a liberal concept evolved in response to changing political and economic circumstances. Paul Lafargue states that property 'is not immutable and always the same, but the contrary, it, like all material and intellectual phenomena, incessantly evolves and passes through a series of forms which differ, but are derived from one another'.[4] Thus in Britain, the United States and Germany both the ideas about property and the institutional arrangements concerned with it changed with the development of industrialisation. A conscious effort was, however, made by liberal theorists in these three countries to find a broader basis for law and order, where private property could be protected. What evolved from these liberal theories of property was a specific variant of property – private property – which became a central part of neo-liberalism's ideological configuration in the twentieth century. The evolution of different national conceptions of property, the chapter will later argue, influenced the shape and form of the variants of neo-liberalism that emerged in the twentieth century.

Britain: Natural rights of ownership

In Britain, John Locke set out the natural rights theory of property the seventeenth century in his *Two Treaties on Government*. Locke claimed that the sole purpose of government in civil society is to defend the property of its subjects, that is, their 'lives, liberties and estates'. Individuals, he argued, possessed natural rights determined by reason, rather than rights granted by an arbitrary power, and it is the role of government to secure these rights. What Locke advocated is constitutional government with a separation of powers between legislative and executive bodies, which is capable of protecting the property rights of individuals. He claimed that, when a government fails to carry out its function and tries to take absolute power, individuals possess the natural right to rebel, as an act of 'lawful self-defence'.[5]

Locke's conception of property was a negative one. Adopting medieval and seventeenth-century Puritan theory, he contended that property originated in the labour and raw materials given to individuals in common by God. Indeed, rights of ownership according to Locke have their roots in a natural relationship that exists between individuals and their environment. With the introduction of money, however, the previous natural limitations, those of rightful appropriation, were overthrown and the natural provision that all individuals should have as much as they could make use of was invalidated. Locke proceeded to show how the introduction of money removed the limitations inherent in his initial justification of individual appropriation. He defended the capitalist interpretation of ownership as a legalistic form, independent of any kind of conventions.[6] As a result of this interpretation, C. B. Macpherson argues that Locke's theory of property was deeply imbued with possessive assumptions about market society. Macpherson points out that Locke defended the inalienable rights of the property-owning capitalist class and excluded those of labourers, who were landless and unpropertied. Thus he contends that, far from being a common natural right, property in Locke's account is seen as a consequence of 'individual economic enterprise'.[7] As a consequence, Macpherson maintains that property in Britain in the seventeenth century came almost exclusively to mean private property; property conceived as 'common property' 'virtually dropped out of sight' and was treated as a 'contradiction in terms'.[8]

In the eighteenth century, theorists of the Scottish Enlightenment developed a 'natural' history account of private property and its role in capitalism. Economists such as Adam Smith associated the rise of private property with social and economic development. In his *Lectures on Jurisprudence*, Smith argued that the social development from early 'hunter-gather' society to agricultural society and finally to modern industrial society extended the concept of property beyond that of mere possession. In the earliest hunter-gather societies, Andrew Reeve points out that Smith questioned whether property existed; a hunter, Smith claimed, 'may have a right to his prey, but this was not a natural right to property because the hunter was treated as having only an exclusive privilege'.[9] The transition to agricultural society, Smith argued, introduced the concept of property and notions of ownership of animals and land. Smith, however, contended that the most significant transition for the concept of property was from late feudal society to commercial society, which paved the way for notions of private possession and economic individualism. In commercial society he contended that property is diffused and its connections with power are subsequently defused. He tied ownership, management and entrepreneurship together; they enabled all individuals to possess the 'natural liberty' to participate in the market economy. Well-constructed commercial policy, Smith maintained, would enable all individuals to use their property in their labour and would inhibit those institutions that keep landed property in the hands of the few.[10]

Smith's interpretation of property provided one of the foundations for classical liberalism's and, later, neo-liberalism's claim that private property sits at the core of liberty – that is, negative liberty understood as non-interference. Classical liberals like Herbert Spencer in the nineteenth century, drawing on Smith's ideas, came to see property as an economic resource that encouraged individualism, natural possessiveness, entrepreneurship and self-reliance. There was a strong association between negative liberty and an attachment to private property which entailed the acceptance of markets. The utilitarians in nineteenth-century Britain, such as Jeremy Bentham and John Stuart Mill, were, like the classical liberals, deeply committed to capitalism and therefore to unfettered property rights. The basis of the utilitarian position, however, was not in rights, as it was for Locke and the classical liberals, but was determined by the consequences of property. The utilitarian arguments of Bentham and Mill claimed that private property acts as a reward for, and incentive to, labour which guarantees security. Government interference, they claimed, must not frustrate expectations of the enjoyment of property. Security of property in civil society requires that government should respect the individual's private property.[11] Alan Ryan, however, points out that the concept of utility and private property were not entirely 'happy allies'. He points to Bentham's claim that the security of private property would be dependent on taxes 'on the productive property of everyone else' to maintain law and order and defence in civil society.[12] Another source of conflict in the utilitarian theory of property was between private property and equality. For Bentham and Mill, property was about expectations determined by law, which create happiness directly. Yet Bentham and Mill observed that private property, whilst promoting the great happiness, could at the same time be a source of great misery for many individuals in society when their expectations were frustrated. As a solution, they claimed that 'the state may, without impairing security, aid the non-propertied by providing them with education in order to give them a start in life and by creating a welfare safety-net beneath them'.[13] Unsurprisingly, neo-liberals were critical of this position and saw it as a diversion from the tenets of classical liberalism and a move in the direction of socialism.

The United States: Freedom and industry

In American society, the most important liberal defense of property stemmed from the revolutionary era and the framing of the American

Constitution. The American colonial rebels argued that the British parliament's 'taxation without representation' constituted an attempt to deny them of their property rights. American revolutionaries placed emphasis upon the value of property in land as a source of personal independence. An individual with direct access to the production of resources in land need not rely on any other individual for their basic means of existence. In addition, Drew McCoy points out:

> The personal independence that resulted from the ownership of land permitted a citizen to participate responsibly in the political process, for it allowed him to pursue spontaneously the common or public good, rather than the narrow interest of men – or the government – on whom he depended for his support.[14]

Thus the revolutionaries did not encourage individuals to attain property so as to be able to avoid public responsibility and pursue their own private self-interests, but rather in order to enable them to become part of a 'committed republican citizenry'.[15] The notion of an alert and active citizenry formed an integral part of conceptions of property ownership in Jeffersonian America. Property in land, the republicans argued, stimulated productivity and led to prosperity. The framers of the American Constitution upheld this ideal of private property by referring to it as a natural right as defined by Locke. They contended that granting individuals the natural right to own private property provided a means through which they could find their place in society and determine the future direction of their lives. The objective of securing and protecting private property, for the framers of the Constitution, was as important as that of safeguarding individual liberty. Indeed, John Adams wrote in 1778: 'Property is surely a right of mankind as really as liberty.'[16] The Fifth Amendment of the American Constitution thus proclaimed that: 'No person shall be deprived of life, liberty or property, without due process of law; nor shall private property be taken for public use without just compensation.'[17]

Property in the United States in the nineteenth century formed the basis of republican government. Republicans, who were eager to create a propertied class within a propertied nation, defended traditional rights to private ownership. The revolutionaries' original notion of the untrammelled rights of property-holders to control, utilise, sell and make profit from private property prevailed. Unlike in aristocratic European society, where property was founded on force and 'unjust military violence', in American republican society property was 'earned by industry and frugality'. Thus the orator, statesman and Whig luminary Edward Everett proclaimed in 1838: 'It is not surprising that the acquisition of property by one's own labour and skill should be held in equal, or even higher estimation, than the inheritance by accident of birth.'[18] Jacksonian democrats held a similar conception of property. They maintained that the main duty of government was to protect individual property rights from both 'domestic and foreign enemies'.[19]

Since the revolutionary period, three principles had underpinned the concept of property in American society: the sanctity of individual property rights, the attainment of personal property through individual labour and the repudiation of aristocratic privileges. Property thus acted as bulwark against the wealth of the aristocracy, and a means of creating a greater degree of social equality. Yet John Adams was aware, by the early nineteenth century, that the acquisition of private property might produce a new elite class. He raised concerns that, 'as the idea and existence of property is admitted and established in society, accumulations of it will be made; the snowball will grow as it rolls'.[20] The problem of defining what constituted personal property became one of the core issues in the debate on slavery. Thomas Jefferson had largely ignored the question of slavery in his discussion of property rights. His Lockean vision of a natural order of individual property owners made no explicit definition of what should constitute 'personal property'.[21] Huston points out that 'property was an object of possession that the law protected; yet possession was secured by the right to property. Neither possession nor property were defined separately.'[22] The notion of property as a 'right to the fruits of his labour', which was one of the most widely held definitions of property in revolutionary American society, became overshadowed in the nineteenth century by the rise of vast accumulations of property within the aristocratic class. In the southern states, the aristocracy defined slaves as it that had been handed down from generation to generation. Critics of slavery contended that this notion of property contradicted the traditional American conception of it as the fruits of one's labour. The aristocracy, they contended, segregated society by 'stealing' the fruits of others' labours rather than by labouring themselves.[23]

Republican government argued that the American Constitution recognised freedom rather than slavery, and its founding fathers assumed that slavery was an institution that would die out over time. In northern America, slavery was seen as a violation of natural rights. Following the civil war, in 1865 President Andrew Johnson and the Republican Congress enacted laws and introduced constitutional amendments that redrew the boundaries of citizenship and expanded the definition of freedom to all Americans. By 1866, a new consensus within the Republican Party, that 'civil equality was an essential attribute to freedom', culminated in the Civil Rights Act. Eric Foner states that 'equality before the law was central to the measure, as were free labour values: no state could deprive any citizen of the right to make contracts, bring lawsuits, or enjoy the protection of the security of person and property'.[24] Neo-liberals like Hayek supported the republican argument that slavery represents coercion and an infringement of individual liberty. Hayek argued that its abolition would require the granting of significant freedoms, most fundamentally the right to own property. Indeed, he wrote that:

> Clearly, a slave will not become free if he obtains merely the right to vote, nor will any degree of 'inner freedom' make him anything but a slave – however much idealist philosophers have tried to convince us to the contrary . . . But if he is subject only to the same laws as all his fellow citizens, if he is immune from arbitrary confinement and free to choose his work, and if he is able to own and acquire property, no other men or group of men can coerce him to do their bidding.[25]

Germany: Property as fulfilment

The historical development of the concept of property in Germany was less contentious than in the United States. Unlike British interpretations of property, which were distinctively objective – utilitarian and economic – German interpretations were characteristically subjective. Indeed, George Newcomb states that 'the subjectivism of the German mind led it naturally to approach the problem of the right to private property through the consideration of will and the requirements of personality'. German theorists favoured the 'highest individualism' in their interpretation of property rights, yet at the same viewed personality in terms of its needs, which were 'truly developed through the state'.[26] Two German theorists in particular, Immanuel Kant and G. W. F. Hegel, came to embody the German tradition of property and ownership.

One of the earliest and most prominent accounts of property rights in Germany was Kant's. Kant's theory of property drew on his 'unsocial sociability' interpretation of historical progress. Alan Ryan states that property, for Kant, was an integral part of human development and progress, one that must become more 'flexible' and more 'usable in the marketplace'; 'mankind must treat their abilities as 'property' if they were to have a motive for developing them'.[27] Kant's understanding of historical progress had a profound impact on his interpretation of possession and the nature of private ownership. What Kant found most striking about the concept of property was that its essence was 'the mode of having external to myself as my own'.[28] He viewed possession both as the physical or 'sensible' possession of an object, and also as what he called the 'intelligible' possession of an object. Howard Williams states that 'the 'sensible possession' of an object simply signifies its bodily appropriation, whereas 'intelligible possession' signifies a possession which is not dependent on actual physical appropriation.[29] It is intelligible possession which is the most fundamental for Kant and for the neo-liberals, as it signifies the legal possession of an object, or 'ownership'.

Kant saw ownership as a fundamental right. He was convinced of the necessity of private property, and thus argued that the property rights of individuals should predominate over their social obligations. The private ownership of property, in Kant's account, was sacred; it embodied the rights, dignity and personality of the individual. As Kant stated himself: 'Property is but the periphery of my person extended to things'.[30] He did not, however, view property as simply a selfish right, but rather as a legal right. Property, he argued, fulfils the ends of law. Thus neo-liberal limits to state interference and the sacredness of free contract and unlimited competition derived support from his doctrines on property. Newcomb states that, for Kant and, later, for Wilhelm von Humboldt, the German state was a legal state (or *Rechtsstaat*), 'in the sense that its sole duty was the maintenance of the legal security of each individual'.[31] Property was to be absolutely immune from interference except by the state, on the exceptional grounds of 'public necessity'.

Hegel, unlike Kant, saw property as 'the embodiment of personality', as 'the essential element of self-consciousness', and the source of 'human fulfilment'.[32] Indeed, in his *Philosophy of Right*, Hegel put forward the case for the genesis of property as an expression of personality. Like the English Idealists, property, he argued, served as a means to a particular end – the fulfilment of the will without which individuals are not fully human. Hegel treated the right to the unlimited accumulation of property as an individual's ultimate moral end – the realisation of the human will or the consciousness of oneself as a moral purposive being. As Hegel put it: 'The rationale of property is to be found not in the satisfaction of needs but in the supersession of the pure objectivity of personality. In his property a person exists for the first time as reason.'[33]

Hegel made it clear that property was, in essence, individual private property, and that, as the modern state advanced, ownership became lodged in individual hands. Thus in Hegel's philosophy property is necessary to freedom, realised through labour and work. Property is not merely a desirable means of facilitating the satisfaction of needs; it is an end in itself because it provides freedom. Through the possession of private property individuals are free to develop their personality. Indeed, unlike classical liberals and neo-liberals, Hegel defined freedom as the realisation of personality rather than as individual economic liberty. Any form of common property arrangement would 'violate the right of personality'.[34] Hegel's unfettered individualism derived from his acceptance of Roman law notions of property. Ryan, however, points out that, while Hegel may have supported a form of individualism, he never accepted the notion of 'absolute owners'. He contends that 'Hegel was bourgeois and anti-feudal, rather than individualist and pro-capitalist'. For Hegel, 'it is because the modern world places so much emphasis on individual responsibility that private property is sacrosanct, rather than because *laissez-faire* makes for tremendous prosperity'.[35]

PRIVATE PROPERTY AND GOVERNMENT

The different national conceptions of property outlined above are fundamental for understanding neo-liberalism's distinctive approaches to the question of property in Britain, the United States and Germany in the twentieth century. As it is argued throughout this book, neo-liberalism is an ideology whose ideas are drawn from several different intellectual and historical contexts. These distinct strands represent a family of ideas and concepts that come together to form neo-liberalism. Thus neo-liberalism draws on a wide variety of sources of inspiration for its interpretation of property: Roman law's emphasis on individual ownership, classical liberalism's defence of private property as an integral part of the market order, utilitarianism's consequentialist position, the American correlation between freedom and private possession and the German conception of property as the embodiment of legality. The most important issue for neo-liberals, however, concerns the relationship between private property and government: the distinction that is made between common property and private property, the emphasis that is placed on the division of labour as the private ownership of the means of production, and the freedom, justice and prosperity that represents an integral part of private ownership.

Common property and private property

A fundamental distinction that neo-liberals make is that which exists between common property and private property. Private property, according to neo-liberals like Mises, is 'where the individual can deal with his private ownership in the means of production the way he considers most advantageous'.[36] Common property, in contrast, is 'where all the means of production belong to society and all income finds its way in the first place to the state coffers'.[37] Neo-liberals argue that property was, and still is, principally private rather than common property. Austrian economists like Mises and Hayek denied socialist and Marxist claims that private property has not always existed and they stress the important role that it has played in the evolution of civilisation. Mises and Hayek argued that private property, unlike common property, is not simply a constructed institution that could easily be abolished, but is an integral part of the evolution of market society.[38]

What makes private property, for neo-liberals, essential to the extended order of the market society is its centrality to the practice of free trade and to the advancement of civilisation. Hayek pointed out that individual property 'is indispensable for the development of trading, and thereby the formation of larger coherent and co-operating structures, and for the appearance of those signals we call prices'.[39] This practice, he maintained, was part of the classical heritage of European civilisation. He observed that it originated with the ancient Greeks, especially with the cosmopolitan outlook of the Stoic philosophers, and was later adopted by the Romans, who propagated it throughout their Empire. An ancient Roman prototype of law based on private property, Hayek argued, provided the foundations for the development of modern civilisation. Indeed, he wrote that:

> It seems that no advanced civilisation has yet developed without a government which saw its chief aim in the protection of property, but that again and again the further evolution and growth to which this gave rise was halted by a 'strong' government. Governments strong enough to protect individuals against the violence of their fellows make possible the evolution of an increasingly complex order of spontaneous and voluntary co-operation.[40]

Hayek, however, stated that, when governments extend beyond these duties and abuse their power, common property comes into being. Through enforcing their supposedly superior wisdom, governments in medieval European feudal systems and in parts of Asia, Hayek maintained, suppressed individual initiatives and directed the use of property to their own ends. It was not until the growth of modern industrialism and the subsequent decline of the powerful state in Britain, and of the towns of the Italian Renaissance, of South Germany and of the Low Countries that the concept of private property was resurrected and the foundations for the modern extended order of market society were laid down.[41]

In neo-liberalism, therefore, there is a strict dichotomy between common property and private ownership: there can be no compromise between the two. Indeed, Mises made it explicit that:

> It is not possible to compromise by putting part of the means of production at the disposal of society and leaving the remainder to individuals. Such systems simply stand unconnected, side by side, and operate fully only within the space they occupy . . . Compromise is always a momentary lull in the fight between the two principles, not the result of a logical thinking out of the problem. Regarded from the standpoint of each side, half-measures are a temporary halt on the way to complete success.[42]

Thus he referred to the land reforms that aimed to socialise the natural factors of production whilst leaving the rest to the private ownership in the means of production as 'senseless'. The principle which individuals hold to be right, Mises asserted, should always be carried through to the end. He maintained that land ownership as the most important means of production should always be private, as it is the 'superior economic form'.[43]

Liberty and individualism

Private rather than common property is fundamental to neo-liberal ideology, as it forms the basis of liberty. Neo-liberals like Milton Friedman argued that freedom and individualism are only possible through the private ownership of the means of production.[44] Jeremy Waldron contends that private property for neo-liberals serves negative liberty, because the nature of individually owning something is a matter of being free to use it without the inference of others.[45] Liberty therefore primarily means non-interference and ownership rights to the resources that an individual possesses without interference. Hayek avowedly disbelieved in the natural rights theory of Locke. Hayek's general line of thought was strictly utilitarian. Freedom, he argued, is not simply a matter of securing an individual's natural right to property. Individuals, he claimed, possess freedom only when the range of decisions taken on the basis of exchange between proprietors of property is maximised, and coercive decisions are confined to those operations of the judiciary and the police that are required to uphold the market order. Thus the recognition of private property, Hayek wrote in his *Constitution of Liberty*, is 'essential for the prevention of coercion'.[46]

Mises followed a similar line of argument in his defense of private property in his *Liberalism*. Private property, Mises argued, more than any other institution, restrains the power of government and creates a sphere in which the individual can be free of the state. It prevents dictatorship by allowing 'other forces to arise side by side with and in opposition to political power'.[47] Private property thus becomes the basis for all those activities that are free of the arbitrary will of the state. 'It is', Mises wrote, 'the soil in which the seeds of freedom are nurtured and in which the autonomy of the individual and ultimately all intellectual and material progress are rooted.' Governments, he proclaimed, tolerate private property where they are compelled to do so, 'but they do not acknowledge it voluntarily in recognition of its necessity'.[48] Even so-called liberal governments, Mises contended, have been unwilling to acknowledge private property and have relegated it to the background. He stated that:

> The tendency to impose oppressive restraints on private property, abuse political power, and to refuse to respect or recognise any free sphere outside or beyond the dominion of the state is too deeply ingrained in the mentality of those who control the government apparatus of compulsion and coercion for them to ever be able to resist it voluntarily.[49]

Thus Mises maintained that 'governments must be forced into adopting liberalism by the power of the unanimous opinion of the people; that they could voluntarily become liberal is not expected'.[50]

Law and justice

Property in neo-liberal ideology is part of legal order; it is protected by abstract rules within a specific legal constitution or *Rechtsstaat* that define the authority of the state and guarantee individual liberty. Abstract rules of property or the rule of law make it possible to determine which specific possessions an individual may command for his/her purposes. It is on this basis that Hayek claimed that 'law, liberty and property are an inseparable trinity'. 'There can be no law', he argued, 'in the sense of universal rules of conduct which does not determine boundaries of the domains of freedom by laying down rules that enable each to ascertain where he is free to act'.[51] It is this unity between law, liberty and property that makes a system of private rather than common ownership the most just system for neo-liberals. Individual liberty and private property are inseparable elements within the neo-liberal conception of justice. For neo-liberals, therefore, 'where there is no property there is no justice'.[52] Justice for neo-liberals is negative justice; it is concerned with conformity to abstract rules. The purpose of justice in liberal society, Hayek contended, is 'to tell each what he can count upon to promote the stability of the expectations upon which the spontaneous order depends'.[53] Justice thus tells individuals not what they must do, but rather what they should not do. This neo-liberal conception of justice is adapted from David Hume's principles of justice. Indeed, Hayek cited with approval Hume's *History of England* (Volume 5) which ascribed the country's greatness to restrictions on government power to interfere with property.[54]

It is the general rules of conduct that make the institution of private property for neo-liberals the most efficient form of resource allocation. An essential part of liberal justice is the freedom of all individuals to be able to act upon their own knowledge in pursuit of their own goals. The rules of the market order, neo-liberals claim, work to everyone's benefit, and all individuals must accept occasional losses as the price of these more general benefits. Their central argument is that private property, unlike common property, encourages a selection process that tends to direct resource use to productive ends. Mises, for instance, in his theory of entrepreneurship, argued that in a system of private property the incentives facing private owners will be based on those of speculation and change. Private owners realise they will either lose or gain from their speculation and thus they have strong incentives to speculate sensibly. To the extent that they fail, ownership of resources will pass out of their hands and into the hands of those who have proven themselves to be worthy of those resources. Under all circumstances, Mises contended that society benefits from the incentives of private individuals.[55]

On similar grounds, Hayek defended a system of private inheritance even though it would generate substantial and unmerited inequalities. His main argument was that leaving one's property to one's children has a useful incentive effect. The transition of material property from parents to children, Hayek argued, is as advantageous to the community as a whole as the transition of immaterial possessions, such as moral values and intelligence. Private inheritance is not only 'essential as a means to preserve the dispersal in the control of capital and as an inducement to accumulation', but is also an important means of harnessing 'the natural instincts of parents to equip the new generations as well as they can'.[56] To prohibit the inheritance of private property, Hayek contended, would 'cause a waste of resources and an injustice much greater than is caused by the inheritance of property'.[57]

Property and the modern corporation

The neo-liberal ideal of a society of individual property owners becomes problematic when applied to modern capitalist economies. In contemporary society, the concept of property has moved away from its classical liberal foundations as the embodiment of individualism and private ownership and has come to be associated with bureaucracy, democratic rule and corporate ownership. In the corporate world, neo-liberals point out that property is diffused into intangible forms such as shares, and the corporation thereby loses sight of its common interest and becomes the source of group conflict. Indeed, Hayek contended that the modern corporation 'turns the institution of property into something quite different from what it is normally supposed to be'.[58] The specific purpose of the modern corporation, neo-liberals argue, should be the pursuit of profit in line with the strict rules of law, rather than the extension of corporate power to achieve a multitude of different ends.

Property and the nature of corporate ownership

In the post-war years, the rise of the modern corporation in capitalist societies generated the view that the main means of production were no longer solely held by private individuals but by large corporations that were managed by executives and boards, which were responsible to a large and dispersed body of shareholders. This led some economists, most notably Joseph Schumpeter, to argue that the rise of corporate ownership represented a movement away from individual private ownership and towards a new, distinct, type of property regime. For Schumpeter, this change amounted to no more than the 'destruction of the institutional framework of capitalist society', and thus the 'evaporation of what we may term the material substance of property – its visible and touchable reality'.[59] Waldron does not go as far as Schumpeter, but views instead corporate property 'rather as a mutation of private property than as a distinct form of property in its own right'.[60] He points out that one of the distinctive features of private property is the ability of property owners to divide up and recombine their rights over resources allocated to them. This, he argues, 'sometimes leads to leasehold arrangements or trusts, and sometimes corporate property'.[61] He argues, however, that these arrangements can still be classified as private property on two grounds. Firstly, he draws attention to the fact that the arrangements were the result of private initiative and were brought about for the purposes of private individuals. Secondly, he observes that 'the corporation, as legal entity, may act as a private owner, using and allocating the resources that 'it' owns as 'it' sees fit rather than on the basis of the common or the collective interest'. On this basis Waldron contends that the corporation can be seen as the *'real* owner' of 'its' assets'.[62]

Corporations, however, can also be seen as a form of common or collective property. Corporations can be constituted not just by individual initiative but also by the state. Government is able to use the private corporations for the performance of what are essentially public functions. Indeed, Mises stated that, in an economy of big business enterprises, 'it is quite possible for those in control of the government to take action against private property'.[63] For example, corporations can be nationalised and made to serve public ends rather than their own or the shareholders' private ends. Thus the role of governments as owners and regulators of large corporations calls into question the validity of market capitalism and free enterprise. This is the principal insight of Adolf A. Berle and Gardiner C. Means in their classic work, *The Modern Corporation and Private Property*, published in 1932. Berle and Means' principal contention was that 'corporations have ceased to be merely legal devices through which the private business transactions of individuals may be carried out. The corporation has, in fact, become both a method of property tenure and a means of organising economic life.'[64] Their main point was that one third of the national wealth in American society lay in the hands of two hundred large corporations, and that individual private property has gone into the hands of 'collective hoppers', which had given rise to industrial oligarchies with tremendous political influence. A new age of the bureaucratised corporation, they argued, was emerging, with a growing division between ownership and management. The entrepreneurial spirit that had guided earlier corporate behaviour was now replaced by that of a managerial class with different incentives.[65]

The proper ends of corporations

The issue of corporate power and private property is a contentious one for neo-liberals. Some neo-liberals, most notably Hayek, adopt Berle and

Means' approach to large managerial corporations. The rise of the corporate economy in the twentieth century, Hayek argued in his essay 'The corporation in democratic society', represents a transition from a property system to a power system, where power follows the control of property and where the control of property is more important than ownership. Property originating in the resources of the millions of shareholders, plus the corporate accumulations, is controlled by the few at the management level. Hayek believed that it is possible to reverse this trend towards 'undesirable and socially dangerous powers' in corporate management through changes in corporate law. Indeed, he stated that:

> The complete separation of management from ownership, the lack of the real power of stockholders, and the tendency of corporations to develop into self-willed and possibly irresponsible empires, aggregates of enormous and largely uncontrollable power, is not a fact that we must accept as inevitable, but largely the result of special conditions which the law has created and the law can change.[66]

His main assertion was that 'if we are to limit the powers of corporations to where they are beneficial, we shall have to confine them to one specific goal, that of the profitable use of the capital entrusted to the management by the stockholders'.[67] Hayek, however, emphasised that corporations, like markets in general, must operate within a framework of rules and regulations that are consistent with the rule of law. While these rules may limit what corporations may do in pursuit of their concrete aims, 'this does not mean that they are entitled to use their resources for particular purposes which have nothing to do with their proper aim'.[68]

Hayek suggested reforms that would entail substantial changes to the corporate world. First, he would give each stockholder a 'legally enforceable claim to his share in the whole profits of the corporation'.[69] Second, he would prohibit corporations from exercising voting rights pertaining to shares they might hold in other corporations. Adopting these reforms, Hayek maintained, would restrain management's freedom to dispose of corporate assets and would give shareholders more control over corporate business.[70] Hayek's suggestions for the reform of corporations are wholly consistent with the immanent principles of the market order. He saw constructs like firms or corporations as tools for human use. It is their purpose is to allow individuals to pool their property for projects that are too large for individual resources. By devoting their resources to the single aim of securing the largest return in long-run profits, corporations are able to curb irresponsible power and make a valuable contribution to the market economy.[71]

Milton Friedman's position on corporations is similar to that of Hayek. Like Hayek, Friedman contended that, in a free-enterprise and private property system the proper end of the corporation should be to 'increase its profits'. Indeed, Friedman expressed the view that,

> [i]f anything is certain to destroy our free society, to undermine its very foundations, it would be a wide-spread acceptance by management of social responsibilities in some sense other than to make as much money as possible. This is a fundamentally subversive doctrine.[72]

Friedman's main concern was with the 'social responsibility' of corporations. Firms or corporations, Friedman maintained, should not be preoccupied with promoting desirable 'social ends': business should have no 'social conscience' where by it might take responsibility for providing employment or eliminating discrimination. For business to have such a conscience would mean that it would be 'preaching pure and unadulterated socialism' and 'undermining the basis of a free society'.[73] The primary responsibility of the corporate executive as an agent of individuals who own the corporation, he argued, should be to them. It is the corporate executive's responsibility 'to conduct the business in accordance with their desires, which generally will be to make as much money as possible while conforming to the basic rules of society, both those embodied in law and those embodied in ethical custom'. Thus the 'social responsibility of business', Friedman claimed, should be to maximise shareholder profit, and long-term economic benefit, he argued, would follow as a natural consequence.[74]

Property and the public interest

Neo-liberalism's interpretation of the relationship that exists between large corporations and private property is based on their conception of the 'public interest'. Neo-liberals reject the popular notion of a public interest that represents the common good or general will of all members of society. In their view, such a concept is constructivist and rational and threatens to undermine the liberal foundations of market society. Thus they are critical of the conception held by management that corporations ought to pursue public as well as private aims. As an aggregate of material assets, corporations, neo-liberals argue, should never be run in the public interest. Hayek for instance contended that deliberately using them in the service of some public interest is as 'dangerous' in the short-run as well as the long-run consequences. He proclaimed that:

> The immediate effect is greatly to extend the powers of the management of corporations over cultural, political, and moral issues for which proven ability to use resources efficiently in production does not necessarily confer special competence; and at the same time to substitute a vague and indefinable 'social responsibility' for a specific and controllable task.[75]

While the short-term effect is to increase irresponsible power, the long-term effect, Hayek maintained, is to increase the power of the state over corporations. It should not be assumed that neo-liberals in their discussion of property dispense with the notion of a public interest altogether. As it has been argued elsewhere in this book, neo-liberals do not deny that it is necessary for the state to provide some form of public good or interest. This public interest is, however, seen as separate from individual private interests. Yet the dilemma for neo-liberals is that private interests must always rely on the existence of a public interest. The notion of a spontaneous order such as the market necessitates the existence of some form of altruistic public interest to safeguard its underlying rules and principles. Andrew Gamble and Gavin Kelly state that the answer to this dilemma it to 'dispense both with the idea that the public good could be objectionable and knowable, and with the idea that the public interest is nothing more than the aggregate of private interests which only individuals can define'.[76] Drawing on Richard Flathman's conception of the public interest,[77] they argue that it is possible to conceive of a public interest that is the result of politics; one that arises through the 'roles, identities, and characteristics' of individuals and the 'history of the communities' that they inhabit. Thus Gamble and Kelly contend that it is possible to have a 'politics of the public interest' that is compatible with neo-liberal ideology: one which arises through the 'sustained negotiation and interaction between all groups in society to establish the principles and institutions through which society should be governed'.[78] Whilst neo-liberals may be unwilling to accept such a definition of the public interest, this conception is more plausible than their ideal of a group of enlightened altruistic politicians that are capable of securing the 'public interest' in order to maintain the market order.

Private monopolies

Many neo-liberals, as it has been argued above, accept giant corporations as private associations. Indeed, they are apologists for big capital and concentrations of property in large companies such as Microsoft. These private monopolies are accepted by neo-liberals like Hayek and Friedman on the grounds that they are simply an inevitable part of economic life in a free enterprise economy. Hayek maintained that monopolies of capital do not represent the same kind of threat to the market economy as monopolies of labour do. Although he acknowledged that he may have in the past 'used the tactical argument that we cannot hope to curb the coercive powers of labour unions unless we at the same time attack enterprise monopoly', he claimed that he had 'become more convinced it would be disingenuous to represent the existing monopolies in the field of labour and those in the field of enterprise as being of the same kind'.[79] Hayek certainly did not view enterprise monopolies as being 'beneficial' or 'desirable', but argued that they do represent only a 'minor problem' in the market system. What he saw as being even more harmful to the market order than private monopolies themselves was 'the arbitrary nature of all policy aimed at limiting the size of individual enterprises'.[80]

Friedman had even fewer reservations than Hayek does about the presence of giant corporations in the free enterprise system. Friedman commented that the long tradition of anti-trust legislation in America has not served to promote more competition, rather on the contrary. He stated that 'instead of promoting competition, anti-trust laws tended to do exactly the opposite, because they tended, like so many government activities, to be taken over by people they were supposed to regulate and control'.[81] He argued that anti-trust laws do 'far more harm than good'. Thus, in relation to Microsoft, Friedman contended that it would not be in the self-interest of Silicon Valley to prosecute Microsoft. He claimed that prosecuting Microsoft under anti-trust laws would be 'suicidal' for the computer industry, as it would impose on an industry which has been relatively free of government intrusion 'a continuous increase in government regulation. Anti-trust very quickly becomes regulation'.[82]

In Germany, however, the ordo-liberals were much more hostile to private monopolies than the neo-liberals in Anglo-America. Germany, unlike Britain and the United States, experienced the compulsory cartelisation of industry under the Third Reich, which crippled competition by creating rigid prices. Thus the ordo-liberals in the post-war years were critical of cartels and monopolies which placed restraints on entrepreneurial freedom. Their policy proposals for reforming German economy included the prevention of unhealthy concentrations of economic power and the prohibition of cartels and other forms of price-fixing. As Wilhelm Röpke proclaimed: 'Monopoly is precisely the worst form of commercialism which we want to combat by trying to mitigate competition by integrating counter-forces.'[83] The ordo-liberals agreed that perfect competition in all markets was impossible to achieve, but argued that restrictions on it by private monopolies could be curtailed by government policy measures. The ordo-liberals, as the 'guardians of competition', proposed that as a corrective force, a form of 'competition administration' should be imposed which is 'guided by the overall economic interest'. Such 'interventionist' measures, they maintained, were consistent with liberal principles as they would lead not only to greater economic freedom, but also to increased productivity and market efficiency.[84]

Conclusion

Private property, this chapter has argued, is fundamental for neo-liberals as it forms the foundation of Western civilisation, it acts as a basis of negative liberty by restraining the powers of government, and it creates the individual initiative that leads to free-market competition and economic efficiency. The chapter has demonstrated that adjacent to the core concept of property are the concepts of ownership, possessive individualism, legal privilege, individual initiative, negative justice and private associations, which are underpinned by peripheral notions such as capital accumulation, voluntary savings, private inheritance and maximised shareholder profits. There is, however, not just one unified concept of property that all neo-liberals subscribe to, but several, which exist within neo-liberalism's family of ideas drawing on different national traditions. Neo-liberalism, as this and previous chapters have demonstrated, is an ideology that draws on a wide variety intellectual movements. In relation to property, neo-liberals, in varying degrees, take their arguments from the Roman conception of private law, Hume's interpretation of justice, the consequentialist position of the British utilitarians, American republicanism's emphasis on property as a basis for freedom and independence and the Kantian notion of legal possession. These diverse sources of influence generate differences between neo-liberal schools with regard to issues such as inheritance rights, the nature of state intervention and competition policy. For all neo-liberals, however, private property is a prerequisite for a functioning market economy. It is a concept and institution that is indispensable to their creed. Without private ownership neo-liberals contend that there would be no means of serving the needs and purposes of an individual's life in society.

Although neo-liberals may look back to the cosmopolitanism of Ancient Greece and Rome with approval, their conception of property is a thoroughly modern one. In the twentieth century the concept of property became diffused with the rise of large corporations. Contemporary neo-liberals accept with approval new types of property in the form of shares. Whilst the ordo-liberals of the post-war years had reservations about the rise of corporations and the concentrations of power that they generated, neo-liberals in Anglo-America are much more willing to accept such monopolistic behaviour. For contemporary neo-liberals, markets, however monopolistic they may appear, are essentially competitive and will continue to grow. As proponents of free trade and free markets, they proclaim that firms or corporations should always be private associations rather than agents of the public interest.

Notes

1. F. A. Hayek, *The Road to Serfdom* (London: Routledge, 1944).
2. Ludwig von Mises, *Liberalism: In the Classical Tradition* (New York: Foundation for Economic Education, 1985), p. 19.
3. G. B. Newcomb, 'Theories of property', *Political Science Quarterly*, 1: 4 (1886), p. 597.
4. Paul Lafargue, *The Evolution of Property from Savagery to Civilisation* (London: New Park Publications, 1975), p. 3.
5. Alan Ryan, *Property and Political Theory* (Oxford: Blackwell, 1984), p. 16.
6. Andrzej Rapaczynski, 'Locke's conception of property and the principle of sufficient reason', *Journal of the History of Ideas*, 42: 2 (1995), pp. 305–15.
7. C. B. Macpherson, *The Political Theory of Possessive Individualism: From Hobbes to Locke* (Oxford: Oxford University Press, 1962), p. 205.
8. C. B. Macpherson, *Property: Mainstream and Critical Positions* (Toronto: Toronto University Press, 1978), p. 10.
9. Andrew Reeve, *Property* (Basingstoke: Macmillan, 1986), p. 57.
10. Adam Smith, *Lectures on Jurisprudence* (Oxford: Oxford University Press, 1978).
11. Jeremy Bentham's classic arguments in his *Theory of Legislation*, trans. R. Hildreth (London: Kegan Paul, 1974) and John Stuart Mill's *The Principles of Political Economy*, Vol. 1 (London: Hodge, 1987).
12. Ryan, *Property and Political Theory* pp. 100–1.
13. Ibid., p. 116.
14. Drew R. McCoy, *The Elusive Republic: Political Economy in Jeffersonian America* (Williamsburg, VA: The Institute of Early American History and Culture, 1980), p. 68.
15. Ibid., p. 68.
16. Quoted in James L. Huston, *Calculating the Value of the Union: Slavery, Property Rights and the Economic Origins of the Civil War* (Chapel Hill: University of North Carolina Press, 2003), p. 8.
17. Quoted in Eric Foner, *The Story of American Freedom* (Basingstoke: Macmillan, 1999), p. 73.

18. Quoted in Huston, *Calculating the Value of the Union*, p. 11.
19. Huston, *Calculating the Value of the Union*, p. 11.
20. Quoted in Huston, *Calculating the Value of the Union*, p. 12.
21. Stanley N. Katz, 'Thomas Jefferson and the right to property in revolutionary America', *Journal of Law and Economics*, 19: 3 (1976), p. 475.
22. Huston, *Calculating the Value of the Union*, p. 13.
23. Ibid., p. 16.
24. Eric Foner, *The Story of American Freedom*, p. 105.
25. F. A. Hayek, *The Constitution of Liberty* (London: Routledge, 1960), p. 20.
26. George B. Newcomb, 'Theories of property', p. 603.
27. Alan Ryan, *Property* (Milton Keynes: Open University Press, 1987), p. 100.
28. Quoted in Howard Williams, 'Kant's concept of property', *The Philosophical Quarterly*, 27: 106 (1977), p. 32.
29. Williams, 'Kant's concept of property', p. 32.
30. Quoted in S. M. Shell, 'Kant's theory of property', *Political Theory*, 6: 1 (1978), p. 79.
31. Newcomb, *Theories of Property*, p. 603.
32. Dudley Knowles, 'Hegel on property and personality', *The Philosophical Quarterly*, 33: 130 (1983), pp. 45–62.
33. G. W. F. Hegel, *The Philosophy of Right* (Oxford: Clarendon Press, 1941), pp. 235–6, quoted in C. B. Macpherson, 'Property as a means or ends', in A. Parel and T. Flanagan (eds), *Theories of Property from Aristotle to the Present* (Waterloo, ON: Wilfred Laurier University Press, 1979), p. 6.
34. T. M. Knox, *Hegel's Philosophy of Right* (Oxford: Clarendon Press, 1952), p. 46.
35. Ryan, *Property and Political Theory*, p. 129.
36. Ludwig von Mises, *Socialism: An Economic and Sociological Analysis* (Indianapolis: Liberty Fund, 1981), p. 254.
37. Ibid., p. 445.
38. See F. A. Hayek, *The Fatal Conceit: The Errors of Socialism* (London: Routledge, 1988), pp. 29–37, and Mises, *Socialism*, pp. 41–4.
39. Hayek, *The Fatal Conceit*, p. 31.
40. Ibid., p. 32.
41. Ibid., pp. 31–3.
42. Mises, *Socialism*, p. 245.
43. Ibid.
44. Milton Friedman, *Capitalism and Freedom* (Chicago: University of Chicago Press, 1962).
45. Jeremy Waldron, *The Right to Private Property* (Oxford: Clarendon Press, 1988), p. 410.
46. Hayek, *The Constitution of Liberty*, p. 140.
47. Mises, *Liberalism*, p. 67.
48. Ibid., p. 67.
49. Ibid., p. 68.
50. Ibid.
51. F. A. Hayek, *Law, Legislation and Liberty: Rules and Order*, Vol. I (Chicago: University of Chicago Press, 1973), p. 107.
52. Hayek, *The Fatal Conceit*, p. 33.
53. F. A. Hayek, *Law, Legislation and Liberty: The Mirage of Social Justice*, Vol. II (Chicago: University of Chicago Press, 1976), p. 37.
54. Hayek, *The Fatal Conceit*, p. 34.

55. Lugwig von Mises, *Theory and History: An Interpretation of Social and Economic Evolution* (New York: Arlington House, 1963), pp. 289–9.
56. Hayek, *The Constitution of Liberty*, p. 90.
57. Ibid., p. 91.
58. F. A. Hayek, 'The corporation in democratic society: In whose interest ought it to and will it be run', in his *Studies in Philosophy, Politics and Economics* (London: Routledge and Kegan Paul, 1967), p. 309.
59. Joseph Schumpeter, *Capitalism, Socialism and Democracy* (London: Allen and Unwin, 1943), pp. 139–42.
60. Waldron, *The Right to Private Property*, p. 57.
61. Ibid., p. 58.
62. Ibid.
63. Mises, *Liberalism*, p. 69.
64. A. A. Berle, Jr and G. C. Means, *The Modern Corporation and Private Property* (New York: Macmillan, 1932), p. 1.
65. Ibid., p. 14.
66. Hayek, 'The corporation in democratic society', p. 311.
67. Ibid., p. 300.
68. Ibid., p. 301.
69. Ibid., p. 307.
70. Ibid., p. 310.
71. T. E. Flanagan, 'F. A. Hayek on property and justice', in Anthony Parel and Thomas Flanagan (eds), *Theories of Property from Aristotle to the Present* (Waterloo, ON: Wilfred Laurier University Press, 1979), pp. 335–60.
72. Quoted in Hayek, 'The corporation in democratic society', p. 312.
73. Milton Friedman, 'The social responsibility of business to increase its profits', *The New York Times Magazine*, 13 September 1970, pp. 3–4.
74. Ibid., pp. 9–10.
75. Hayek, 'The corporation in democratic society', p. 311.
76. Andrew Gamble and Gavin Kelly, 'The politics of the company', in John Parkinson, Andrew Gamble and Gavin Kelly (eds), *The Political Economy of the Company* (Oxford: Hart Publishing, 2000), p. 24.
77. Richard Flathman, *The Public Interest* (New York, 1966).
78. Gamble and Kelly, 'The politics of the company', p. 25.
79. Hayek, *The Constitution of Liberty*, p. 265.
80. Ibid.
81. Milton Friedman, 'The business community's suicidal impulse', *Cato Policy Report*, Vol. 21, No. 2, March/April 1999, pp. 1–2.
82. Ibid., pp. 4–5.
83. Wilhelm Röpke, *A Humane Economy: The Social Framework of the Free Market* (Chicago: Henry Regnery, 1958), p. 128.
84. Norbert Kloten, 'The role of the public sector in the Social Market Economy', in Alan Peacock and Hans Willgerodt, *German Neo-Liberals and the Social Market Economy* (London: Macmillan Trade Policy Research Centre, 1989), pp. 87–8.

Chapter 9

Conclusion

Neo-liberalism was one of the most significant ideological movements of the twentieth century. Its core principles captured the minds of political leaders in the Western world and helped to shape the contours of political debate. Yet the exact nature of neo-liberalism as a universal economic doctrine or ideology remains vague. This book has explored the roots of neo-liberalism and its conceptual configuration in order to uncover its distinctive identity as an ideology. The central contention of the book is that neo-liberalism is a complex ideology with many different strands, but, through their common enemy, collectivism, and through their conceptual boundaries, these strands come together to form a coherent whole. The starting premise of the book, set out in the first half, was that an inquiry into the nature of neo-liberal ideology must first examine the roots of the ideology and identify its place within the wider tradition of liberalism. Utilising Michel Foucault's genealogical method of social inquiry and Terence Ball's conceptual–historical approach to ideologies, this part of the book explored the origins of neo-liberal ideology. Neo-liberalism, it contended, is an ideology that draws on aspects of different liberal movements or traditions, in particular the classical liberalism of Adam Smith and David Hume, the Lockean liberalism of Thomas Jefferson and John Adams, and the German *Liberalismus* of Immanuel Kant and Wilhelm von Humboldt. Rather than simply reviving the core ideas of these liberal movements, neo-liberalism reinterpreted them on a new ideological terrain, in reaction to the various threats it faced both from the inside and from the outside. This book has argued that neo-liberals such as F. A. Hayek, Lionel Robbins and Milton Friedman were not just reacting to the rise of socialism within national economies. Also, and more significantly, they were responding to the 'new' interventionist variants within their own creed, such as the new liberalism advocated by T. H. Green, L. T. Hobhouse and J. A. Hobson in Britain and American progressivism associated with Franklin D. Roosevelt's New Deal administration.

This book has examined how the efforts of neo-liberals in the first half of the twentieth century to revive liberalism were inaugurated at the founding of the Mont Pelerin Society in 1947. Like Marxists of an earlier time, the neo-liberals at Mont Pelerin constructed their own utopia. Their utopian vision of a free-market society influenced national economic programmes in Germany in the 1950s and in Anglo-America in the 1980s. The present book has set out the links between political and economic ideas and policy agendas. It has highlighted the difference in emphasis between neo-liberalism's intellectual agenda and its policy agenda. Neo-liberalism, as an intellectual movement cultivating ideas within think-tanks, was extremely significant in transforming the nature and scope of political debate. However, when these ideas were transformed into policy agendas, they became part of a larger constellation of intellectual ideas competing for influence. There remained a fundamental distinction between neo-liberalism as an ideology and the neo-liberalism that was incorporated into the New Right. Whilst neo-liberal intellectuals were attempting to reconstruct policy agendas to create a new 'liberal' utopia, neo-liberal politicians on the New Right were less willing to implement such extreme measures. As Chapter 6 has demonstrated with reference to welfare policy, neo-liberal politicians in Anglo-America never implemented radical proposals for the reform of the welfare system because these were perceived to be too costly and unpopular with the electorate. In the 1980s, neo-liberalism may have helped to shape the contours of policy debates and to guide proposals for reform, but neo-liberalism was far from being a hegemonic ideology in terms of its influence over the actual policies that were implemented.

Using Michael Freeden's conceptual approach to ideologies, the second half of the book has concentrated on the decontested concepts that are at the core of neo-liberalism – the market, welfare, the constitution and property – and on their accompanying, adjacent and peripheral, concepts. Neo-liberalism, like all ideologies, is a movement of concepts. Its core concepts, that may have been previously adjacent or even peripheral within liberal ideology, were brought back to the core of the ideology with its rise in influence. The book has examined how liberal concepts were reconstructed by neo-liberals onto a new political terrain. Chapters 5, 6, 7 and 8 have mapped out the conceptual histories of neo-liberalism's four core concepts and have analysed the extent to which neo-liberals have drawn on these histories in their own interpretations of the concepts in question. The chapters went on to examine how the four core concepts constitute neo-liberalism's conceptual configuration. In Chapter 5, the core concept of the market or the 'market order' was discussed in relation to adjacent concepts such as evolution, spontaneous order, limited knowledge, free exchange, individualism and entrepreneurship. Peripheral notions such as the enterprise culture, income-tax relief, privatisation, deregulation and share-ownership were also considered. Chapter 6 looked at the core concept of welfare and at the adjacent concepts of equality of opportunity, freedom, personal responsibility, self-reliance and negative rights. It related these concepts to peripheral policy ideas such as reduced social expenditure, education vouchers, private insurance, 'workfare' and negative income-tax. Chapter 7 focused on the core concept of the Constitution and the adjacent concepts of freedom, private law, legal responsibility, abstract order, 'rules of just conduct' and evolution. These concepts were linked with peripheral concepts like the legal state, a separation of powers, administrative courts, a 'fiscal constitution', and balanced budgets. The final core concept, which the book examined in Chapter 8, was property. It connected the concept of property with its accompanying adjacent concepts of ownership, possessive individualism, legal privilege, individual initiative, negative justice and private association, and with peripheral concepts such as capital accumulation, voluntary savings, private inheritance and maximised shareholder profits. It is the ordering of these concepts in this specific configuration that gives neo-liberalism its distinctive identity as an ideology.

Like all other liberal variants, neo-liberalism retains family resemblances with liberalism; it is part of the family continuity of the liberal tradition. It identifies itself in some shape or form with the core concepts of liberalism – liberty, individualism and, to a lesser extent, progress – and shares similarities with other currents of liberal thought.[1] Hayek and other neo-liberals were, however, historically selective in the liberal traditions that they drew on. Neo-liberals only recognised variants of liberalism that were consistent with their view of the course of history, in particular with classical liberalism. They rejected more contemporary liberal concepts of rationality and sociability, and the radical intellectual changes introduced by liberal thinkers such as T. H. Green and Hobson in Britain and John Dewey in the United States. Although theorists such as Freeden may contend that Hayek was more of a conservative than of a liberal, Hayek never identified himself in this way. In his postscript to *The Constitution of Liberty*, 'Why I am not a conservative', Hayek explicitly rejected the label 'conservative' on the grounds that liberals and conservatives hold opposing views on issues such as change, order, authority, morality, religion and knowledge. Liberals, he claimed, do not wish to preserve things, rather on the contrary. 'Liberalism', he argued, 'is not averse to evolution and change; and where spontaneous change has been smothered by government control, it wants a great deal of change of policy.'[2] Hayek supported the creation of new ideas rather than fearing them, and saw conservatism as a weak ideology, lacking in imagination What Hayek espoused was a combination of classical liberalism and German liberalism, rather than a brand of conservatism. Whilst there are unquestionably key conservative principles in evidence in Hayek's, Milton Friedman's and other neo-liberals' thought, they remained foremost liberals. Identifying neo-liberalism with conservatism only serves to blur the liberal and libertarian content of the ideology.

Hayek and other neo-liberal intellectuals, therefore, must be seen as part of the corpus of liberalism. Like the new liberals before them, neo-liberals were successors of liberalism who reinvented liberal ideology. They undertook what Freeden refers to as a 'redecontesting' of liberal concepts due to significant changes in economic, political and cultural assumptions. Concepts that had already been decontested by liberals such as the new liberals were decontested again by neo-liberals, in reaction to the political and economic context within which they were writing.[3] Neo-liberals did not break with core liberal concepts such as liberty and individualism, rather they changed their specific meaning. The movement of marginalised liberal concepts, for instance property and the market, at the core of neo-liberalism redirected the ideology and provided the liberals with a new philosophical language.

Varieties of neo-liberalism

A central argument of this book is that neo-liberalism is a complex ideology with several different strands. In Germany, Britain and the United States different forms of neo-liberalism emerged in intellectual and political debates. Germany was the first country to adopt neo-liberalism in the 1950s. Hayek in his *Road to Serfdom* had despaired about the rise of interventionism in Germany. Yet, as this book has observed, it was in the most illiberal of the three countries that neo-liberalism first came to prominence as an intellectual movement of ideas. Chapter 4 has demonstrated how the rise of the Third Reich and the strident interventionism of the war years created a sense of urgency amongst liberal intellectuals to redirect the German economy and restore liberalism. Indeed, the rise of neo-liberalism was a direct result of the destruction of Nazism, which produced a desire to create a different kind of German state and economy. The German ordo-liberals, drawing on the liberalism of Kant and Humboldt, embraced many of the central tenets of neo-liberalism – open markets, free contracts, private property and a *Rechtsstaat*. The ordo-liberals were, however, unique in the emphasis they placed upon the 'social' element of the market encapsulated in the 'Social Market Economy'. German neo-liberals such as Alexander Rüstow, Walter Eucken, Alfred Müller-Armack and Ludwig Erhard argued that the market should act as a vehicle for 'social justice'. They maintained that free competition, rather than the state, would allow for the formation of a system of private social security. The success of this 'liberal' revival in Germany in the 1950s, a country that had succumbed to tyrannies of National Socialism, was a source of confidence for other nations with a more prominent liberal past.

The German 'social' model of neo-liberalism influenced the tide of thinking in Britain in the 1970s. Whilst in Germany neo-liberalism was a direct reaction to the years under the Third Reich, in Britain its rise stemmed from the power of organised labour. Advocates of neo-liberal policy reform such as Keith Joseph took inspiration from the German example, arguing for a socially responsible market economy created through industry. An important influence over the views of leading neo-liberal politicians in Britain were the free market think-tanks the Institute of Economic Affairs, the Adam Smith Institute and the Centre for Policy Studies. These think-tanks set out to transform the 'climate of opinion', inspiring many of the policy proposals behind the Thatcher government's reform programme in the 1980s.

In the United States the rise in influence of neo-liberal ideas was a direct response to the growth of the illegitimate and unconstitutional powers of compensatory state. American neo-liberalism in the 1970s and 1980s became associated with the upsurge in neo-conservatism, although, as the book has argued, the two are not necessarily the same thing. Whilst neo-liberals prioritise economics and market relations, neo-conservatives emphasise morality and the authority of the state, although there is much common ground between the two ideologies. Discontented Conservatives of the

Great Society programme such as William F. Buckley, Russell Kirk and Irving Kristol attempted to create a conservative 'counter-reformation'. American intellectuals directly identifiable with neo-liberalism, in particular Milton Friedman from the Chicago School and James M. Buchanan from the Virginia School, applied an ultra-free-market ideological stance to economic policy. Their ideas became embedded in the policy agendas set out by right-wing think-tanks such as the Cato Institute, the American Enterprise Institute and the Hoover Institute. In the 1960s and 1970s, many of their proposals were adopted by neo-liberals in the Republican Party, most notably Barry Goldwater and Ronald Reagan, who attempted to establish the credibility of neo-liberalism as a policy agenda.

These three distinct neo-liberal movements in Germany, Britain and the United States did not, however, exist in isolation. There was much common ground between the three; together they can be said to represent a crystallisation of a particular liberal position with specific nuances. This book has pointed to the bridges connecting the three countries. One of the most fundamental of these bridges is the intellectual and historical context within which neo-liberalism arose. The book has highlighted two contexts that are intimately connected with neo-liberal ideology. The first one is that of the 1930s and 1940s, and is associated with the origins of neo-liberalism. As Chapter 3 has demonstrated, neo-liberalism came to prominence at a time when liberal ideas were in decline. Economists such as Joseph Schumpeter and John Maynard Keynes argued that liberalism was no longer a viable philosophy with which to approach the economic problems of the twentieth century. They maintained that the so-called 'age of *laissez-faire*' was over and that collectivism was the future. Liberal intellectuals across the Western world reacted to this pessimism, vowing to fight collectivism and to revive liberal ideology. The Mont Pelerin Society united these isolated liberals. It connected the three national movements by setting out, in its statement of aims, many of the central doctrines of neo-liberalism that were adapted to national contexts. Chapter 3 has highlighted the important role that the Mont Pelerin played in refurbishing and strengthening liberalism in the years after the Second World War. It has pointed out how the society acted as an international meeting ground for scholars, intellectuals and politicians of a 'liberal' persuasion, making them exchange ideas and redirect the future course of liberalism. Consequently, there was a significant transfer of ideas between Germany, Britain and the United States. In Britain, Keith Joseph in the 1970s drew on the German model of neo-liberalism as a source of guidance, and in the

United States and Britain in the 1980s there were exchanges of ideas and policy proposals that led to similar programmes of reform.

The second context of neo-liberalism is that of the 1960s and 1970s, and it is associated with the Keynesian assault and the rise of the modern welfare state. In Anglo-America, the rise of neo-liberalism was a reaction to the dominance of Keynesian demand management and welfare policies. In the United States, Friedman led the assault consigning Keynesian policy prescriptions to the ash heap of economic history. In Britain, similar attacks were made by the Institute of Economic Affairs. The Keynesian orthodoxy passed from complete domination in the 1960s to near irrelevance, with the rise of Friedman's monetarist economic theories in Anglo-America in the early 1980s.

Another common thread between the varieties of neo-liberalism in these three national contexts is the influence of intellectual figures such as Hayek. This book has observed that neo-liberalism was not purely an Anglo-American affair, but was also an ideology with powerful German-Austrian connections. Hayek's thought created a bridge between the different currents of neo-liberalism in Germany, Britain and the United States. Throughout the twentieth century Hayek published a stream of influential articles and books whose impact on the world of ideas was considerable. In particular, his 1944 *Road to Serfdom* was a resounding success in all three countries. Hayek's writing radically deepened the Austrian insights he had inherited from his intellectual forebears. In his writings, Hayek borrowed ideas from the German tradition of liberalism, in particular the *Rechtstaat*, which was fundamental to his liberal programme. In the immediate post-war years, he renewed his acquaintance with the German ordo-liberal Wilhelm Röpke to discuss the future of Germany. The break-up of Germany and the dismantling of German industry subsequently became a central topic of discussion at the Mont Pelerin Society's first meeting in 1947. Hayek was supportive of the ordo-liberals' proposals for the reconstruction of Germany on the basis of an economic model that in many ways was similar to his own market order, although he made it explicit that he had severe reservations about labeling such an economy 'social'.

In Anglo-America, Hayek's role in the rise of neo-liberalism was even more evident. In the United States, Hayek joined the University of Chicago in the 1950s, a bulwark for free-market views, where he spent ten years developing his ideas under the influence of fellow 'liberal' economists Friedman and, later, George Stigler. Throughout the 1960s and 1970s he participated in numerous organisations actively to promote neo-liberal ideas, which included the Foundation for Economic Education, the Philadelphia Society, the American Enterprise Institute, the Cato Institute, the Heritage Foundation and the Hoover Institute, where he became an honorary fellow. He later went on to become a keen supporter of Reagan's campaign for the White House.

Similarly, in Britain, from the 1960s to the 1980s, Hayek became intimately connected with the activities of the free-market think-tank, the Institute of Economic Affairs, which helped to generate ideas that were influential in shaping the policy agendas of the Thatcher government. One of his most important publications through the IEA in 1972, *A Tiger by the Tail*, warned against the dangers of inflation that he saw as being inherent in Keyensiansim. Hayek's philosophy had a lasting impact on the Conservative Party in the 1970s which incorporated many of his ideas into its policy proposals.

Future directions

Neo-liberalism was undoubtedly a significant ideology in the twentieth century, and had a central role to play in intellectual and policy discourses in Germany in the 1950s and in Britain and the United States in the 1970s and 1980s. Its place today as an economic ideology of the Right is, however, less clear. It can be argued that today the ideological context has moved away from neo-liberalism and from questions concerning free enterprise, the rule of law and limited government, towards a neo-conservative agenda. Nowhere is this movement more apparent than in the United States. In contemporary American politics, neo-conservatism has surfaced as an intellectual current that aims to transform the Republican Party, and American conservatism in general, into a new type of conservative politics. At the most basic level, neo-conservatism stands for moral values and religion, the authority of the state, and national security – all tenets that neo-liberals would find it hard to identify with. Irving Kristol points out that neo-conservatism is 'impatient with the Hayekian notion that we are on a "road to serfdom". Neo-cons do not feel that kind of alarm or anxiety about the growth of the state in the past century, seeing it as natural, indeed inevitable.'[4] Certainly neo-conservatives draw on many thinkers and politicians such as Herbert Hoover, Russell Kirk and Barry Goldwater, whom, as this book has demonstrated, neo-liberals themselves took inspiration from. The book has pointed out that neo-liberalism and various forms of neo-conservatism existed amicably side-by-side in American society in the twentieth century. It has contended that neo-conservatives and neo-liberals do have much common ground, such as a desire to promote free markets and an opposition to government regulation and social spending. Unlike the conservatism of the past, however, the neo-conservatism of the twenty-first century is guided by a new radicalism and sense of urgency following threats to national and international security.

Neo-conservatism has rose to prominence in the United States following the terrorist attacks of September 11 and has since eclipsed neo-liberalism as the overriding discourse in American politics. Indeed, President George W. Bush's new security agenda aims to replace neo-liberalism with neo-conservatism using American military power. Neo-conservatives reject the neo-liberal policy of minimal government, and instead adopt an 'aggressive' foreign policy stance against 'rogue states'. In response to international terrorism, they have embraced an 'imperial role' of pre-emptive war and regime change.[5] It would, therefore, appear as though neo-liberals have more in common with the paleo-conservatives who stood in opposition to the New Deal than with the neo-conservatives that are in power today. The rise of neo-conservatism does not, however, signal the end of neo-liberalism. Neo-liberalism is alive and well, embedded in the discipline of economics, and continues to dominate discussions about the future course of the global economy. Yet, whilst there is still a very clear neo-liberal agenda, it is one that has become increasingly defused. In the twenty-first century, neo-liberalism no longer has an overriding influence on policy agendas in Germany, Britain and the United States, as it did in second part of the twentieth century, and the prominence of an intellectual community of neo-liberals based around the Mont Pelerin Society and free-market think-tanks has faded. The question, however, should not be 'What comes after neo-liberalism?', but, rather, 'What do neo-liberalism and neo-conservatism have in common?'. Neo-liberalism remains one of the most influential streams of thought on the Right, informing both republican policy and conservative ideology in general. Neo-liberalism and neo-conservatism share much common ground. One of the great ideological projects of the twenty-first century, therefore, will be to find a way of reconciling the two.

Notes

1. Michael Freeden, *Ideologies and Political Theory* (Oxford: Oxford University Press, 1996), p. 145.

2. F. A. Hayek, 'Why I am not a conservative', in his *The Constitution of Liberty* (London: Routledge, 1960), p. 399.
3. Freeden writes about the 'redecontesting' of liberal concepts in relation to the new liberalism in his *Ideologies and Political Theory*, ch. 5. This can equally be applied to neo-liberalism.
4. Irving Kristol, 'The neo-conservative persuasion, what it was, and what it is', in Irwin Stelzer (ed.), *Neo-Conservatism* (London: Atlantic Books, 2004), p. 35.
5. S. Halper and J. Clarke, *America Alone: The Neo-Conservatives and the Global Order* (Cambridge: Cambridge University Press, 2004).

Bibliography

Abelshauser, Werner, 'The first post-liberal nation: Stages in the development of modern corporatism in Germany', *European History Quarterly*, Vol. 14 (1984), pp. 285–318.
Abromeit, H., 'Government–industry relations in West Germany', in M. Chick (ed.), *Governments, Industries and Markets* (London: Edward Elgar, 1990), pp. 54–68.
Adam Smith Institute, *The Omega Report: Local Government* (London: ASI, 1983).
Albert, Michel, *Capitalism Against Capitalism* (London: Whurr Publishers, 1994).
Amenta, Edwin and Skocpol, Theda, 'Redefining the New Deal: World War II and the Development of social provision in the United States', in M. Weir, A. S. Orloff and T. Skocpol (eds), *The Politics of Social Policy in the United States* (Princeton: Princeton University Press, 1988), pp. 81–122.
Appleby, Joyce, *Liberalism and Republicanism in the Historical Imagination* (Cambridge, MA: Harvard University Press, 1992).
Ashford, Nigel, *Consensus and Conflict Within Neo-Liberalism* (Strathclyde: Papers on Government and Politics, 1985).
Bailyn, Bernard, *The Ideological Origins of the American Revolution* (Cambridge, MA: Harvard University Press, 1967).
Ball, Terence, 'Political theory and conceptual change' in A. Vincent (ed.), *Political Theory: Tradition and Diversity* (Cambridge: Cambridge University Press, 1997), pp. 28–44.
Ball, Terence, *Transforming Political Discourse: Political Theory and Critical Conceptual History* (Oxford: Blackwell, 1988).
Banning, Lance, 'Jeffersonian ideology revisited: liberal and classical ideas in the new American republic', *William and Mary Quarterly*, Vol. 43 (1986), pp. 1–28.
Barker, Rodney, *Political Ideas in Modern Britain* (London: Methuen, 1978).
Barry, Norman, 'Commentary: markets and regulation', in J. Blundell and C. Robinson (eds), *Regulation Without the State . . . The Debate Continues* (London: IEA, 2000), pp. 112–19.

Barry, Norman, 'Economic liberalism, ethics and the social market economy', in James Meadowcroft (ed.), *The Liberal Political Tradition*, pp. 64–79.
Barry, Norman, *Hayek's Social and Economic Philosophy* (London: Macmillan, 1979).
Barry, Norman, *The New Right* (London: Croom Helm, 1987).
Barry, Norman, 'Political and economic thought of German neo-liberals', in A. Peacock and H. Willgeradot (eds), *German Neo-Liberals and the Social Market Economy* (London: Macmillan, 1989), pp. 105–24.
Barry, Norman, 'Review article: The new liberalism', *British Journal of Political Science*, 13 (1983), pp. 93–123.
Barry, Norman, 'Understanding the market', in Loney, M. (ed.), *The State or the Market: Politics and Welfare in Contemporary Britain* (London: Sage, 1996).
Barry, Norman, *Welfare* (Buckingham: Open University Press, 1999).
Baylin, Bernard, *The Ideological Origins of the American Revolution* (Cambridge, MA: Harvard University Press, 1967).
Beck, K. N., 'What was liberalism in the 1950s?', *Political Science Quarterly*, 102: 2 (1987), pp. 233–58.
Beetham, David, *Max Weber and the Theory of Modern Politics* (London: Allen and Unwin, 1974).
Bell, Daniel, *The American New Right* (New York: Anchor Doubleday, 1964).
Bell, Daniel, *The End of Ideology* (New York: Free Press, 1962).
Bell, Daniel, 'The prospects of American capitalism: On Keynes, Schumpeter and Galbraith', in his *The End of Ideology: On the Exhaustion of Political Ideas in the 1950s* (New York: Free Press, 1962), pp. 70–85.
Bellamy, Richard, 'Dethroning politics: Liberalism, constitutionalism and democracy in the thought of F. A. Hayek', *British Journal of Political Science*, 24: 3 (1994), pp. 419–32.
Bellamy, Richard, *Liberalism and Modern Society: A Historical Argument* (Cambridge: Polity, 1992).
Bendersky, J. W., *Carl Schmitt* (Princeton: Princeton University Press, 1983).
Bentham Jeremy, *Theory of Legislation*, trans. R. Hildreth (London: Routledge and Kegan Paul, 1974).
Berghahn, V., 'Ideas into politics: The case of Ludwig Erhard', in Bullen et al., *Ideas into Politics*, pp. 168–87.
Berle, A. A. and Means, G. C., *The Modern Corporation and Private Property* (New York: Macmillan, 1932).
Bessel, Richard, *Germany After the First World War* (Oxford: Clarendon Press, 1993).
Bevir, Mark, *The Logic of the History of Ideas* (Cambridge: Cambridge University Press, 1999).
Blumenthal, Sidney, *The Rise of the Counter-Establishment: From Conservative Ideology to Political Power* (New York: Times Books, 1986).
Blundell, John and Robinson, Colin, *Regulation Without the State* (London: IEA, 1999).
Blyth, Mark, *Great Transformations: Economic Ideas and Institutional Change in the Twentieth Century* (Cambridge: Cambridge University Press, 2002).

Bosanquet, Nick, *After the New Right* (London: Heinemann, 1983).
Brazier, R., *Constitutional Practice* (Oxford: Clarendon Press, 1994).
Brebner, J. B., '*Laissez-faire* and state intervention in nineteenth-century Britain', *The Journal of Economic History*, Vol. 8 (1948), pp. 59–73.
Briggs, Asa, 'The welfare state in historical perspective', in C. Pierson and F. G. Castles (eds), *The Welfare State Reader* (Cambridge: Polity, 2000), pp. 18–29.
Brinkley, Alan, 'Historians and the inter-war years', in his *Liberalism and its Discontents*, pp. 111–32.
Brinkley, Alan, 'The late New Deal and the idea of the state', in his *Liberalism and its Discontents*, pp. 37–62.
Brinkley, Alan, *Liberalism and its Discontents* (Cambridge, MA: Harvard University Press, 1998).
Brinkley, Alan, 'The problem of American conservatism', in his *Liberalism and its Discontents*, pp. 277–97.
Brinkley, Alan, 'The two world wars and American liberalism', in his *Liberalism and its Discontents*, pp. 79–93.
Brittan, Samuel, *Government and the Market Economy* (London: IEA, 1971).
Brittan, Samuel, 'The Thatcher government's economic policy', in D. Kavanagh and A. Seldon (eds), *The Thatcher Effect: A Decade of Change* (Oxford: Oxford University Press, 1989), pp. 3–20.
Buchanan, J. M., *Liberty, Market and State: Political Economy in the 1980s* (Sussex: Wheatsheaf, 1986).
Buchanan, J. M., *The Limits of Liberty: Between Anarchy and Leviathan* (Chicago: University of Chicago Press, 1975).
Buchanan, J. M. and Tullock, G., *The Calculus of Consent: Logical Foundations of Constitutional Democracy* (Michigan: University of Michigan Press, 1962).
Buchanan, J. M. and Wagner, R. E., *Democracy in Deficit* (New York: Academic Press, 1977).
Buchanan, J. M., Burton, J. and Wagner, R. E., *The Consequences of Mr. Keynes* (London: IEA, 1978).
Bullen, R. J., Strandmann, H. P. and Polansky, A. (eds), *Ideas into Politics: Aspects of European History, 1880–1950* (London: Croom Helm, 1984).
Caldwell, Bruce, *Hayek's Challenge: An Intellectual Biography of F. A. Hayek* (Chicago: University of Chicago Press, 2004).
Callinicos, Alex, *Against the Third Way: An Anti-Capitalist Critique* (Cambridge: Polity, 2001).
Callinicos, Alex, *The New Mandarins of American Power* (Cambridge: Polity, 2003).
Carr, William, *The Origins of the Wars for Reunification* (London: Longman, 1991).
Clarke, Peter, *The Keynesian Revolution in the Making, 1924–1936* (Oxford: Clarendon Press, 1988).
Clarke, Peter, *Liberals and Social Democrats* (Cambridge: Cambridge University Press, 1978).

Clarke, Peter, 'The politics of Keynesian economics', in M. Bentley and J. Stevenson (eds), *High and Low Politics in Modern Britain* (Oxford: Clarendon Press, 1983), pp. 231–49.

Coates, David, *Models of Capitalism: Growth and Stagnation in the Modern Era* (Cambridge: Polity, 2000).

Cockett, Richard, *Thinking the Unthinkable: Think-Tanks and the Economic Revolution, 1931–1983* (London: HarperCollins, 1994).

Connolly, William E., *The Terms of Political Discourse* (Oxford: Blackwell, 1993).

Cowling, Maurice, 'The sources of the New Right', reprinted in his *Mill and Liberalism* (Cambridge: Cambridge University Press, 1990), pp. 31–40.

Cristi, Renato, *Carl Schmitt and Authoritarian Liberalism* (Cardiff: The University of Wales Press, 1998).

Dangerfield, G., *The Strange Death of Liberal England* (New York: Capricorn, 1935).

Deane, P., *The Evolution of Economic Ideas* (Cambridge: Cambridge University Press, 1978).

Denham, Andrew and Garnett, Mark, 'From guru to godfather: Keith Joseph, "New" Labour and the British conservative tradition', *The Political Quarterly*, 72: 1 (2001), pp. 99–110.

Denham, Andrew and Garnett, Mark, *Keith Joseph* (Chesham: Acumen, 2001).

Dicey, A. V., *Introduction to the Study of the Law of the Constitution* (London: Macmillan, 1905).

Dicey, A. V., *Lectures on the Relation Between Law and Public Opinion in England During the Nineteenth Century* (London: Macmillan, 1905).

Dietze, G., 'Hayek on the rule of law', in F. Machluo (ed.), *Essays on Hayek* (London: Routledge and Kegan Paul, 1977), pp. 129–38.

Diggins, John Patrick, *The Lost Soul of American Politics: Virtue, Self-Interest and the Foundations of Liberalism* (New York: Basic Books, 1984).

Douglas, P. and Powell, J. E., *How Big Should Government Be?* (London: Macmillan, 1968).

Ebenstein, Alan, *Friedrich Hayek: A Biography* (New York: St Martin's Press, 2001).

Ebenstein, Alan, *Hayek's Journey: The Mind of Friedrich Hayek* (New York: Palgrave Macmillan, 2003).

Edwards, Lee, *Goldwater: The Man Who Made a Revolution* (Washington, DC: Regnery, 1995).

Evans, Brendan, and Taylor, Andrew, *From Salisbury to Major: Continuity and Change in Conservative Politics* (Manchester: Manchester University Press, 1996).

Finer, Herman, *The Road to Reaction* (London: Dennis Doleson, 1946).

Flanagan, T. E., 'F. A. Hayek on property and justice', in A. Parel and T. E. Flanagan (eds), *Theories of Property from Aristotle to the Present* (Waterloo, ON: Wilfred Laurier University Press, 1979), pp. 335–60.

Flathman, Richard, *The Public Interest* (New York: Free Press, 1966).

Foley, Michael, *The Politics of the British Constitution* (Manchester: Manchester University Press, 1999).
Foner, Eric, *The Story of American Freedom* (London: Picador, 1999).
Foot, Michael and Kramnick, Isaac, *Thomas Paine Reader* (Harmondsworth: Penguin, 1987).
Foucault, Michel, *Discipline and Punishment: The Birth of the Modern Prison* (New York: Vintage, 1979).
Foucault, Michel, 'Nietzsche, genealogy and history', in P. Rainbow (ed.), *The Foucault Reader: An Introduction to Foucault's Thought* (London: Penguin, 1991), pp. 80–97.
Fraser, D., *The Evolution of the British Welfare State: A History of Social Policy since the Industrial Revolution* (London: Macmillan, 1973).
Freeden, Michael, 'The family of liberalisms: A morphological analysis', in Meadowcroft, *The Liberal Political Tradition*, pp. 14–39.
Freeden, Michael, *Ideologies and Political Theory* (Oxford: Oxford University Press, 1996).
Freeden, Michael, *Liberalism Divided: A Study in British Political Thought, 1914–1939* (Oxford: Clarendon Press, 1986).
Freeden, Michael, *The New Liberalism: An Ideology of Social Reform* (Oxford: Clarendon Press, 1978).
Freeden, Michael, 'The new liberalism and its aftermath', in Bellamy (ed.), *Victorian Liberalism*, pp. 171–90.
Freeden, Michael, 'Political concepts and ideological morphology', *The Journal of Political Philosophy*, 2: 2 (1994), pp. 145–61.
Freeden, Michael, 'The stranger at the feast: Ideology and public policy in twentieth-century Britain', *Twentieth Century British History*, 1. 1 (1990), pp. 32–51.
Friedman, Milton, 'The business community's suicidal impulse', *Cato Policy Report*, Vol. 21, No. 2, March/April 1999, pp. 1–8.
Friedman, Milton, *Capitalism and Freedom* (Chicago: University of Chicago Press, 1962).
Friedman, Milton, *The Counter-Revolution in Monetary Theory* (London: IEA, 1970).
Friedman, Milton, 'The social responsibility of business to increase its profits', *The New York Times Magazine*, 13 September 1970, pp. 3–10.
Friedman, Milton, and Friedman, Rose, *Free to Choose* (Harmondsworth: Penguin, 1980).
Friedman, Milton and Schwartz, Anna, *A Monetary History of the United States, 1867–1960* (Princeton: Princeton University Press, 1963).
Friedrich, Carl J., 'The political thought of neo-liberalism', *The American Political Science Review*, 49: 2 (1955), pp. 502–29.
Frost, Gerald, *Antony Fisher: Champion of Liberty* (London: Profile Books, 2002).
Galbraith, John Kenneth, *The Affluent Society* (Boston, MA: Houghton-Mifflin, 1958).
Galbraith, John Kenneth, *The World Economy Since the Wars: A Personal View* (London: Sinclair Stevenson, 1994).

Gallie, W. B., 'Essentially contested concepts', *Proceedings of the Aristotelian Society*, 56 (1955–6), pp. 197–8.
Gamble, Andrew, *The Conservative Nation* (London: Routledge and Kegan Paul, 1974).
Gamble, Andrew, 'Economic decline and the crisis of legitimacy', in C. Graham and T. Prosser (eds), *Waving the Rules: The Constitution under Thatcherism* (Milton Keynes: Open University Press, 1988), pp. 25–37.
Gamble, Andrew, 'The free economy and the strong state: The rise of the social market economy', *Socialist Register* (1979), pp. 1–17.
Gamble, Andrew, 'Neo-liberalism', *Capital and Class*, 75 (Autumn, 2001), pp. 127–34.
Gamble, Andrew, *Politics and Fate* (Cambridge: Polity, 2000).
Gamble, Andrew, 'The weakening of social democracy', in M. Loney et al., *The Market or the State: Politics and Welfare in Contemporary Britain* (London: Sage, 1996).
Gamble, Andrew and Kelly, Gavin, 'The politics of the company', in John Parkinson, Andrew Gamble and Gavin Kelly (eds), *The Political Economy of the Company* (Oxford: Hart Publishing, 2000), pp. 22–31.
Geertz, Clifford, *The Interpretation of Cultures: Selected Essays* (New York: Frank Cass, 1973).
George, Vic and Wilding, Paul, *Welfare and Ideology* (Hemel Hempstead: Harvester Wheatsheaf, 1993).
Gerring, John, 'The neo-liberal epoch (1928–1992)', in his *Party Ideologies in America, 1828–1996* (Cambridge: Cambridge University Press, 1998), pp. 125–58.
Goldberg, R. A., *Barry Goldwater* (New Haven: Yale University Press, 1995).
Goldwater, Barry, *The Conscience of a Conservative* (Shepardsville: Victor, 1960).
Graham, David and Clarke, Peter, *The New Enlightenment: The Rebirth of Liberalism* (London: Macmillan, 1986).
Gray, John, *False Dawn: The Delusions of Global Capitalism* (London: Granta Books, 1998).
Gray, John, *Hayek on Liberty* (London: Routledge, 1988).
Gray, John, 'Hayek on the market economy and the limits of state action', in David Helm (ed.), *The Economic Borders of the State* (Oxford: Oxford University Press, 1989), pp. 127–39.
Gray, John, *Liberalism* (Oxford: Oxford University Press, 1986).
Gray, John, *Limited Government: A Positive Agenda* (London: IEA, 1989).
Gray, John, *The Moral Foundations of Market Institutions* (London: IEA, 1992).
Green, David, *Community Without Politics: A Market Approach to Welfare Reform* (London: IEA, 1996).
Green, David, *The New Right: The Counter-Revolution in Political, Economic and Social Thought* (Brighton: Wheatsheaf, 1987).
Green, David, *Reinventing Civil Society: The Rediscovery of Welfare Without Politics* (London: IEA, 1993).

Greenleaf, W. H., *The British Political Tradition: The Rise of Collectivism*, Vol. I (London: Methuen, 1983).
Greenleaf, W. H., *The British Political Tradition: The Ideological Heritage*, Vol. II (London: Methuen, 1983).
Grimes, Alan P., *American Political Thought* (New York: Holt, Rinehart and Winston, 1955).
Halevy, E., *A History of the English People in the Nineteenth Century* (London: Macmillan, 1961).
Hall, Stuart, 'The great moving right show', in S. Hall and M. Jacques (eds), *The Politics of Thatchersim* (London: Lawrence and Wishart, 1983), pp. 19–39.
Hall, Stuart, 'Variants of liberalism', in James Donald and Stuart Hall (eds), *Politics and Ideology* (Milton Keynes: Open University Press, 1986).
Hallowell, John H., *The Decline of Liberalism as an Ideology: With Particular Reference to Germany* (London: Kegan Paul, 1946).
Halper, S. and Clarke, J., *America Alone: The Neo-Conservatives and the Global Order* (Cambridge: Cambridge University Press, 2004).
Hampsher-Monk, Iain, 'British and European background to the ideas of the constitution', in Joseph Smith (ed.), *The American Constitution: The First 200 Years* (Exeter: Exeter University Publications, 1992), pp. 1–16.
Hardach, Karl, *The Political Economy of Germany in the Twentieth Century* (Berkeley: University of California Press, 1976).
Harris, J., 'Some aspects of social policy in Britain during the Second World War', in Mommsen, *Emergence of the Welfare State in Britain and Germany*, pp. 247–62.
Harris, J., *William Beveridge: A Biography* (Oxford: Oxford University Press, 1977).
Harris, N., *Competition and the Corporate Society: British Conservatives, The State and Industry, 1945–1964* (London: Methuen, 1972).
Harris, Ralph and Sewill, Brendon, *British Economic Policy 1970–74: Two Views* (London: IEA, 1975).
Harrison, Graham, *The World Bank and Africa: The Construction of Governance States* (London: Routledge, 2004).
Hartwell, Max, *A History of the Mont Pelerin Society* (Indianapolis: Liberty Fund Inc., 1995).
Hartz, Louis, *The Liberal Tradition in America: An Interpretation of American Political Thought since the Revolution* (New York: Harcourt, Brace and World, 1955).
Harvey, David, *A Brief History of Neo-Liberalism* (Oxford: Oxford University Press, 2005).
Harvey, David, *The New Imperialism* (Oxford: Oxford University Press, 2003).
Hayek, F. A., 'An Anglo-American federation', letter to *The Spectator*, 15 December 1939, in Bruce Caldwell (ed.), *The Collected Works of F. A. Hayek*, Vol. 10, *Socialism and War: Essays, Documents, Reviews* (Chicago: Chicago University Press, 1997), pp. 162–4.
Hayek, F. A., 'The constitution of a liberal state', in his *New Studies in Philosophy, Politics, Economics and the History of Ideas*, pp. 98–104.

Hayek, F. A., *The Constitution of Liberty* (London: Routledge, 1960).
Hayek, F. A., 'The corporation in democratic society: In whose interest ought it to and will it be run', in his *Studies in Philosophy, Politics and Economics*, pp. 300–12.
Hayek, F. A., 'Dr. Bernard Mandeville', in his *New Studies in Philosophy, Politics, Economics and the History of Ideas* (London: Kegan Paul, 1978), pp. 249–61.
Hayek, F. A., *Economic Freedom and Representative Government* (London: IEA, 1973).
Hayek, F. A., *The Fatal Conceit: The Errors of Socialism*, ed. by W. W. Bartley (London: Routledge, 1988).
Hayek, F. A., 'The historians and the future of Europe', in his *Studies in Philosophy, Politics and Economics*, pp. 135–47.
Hayek, F. A., 'History and politics', in F. A. Hayek (ed.), *Capitalism and the Historians* (Chicago: University of Chicago Press, 1954), pp. 3–29.
Hayek, F. A., 'The intellectuals and socialism', in his *Studies in Philosophy, Politics And Economics*, pp. 178–94.
Hayek, F. A., *Law, Legislation and Liberty: Rules and Order*, Vol. I (Chicago: Chicago University Press, 1973).
Hayek, F. A., *Law, Legislation and Liberty: The Mirage of Social Justice*, Vol. II (Chicago: Chicago University Press, 1976).
Hayek, F. A., *Law, Legislation and Liberty: The Political Order of a Free People*, Vol. III (Chicago: University of Chicago Press, 1979).
Hayek, F. A., 'Liberalism', in his *New Studies in Philosophy, Politics, Economics And the History of Ideas*, pp. 119–51.
Hayek, F. A., 'The nature and history of the problem', in F. A. Hayek (ed.), *Collectivist Economic Planning: Critical Studies on the Impossibilities of Socialism* (London: Routledge, 1935).
Hayek, F. A., *New Studies in Philosophy, Politics, Economics and the History of Ideas* (London: Kegan Paul, 1978).
Hayek, F. A., 'Opening address of the Mont Pelerin Society', in his *Studies in Philosophy, Politics and Economics*, pp. 148–59.
Hayek, F. A., 'The principles of a liberal social order', in his *Studies in Philosophy, Politics and Economics*, pp. 160–77.
Hayek, F. A., 'The results of human action but not of human design', in his *Studies In Philosophy, Politics and Economics*, pp. 96–105.
Hayek, F. A., *The Road to Serfdom* (London: Routlegde, 1944).
Hayek, F. A., 'The Road to Serfdom *after* twelve years', in his *Studies in Philosophy, Politics and Economics*, pp. 216–28.
Hayek, F. A., *Studies in Philosophy, Politics and Economics* (London: Routledge, 1967).
Hayek, F. A., *A Tiger by the Tail* (London: IEA, 1972).
Hayek, F. A., 'The use of knowledge in society', in his *Individualism and Economic Order* (London: Routledge, 1948).
Hayek, F. A., 'What is "social"? – What does it mean?', in his *Studies in Philosophy, Politics and Economics*, pp. 237–50.

Hayek, F. A., 'Why I am not a conservative', in his *Constitution of Liberty*, pp. 397–414.

Hayward, Steven F., *The Age of Reagan: The Fall of the Old Liberal Order, 1964–1980* (Roseville, CA: Prima Publishing, 2001).

Heffer, Simon, *Like the Roman: The Life of Enoch Powell* (London: Weidenfeld and Nicolson, 1998).

Hegel, G. W. F., *The Philosophy of Right* (Oxford: Clarendon Press, 1941).

Held, David, *Democracy and the Global Order: From Modern State to Cosmopolitan Governance* (Cambridge: Polity, 1996).

Hennock, E. P., 'The origins of British National Insurance and the German precedent, 1880–1914', in Mommsen, *The Emergence of the Welfare State in Britain and Germany*, pp. 82–96.

Higgs, Robert, 'Fifty years of the Mont Pelerin Society', *Independent Review*, 1: 4 (1997), pp. 623–30.

Hill, D., 'Neo–liberalism and hegemony revisited', *Educational Philosophy and Theory*, 30: 1 (1998), pp. 69–83.

Hills, J. (ed.), *The State of Welfare: The Welfare State in Britain since 1974* (Oxford: Oxford University Press, 1990).

Hobhouse, T. L., *Liberalism and Other Writings*, in Meadowcroft, James (ed.), (Cambridge: Cambridge University Press, 1994).

Hobson, J. A., *The Crisis of Liberalism* (London: King, 1909).

Hockerts, H. G., 'German post-war social policies against the background of the Beveridge Plan', in Mommsen, *Emergence of the Welfare State in Britain and Germany*, pp. 315–28.

Hodgson, Geoffrey, *The Democratic Economy* (Harmondsworth: Penguin, 1984).

Hodgson, Geoffrey, *Economics and Evolution: Bringing Life Back into Economics* (Cambridge: Polity, 1993).

Hodgson, Geoffrey, *Economics and Utopia: Why the Learning Economy is not the End of History* (London: Routledge, 1999).

Hodgson, Godfrey, 'The ideology of the liberal consensus', in W. H. Chafe and A. Stikoff, *A History of Our Time: Readings on Post-War America* (Oxford; Oxford University Press, 1987), pp. 57–71.

Hoffman, J. D., *The Conservative Party in Opposition, 1945–51* (London: Macgibbon and Kee, 1964).

Hofstadter, Richard, *The Age of Reform* (New York: Vintage Books, 1955).

Hofstadter, Richard, *The American Political Tradition* (London: Jonathan Cape, 1962).

Hoover, Kenneth and Plant, Raymond, *Conservative Capitalism in Britain and the United States* (London: Routledge, 1989).

Huston, James L., *Calculating the Value of the Union: Slavery, Property Rights and the Economic Origins of the Civil War* (Chapel Hill: University of North Carolina Press, 2003).

Isserman, M. and Kazin, M., *America Divided: The Civil War of the 1960s* (Oxford: Oxford University Press, 2000).

Jeffries, John W., 'The "New" New Deal: FDR and American liberalism, 1937–1945', *Political Science Quarterly*, 105: 2 (1990), pp. 387–410.
Jennings, I., *The Law and the Constitution* (London: University of London Press, 1967).
Jewkes, John, *Ordeal by Planning* (London: Macmillan, 1948).
Jones, L. E., *German Liberalism and the Dissolution of the Weimar Party System, 1918–1933* (London: Chapel Hill, 1988).
Jordan, B., *Freedom and the Welfare State* (London: Routledge, 1976).
Joseph, Keith, *Monetarism Is Not Enough* (London: Centre for Policy Studies, 1976).
Joseph, Keith, *Stranded on the Middle Ground* (London: Centre for Policy Studies, 1976).
Joseph, Keith, *Why Britain Needs a Social Market Economy* (London: Centre for Policy Studies, 1975).
Judis, John B., *William F. Buckley Jr.: Patron Saint of the Conservatives* (New York: Simon and Schuster, 1988).
Katz, Stanlet N., 'Thomas Jefferson and the right to property in revolutionary America', *Journal of Law and Economics*, 19: 3 (1976), pp. 475–99.
Keane, John, *Tom Paine: A Political Life* (London: Bloomsbury, 1995).
Kelly, A. H., *Foundations of Freedom in the American Constitution* (New York: Free Press, 1958).
Ketcham, R., *Framed for Prosperity: The Enduring Philosophy of the Constitution* (Lawrence: University Press of Kansas, 1993).
Keynes, J. M., 'The end of *laissez-faire*', in his *Essays in Persuasion* (London: Rupert Hart Davis, 1952), pp. 293–9.
Keynes, J. M., *The General Theory of Unemployment, Interest and Money* (London: Macmillan, 1936).
King, Desmond S., *The New Right: Politics, Markets and Citizenship* (Basingstoke: Macmillan, 1987).
Kloten, Norbert, 'The role of the public sector in the social market economy', in Peacock and Willgerodt, *German Neo-Liberals and the Social Market Economy*, pp. 69–104.
Knowles, Dudley, 'Hegel on property and personality', *The Philosophical Quarterly*, 33: 130 (1983), pp. 45–62.
Knox, T. M., *Hegel's Philosophy of Right* (Oxford: Clarendon Press, 1952).
Krieger, Leonard, *The German Idea of Freedom: The History of a Political Tradition* (Boston, MA: Beacon Press, 1957).
Krieger, Loenard, 'The idea of the welfare state in Europe and the United States', *Journal of the History of Ideas*, 24: 4 (1963), pp. 551–65.
Kristol, Irving, 'The neo-conservative persuasion: What it is and what it was', in Irwin Stelzer (ed.), *Neo-Conservatism* (London: Atlantic Books, 2004), pp. 31–8.
Kristol, Irving, *Two Cheers for Capitalism* (New York: Basic Books, 1978).
Lafargue, Paul, *The Evolution of Property from Savagery to Civilisation* (London: New Park Publications, 1975).

Lane, Jan-Erik, *Constitution and Political Theory* (Manchester: Manchester University Press, 1996).
Laski, Harold, *Reflections on the Constitution: The House of Commons, the Cabinet, the Civil Service* (Manchester: Manchester University Press, 1951).
Laski, Harold J., *The Rise of European Liberalism: An Essay in Interpretation* (London: Allen and Unwin, 1936), p. 9.
Lawson, Nigel, *The New Conservatism* (London: Centre for Policy Studies, 1980).
Lawson, R., 'Germany: Maintaining the middle way', in P. Taylor and V. George (eds), *European Social Policy* (Basingstoke: Macmillan, 1996), pp. 231–52.
Le Grand, J., 'The welfare state', in Hills, *The State of Welfare*, pp. 347–61.
Leach, Richard, *British Political Ideologies* (Hemel Hempstead: Philip Allan, 1991).
Leaman, Jeremy, *The Political Economy of West Germany, 1945–1985* (Basingstoke: Macmillan, 1988).
Leftwich, Adrian, *States of Development: On the Primacy of Politics in Development* (Cambridge: Polity, 2000).
Lekachman, R., *The Age of Keynes* (New York: McGraw Hill, 1975).
Lindblom, Charles E., *Politics and Markets: The World's Politico-Economic Systems* (New York: Basic Books, 1977).
Lindsay, T. F. and Harrington, M., *The Conservative Party 1918–1970* (London: Macmillan, 1974).
Lindsey, Brink, *Against the Dead Hand: The Uncertain Struggle for Global Capitalism* (Washington, DC: Cato Institute, 2002).
Link, Arthur S., 'What happened to the progressive movement in the 1920s?', *American Historical Review*, 4 (July 1959), pp. 833–51.
Lippmann, Walter, *Essays in the Public Philosophy* (London: Hamilton, 1955).
Lippmann, Walter, *The Good Society* (London: Allen and Unwin, 1937).
Locke, John, *Two Treaties on Government*, ed. by P. Laslett (ed.) (Cambridge: Cambridge University Press, 1989).
Loughlin, M., *Public Law and Political Theory* (Oxford: Oxford University Press, 1992).
Lowi, T. J., *The End of Liberalism* (New York: Fontana, 1979).
Lowi, T. J., *The End of the Republican Era* (Norman: University of Oklahoma Press, 1995).
Macpherson, C. B., *The Political Theory of Possessive Individualism: From Hobbes to Locke* (Oxford: Oxford University Press, 1962).
Macpherson, C. B., *Property: Mainstream and Critical Positions* (Toronto: Toronto University Press, 1978).
Macpherson, C. B., 'Property as a means or ends', in Parel and Flanagan, *Theories of Property: From Aristotle to the Present*, pp. 5–16.
Mandeville, Bernard, *The Fable of the Bees* (Harmondsworth: Penguin, 1970).
Marshall, Alfred, *Principles of Economics* (London: Macmillan, 1987).
Marshall, T. H., *Citizenship and Social Class* (Cambridge: Cambridge University Press, 1950).

Marx, K. and Engels, F., *The German Ideology* (London: Lawrence and Wishart, 1970).
McCoy, Drew R., *The Elusive Republic: Political Economy in Jeffersonian America* (Williamsburg, VA: Institute of Early American History and Culture, 1980).
McGirr, Lisa, *Suburban Warriors: The Origins of the New American Right* (Princeton: Princeton University Press, 2001).
Mcquaid, K., *Uneasy Partners: Big Business in American Politics, 1945–1990* (New York: Johns Hopkins University Press, 1994).
Mead, Lawrence M., *Beyond Entitlement: The Social Obligations of Citizenship* (London: Free Press, 1986).
Meadowcroft, James, *Conceptualizing the State: Innovation and Dispute in British Political Thought, 1880–1914* (Oxford: Clarendon Press, 1995).
Meadowcroft, James, 'Introduction', in his *Liberal Political Tradition*, pp. 1–16.
Meadowcroft, James (ed.), *The Liberal Political Tradition: Contemporary Reappraisals* (Cheltenham: Edward Elgar, 1996).
Megay, Edward, 'Anti-pluralist liberalism: The German neo-liberals', *Political Science Quarterly*, 85: 3 (1970), pp. 418–39.
Megay, Edward, 'Treitschke reconsidered: The Hegelian tradition of German liberalism', *Midwest Journal of Political Science*, 2: 3, 1958, pp. 278–304.
Menger, Carl, 'On the origin of money', *Economic Journal*, 4 (June 1892), pp. 239–55.
Mill, John Stuart, *On Liberty* (Harmondsworth: Penguin, 1982).
Mill, John Stuart, *The Principles of Political Economy*, Vol. 1 (London: Hodge, 1987).
Mill, John Stuart, *On Representative Government* (Harmondsworth: Penguin, 1987).
Mirsha, Ramesh, *The Welfare State and Capitalist Society* (Hemel Hempstead: Harvester Wheatsheaf, 1990).
Mirsha, Ramesh, *The Welfare State in Crisis: Social Thought and Social Change* (Hemel Hempstead: Harvester Wheatsheaf, 1984).
Mises, Ludwig von, 'Economic calculation in the socialist commonwealth', in A. Nove and D. M. Nuti (eds), *Socialist Economics: Selected Readings* (Harmondsworth: Penguin, 1972), pp. 67–90.
Mises, Ludwig von, *Liberalism: In the Classical Tradition* (New York: Foundation for Economic Education, 1985).
Mises, Ludwig von, *Socialism: An Economic and Sociological Analysis* (Indianapolis: Liberty Fund, 1981).
Mises, Ludwig von, *Theory and History: An Interpretation of Social and Economic Evolution* (New York: Arlington House, 1963).
Modderidge, D. E., *Keynes* (London: Macmillan, 1993).
Mommsen, W. J., 'History of political theory in the Federal Republic of Germany: Strange death and slow recovery', in D. Castiglione and I. Hampshire-Monk (eds), *The History of Political Thought in National Contexts* (Cambridge: Cambridge University Press, 2001), pp. 36–51.

Mommsen, W. J. (ed.), *Emergence of the Welfare State in Britain and Germany 1850–1950* (London: Croom Helm, 1981).

Montesquieu, C., *The Spirit of Laws* (Cambridge: Cambridge University Press, 1989).

Morrison, Herbert, *Can Planning be Democratic?* (London: Routledge, 1944).

Müller-Armack, A., 'The principles of the social market economy', *The German Economic Review*, 3: 2 (1965), pp. 87–114.

Murray, Charles, *Losing Ground: American Social Policy, 1950–1980* (New York: Basic Books, 1984).

Nash, George, *The Conservative Intellectual Tradition in America since 1945* (Wilmington: Intercollegiate Studies Institute, 1996).

Neumann, Franz, *The Rule of Law: Political Theory and the Legal System in Modern Society* (Leamington Spa: Berg, 1986).

Newcomb, George, 'Theories of property', *Political Science Quarterly*, 1: 4 (1886), pp. 494–509.

Nicholls, A. J., *Freedom with Responsibility: The German Social Market Economy, 1918–1963* (Oxford: Oxford University Press, 1994).

Nicholls, A. J., 'Ludwig Erhard and German liberalism – An ambivalent relationship', in K. H. Jarausch and L. E. Jones (eds), *In Search of Liberal Germany: Studies in the History of German Liberalism 1789 to the Present* (New York: St Martin's Press, 1996), pp. 379–98.

Nicholls, A. J., 'The other Germany – The neo-liberals', in Bullen et al., *Ideas into Politics*, pp. 160–79.

Oakeshott, Michael, 'The political economy of freedom', in his *Rationalism in Politics and other Essays* (London: Methuen, 1962), pp. 37–58.

O'Brien, M. and Penna, S., *Theorising Welfare: Enlightenment and Modern Society* (London: Sage, 1998).

Ohmae, Kenichi, *The End of the Nation State: The Rise of Regional Economics* (London: HarperCollins, 1996).

Oliver, H. M., 'German neo-liberalism', *The Quarterly Journal of Economics*, 74: 1 (1960), pp. 110–27.

Orwell, George, 'Review: *The Road to Serfdom* by F. A. Hayek', in S. Orwell and I. Angus (eds), *George Orwell: The Collected Essays, Journalism and Letters of Orwell, Vol. 3, 1943–1945* (London: Secker and Warburg, 1968), pp. 118–21.

Parel, A. and Flanagan, T. (eds), *Theories of Property from Aristotle to the Present* (Waterloo, ON: Wilfred Laurier University Press, 1979).

Peacock, Alan and Willgerodt, Hans (eds), *German Neo-Liberals and the Social Market Economy* (Basingstoke: Macmillan, 1989).

Peele, Gillian, *Revival and Reaction: The Right in Contemporary America* (Oxford: Clarendon Press, 1984).

Peterson, George, E., 'Federalism and the state', in J. Palmer and I. V. Sawhill (eds), *The Reagan Record* (Washington, DC: The Urban Institute, 1984).

Pierre, J. and Peters, B. G. (eds), *Governance, Politics and the State* (Basingstoke: Macmillan, 2000).

Pierson, Paul, *Dismantling the Welfare State?: Reagan, Thatcher and the Politics of Retrenchment* (Cambridge: Cambridge University Press, 1994).

Plotke, David, *Building a Democratic Political Order: Reshaping American Liberalism in the 1930s and 1940s* (Cambridge: Cambridge University Press, 1996).

Pocock, J. G. A., *The Machiavellian Movement: Florentine Political Thought and the Atlantic Republican Tradition* (Princeton: Princeton University Press, 1975).

Polanyi, Karl, *The Great Transformation* (Boston, MA: Beacon Press, 1944).

Powell, J. E., *Saving in a Free Society* (London: IEA, 1960).

Quick, P. D., 'Business: Reagan's industrial policy', in J. L. Palmer and I. V. Sawhill (eds), *The Reagan Record* (Washington, DC: The Urban Institute, 1984), pp. 287–308.

Rae, N. C., *The Decline and Fall of the Liberal Republicans: From 1952 to the Present* (New York: Oxford University Press, 1989).

Raison, T., *Tories and the Welfare State: A History of Conservative Social Policy since the Second World War* (Basingstoke: Macmillan, 1990).

Ranelagh, John, *Thatcher's People* (London: HarperCollins, 1991).

Rapaczynski, Andrzej, 'Locke's conception of property and the principle of sufficient reason', *Journal of the History of Ideas*, 42: 2 (1981), pp. 305–15.

Raphael, D. D., *Adam Smith* (Oxford: Oxford University Press, 1985).

Reeve, Andrew, *Property* (Basingstoke: Macmillan, 1986).

Ricardo, David, *On the Principles of Political Economy and Taxation* (Harmondsworth: Penguin, 1974).

Ricci, D. M., *The Transformation of American Politics: The New Washington and the Rise of Think-Tanks* (New Haven: Yale University Press, 1993).

Rieter, Heinz, and Schmolz, Matthias, 'The ideas of German ordo-liberalism 1938–45: Pointing the way to a new economic order', *The European Journal of the History of Economic Thought*, 1: 1 (1993), pp. 83–108.

Ritschel, Daniel, *The Politics of Planning: The Debate on Economic Planning in Britain in the 1930s* (Oxford: Oxford University Press, 1997).

Ritter, G. A., *Social Welfare in Germany and Britain: Origins and Development* (Leamington Spa: Berg, 1986).

Robinson, Richard, 'Neo-liberalism and the future world: Markets and the end of politics', Inaugural Lecture, Institute of Social Studies, The Hague, The Netherlands, 5 February 2004.

Roche, G. C., 'The relevance of Friedrich A. Hayek', in F. Machlup (ed.), *Essays on Hayek* (New York: New York University Press, 1976), pp. 5–19.

Röpke, Wilhelm, *A Humane Economy: The Social Framework of the Free Market* (Chicago: Henry Regnery, 1958).

Rose, Richard, *Understanding Big Government* (London: Sage, 1984).

Rosenberg, Hans, 'Political and social consequences of the Great Depression of 1873–1896 in Central Europe', *Economic History Review* (1943), pp. 296–331.

Ruggiero, Guido de, *The History of European Liberalism* (Oxford: Oxford University Press, 1927).

Ryan, Alan, *Property* (Milton Keynes: Open University Press, 1987).

Ryan, Alan, *Property and Political Theory* (Oxford: Blackwell, 1984).
Ryan, Alan, *John Dewey and the High Tide of American Liberalism* (New York: Norton and Company, 1995).
Schmitter, Philippe, 'Still the century of corporatism?' in Schmitter, P. and Lehmbruch, G (eds), *Trends Towards Corporatist Intermediation* (London: Sage, 1979), pp. 56–75.
Schoenwald, J. M., *A Time for Choosing: The Rise of Modern American Conservatism* (New York: Oxford University Press, 2001).
Schumpeter, Joseph A., *Capitalism, Socialism and Democracy* (London: Allen and Unwin, 1943).
Schumpeter, Joseph, *History of Economic Analysis* (London: Routledge, 1954).
Schumpeter, Joseph A., 'The instability of capitalism', *Economic Journal*, 38 (September 1928), pp. 376–89.
Seldon, Arthur, *After the NHS* (London: IEA, 1968).
Seldon, Arthur, *Not Unanimous: A Rival Verdict to the Radcliffe Report on the Workings of the Monetary System* (London: IEA, 1960).
Shearmur, Jeremy, *Hayek and After: Hayekian Liberalism as a Research Programme* (London: Routledge, 1996).
Shearmur, Jeremy, *The Politics of Karl Popper* (London: Routledge, 1988).
Sheehan, James J., *German Liberalism in the Nineteenth Century* (Chicago: University of Chicago Press, 1978).
Shell, S. M., 'Kant's theory of property', *Political Theory*, 6: 1 (1978), pp. 73–89.
Shonfield, Andrew, *Modern Capitalism: The Changing Balance of Public and Private Power* (Oxford: Oxford University Press, 1965).
Showronek, Stephen, *Building a New American State: The Expansion of Administrative Capacities, 1877–1920* (Cambridge: Cambridge University Press, 1982).
Skidelsky, Robert, 'The political meaning of the Keynesian Revolution', in R. Skidelsky (ed.), *The End of the Keynesian Era: Essays on the Disintegration of the Keynesian Political Economy* (London: Macmillan, 1977), pp. 31–54.
Skidelsky, Robert, 'The reception of the Keynesian Revolution', in Milo Keynes (ed.), *Essays on John Maynard Keynes* (Cambridge: Cambridge University Press, 1975), pp. 89–107.
Skidelsky, Robert, *The World After Communism: A Polemic for Our Time* (Basingstoke: Macmillan, 1995).
Skocpol, Theda, *Social Policy in the United States: Future Possibilities in Historical Perspective* (Princeton: Princeton University Press, 1995).
Smith, Joseph (ed.), *The American Constitution: The First 200 Years* (Exeter: Exeter University Publications, 1992).
Smith, Adam, *Lectures on Jurisprudence* (Oxford: Oxford University Press, 1978).
Smith, Adam, *The Wealth of Nations* (Harmondsworth: Penguin, 1976).
Stapleton, Julia, 'Resisting the centre at the extremes: English liberalism in the political thought of inter-war Britain', *British Journal of Politics and International Relations*, 1: 3 (1999), pp. 273–303.

Steel, Ronald, *Walter Lippmann and the American Century* (Boston, MA: Little, Brown and Company, 1980).
Stockman, David A., *The Triumph of Politics* (London: Bodley Head, 1986).
Stolper, Gustav, *The German Economy, 1870 to the Present* (London: Weidenfeld and Nicolson, 1967).
Streit, M. E. and Wohlgemuth, M., 'The market economy and the state: Hayekian and ordo-liberal conceptions', in P. Koslowski (ed.), *The Theory of Capitalism in German Economic Tradition: Historicism, Ordo-Liberalism and Critical Theory* (Berlin: Springer-Verlag, 2000), pp. 224–71.
Sugden, Robert, 'Naturalness and the spontaneous order of the market', in S. H. Heap and Ross, A. (eds), *Understanding the Enterprise Culture* (Edinburgh: Edinburgh University Press, 1992), pp. 161–81.
Swedberg, Richard, *Joseph A. Schumpeter: His Life and Works* (Cambridge: Polity, 1991).
Swedberg, Richard, *Max Weber and the Idea of Economic Sociology* (Princeton: Princeton University Press, 1998).
Taylor, A. J., *Laissez-Faire and State Intervention in Nineteenth-Century Britain* (Basingstoke: Macmillan, 1972).
Thatcher, Margaret, *The Downing Street Years* (New York: HarperCollins, 1993).
Timmins, N., *The Five Giants: A Biography of the Welfare State* (London: Fontana, 1996).
Tocqueville, Alexis de, *Democracy in America* (New York: Basic Books, 1956).
Tomlinson, Jim, *Hayek and the Market* (London: Pluto Press, 1990).
Trattner, W. I., *From Poor Law to Welfare State: A History of Social Welfare in America* (New York: Free Press, 1979).
Tribe, Keith, 'Genealogy of the social market economy', in his *Strategies of Economic Order: German Economic Discourse, 1750–1950* (Cambridge: Cambridge University Press, 1995), pp. 231–54.
Tullock, Gordon, *The Politics of Bureaucracy* (Washington, DC: Public Affairs Press, 1965).
Tumlir, Jan, 'Franz Böhm and economic–constitutional analysis', in Peacock and Willgerodt, *German Neo-Liberals and the Social Market Economy*, pp. 125–41.
Utley, T. E., *Enoch Powell: The Man and his Thinking* (London: William Kimber, 1968).
Vincent, Andrew, 'Classical liberalism and its crisis of identity', *History of Political Thought*, 11: 1 (1990), pp. 143–61.
Vincent, Andrew, 'New ideologies for old?', *Political Quarterly*, 69: 1 (1998), pp. 48–58.
Viner, J., 'The intellectual history of *laissez-faire*', *Journal of Law and Economics*, Vol. 3 (1960), pp. 45–69.
Vorländer, Hans, 'Is there a liberal political tradition in Germany?', in Meadowcroft, *The Liberal Political Tradition*, pp. 87–109.
Wainwright, Hilary, 'Hayek and the social-engineering state', in her *Arguments for a New Left* (Oxford: Blackwell, 1994), pp. 49–67.

Waldron, Jeremy, *The Right to Private Property* (Oxford: Clarendon Press, 1988).
Waldron, Jeremy, 'Theoretical foundations of liberalism', *Philosophical Quarterly*, 37: 147 (1987), pp. 106–17.
Walras, L., *Elements of Pure Economics, or The Theory of Social Wealth* (New York: Augustus Kelly, 1956).
Ware, Alan and Goodin, R. E. (eds), *Needs and Welfare* (London: Sage, 1990).
Watkins, Susan, 'New Labour: A weightless hegemony', *New Left Review*, 27 May/June (2004), pp. 1–28.
Watson, George, *The English ideology: Studies in the language of Victorian politics* (London: Allen Lane, 1973).
Weber, Max, *Economy and Society* (London: Routledge, 1976).
Weber, Max, *From Max Weber* (London: Routledge, 1948).
Weber, Max, 'The national state and economic policy', in K. Tribe (ed.), *Reading Weber* (London: Longman, 1989).
Weber, Max, *The Protestant Ethic and the Spirit of Capitalism* (London: Routledge, 1978).
Westbrook, Robert, *John Dewey and Democracy* (Cambridge, MA: Harvard University Press, 1991).
Wilding, Paul, 'The welfare state and the Conservatives', *Political Studies*, 45 (1997), pp. 719–31.
Williams, Howard, 'Kant's concept of property', *The Philosophical Quarterly*, 27: 106 (1977), pp. 29–41.
Wiseman, Jack, 'Social policy and the social market economy', in Peacock and Willgerodt, *German Neo-Liberals and the Social Market Economy*, pp. 160–78.
Wittgenstein, L., *Philosophical Investigations* (Oxford: Blackwell, 1972).
Wood, Gordon S., 'Ideology and the origins of liberal America', *William and Mary Quarterly*, 44: 3 (1987), pp. 628–40.
Wootton, Barbara, *Plan or No Plan* (London: Victor Gollancz, 1934).
Zweig, Konrad, *The Origins of the German Social Market Economy: The Leading Ideas and their Intellectual Roots* (London: ASI, 1980).

Index

Adam Smith Institute, 153
Adams, John, 33, 197
Adenauer, Konrad, 88
Allais, Maurice, 71
American Civil War, 34–5
American Enterprise Institute, 102–3, 221, 223
American Public Health Association, 144
American Revolution, 7, 32, 33, 143
Anderson, Martin, 106
Anti-Corn Law League, 25
Aristotle, 29
Aron, Raymond, 64
Association for Improving the Condition of the Poor, 143
Attlee, Clement, 146
Austrian School of Economics, 15, 23, 81, 101, 119–20, 121–6, 136

Baroody, William, 103
Bastiat, Frederic, 25
Benn, Ernest, 65
Bentham, Jeremy, 24, 36, 41, 196
Berlin, Isaiah, 64
Beveridge, William, 57, 148, 156
Beveridge Report, 38, 57, 146
Bill of Rights (Britain), 169
Bill of Rights (United States), 172
Birch Nigel, 91
Bismarck, Otto von, 144
Böhm, Franz, 82, 83, 176–7
Bow Group, 91–2
Bretton Woods, 135
Bright, John, 25
Britain
 and collectivism, 55–7, 68

Constitution, 6, 169–71, 183–4
and classical liberalism, 22–7, 29, 34, 36, 53, 119–20, 130
and European integration, 88
and liberalism, 14, 22–7, 36–8, 41, 42, 133
and neo-liberalism, 3, 65, 84, 89–98, 131–2, 220–1; *see also* New Right
and the new liberalism, 36–8
and private property, 194–6
and social policy, 141–3, 144–6, 152–6, 157–62
Brittan, Samuel, 96
Brookings Institute, 102
Brown, Lewis H., 102
Buchanan, James, 6, 168, 173–4, 182–4, 188–9, 221
Buchanan, Patrick, 99
Buckley, William, F., 100–1, 221
Burton, John, 183–4
Bush, George W., 224
Butler, R. A., 90

capitalism *see* markets
Carr, Robert, 91
Cato Institute, 7, 221, 223
Centre for Policy Studies, 7, 95–7, 159, 220
Chicago School of Economics, 101, 221–2
Christian Democratic Union, 89
Christianity, 83, 100, 143
Civil Rights Act, 199
classical economics *see* classical liberalism
classical liberalism, 1, 7, 8, 14, 22–5, 29, 34, 35, 36–7, 48–9, 50, 53–5, 60, 68, 75, 82, 86, 90, 101, 108, 116–21, 130, 136, 141–3, 153, 163, 196, 201, 216

244

INDEX

Cobden, Richard, 25
Cold War, 146–7, 173
collectivism, 1, 14, 16, 35–43, 47, 49, 50,
    55–69, 74–5, 91–2, 97, 123–4, 137, 143,
    147, 169, 216, 221
Common Agricultural Policy, 88
Common Market *see* European Economic
    Community
company *see* corporations
concepts, 9, 11–14, 216, 219
    adjacent, 11–12, 13, 217–18
    configuration, 12
    core, 9, 11–12, 13, 136, 217–18
    history, 12–13
    morphology, 12
    peripheral, 11–12, 13, 217
Conservative Party, 15, 56, 65, 81, 90–8, 130,
    137, 156–7, 223
conservatism, 42, 99–107, 219, 224
constitution, 13, 16, 167–89, 218
    traditions, 169–77
Corn Laws, 26
corporations, 130, 134, 206–9
corporatism, 59–62, 90, 131, 151
Currency Reform, 85–6

De Gaulle, Charles, 88
Democratic Party (Germany), 39
Democratic Party (United States), 105
Dewey, John, 7, 42, 218
Dicey, A. V., 26, 49, 55, 169–70

Eden, Anthony, 90
Eisenhower, Dwight, 103
English Civil War, 32
English common law, 32
Enlightenment, 24, 32, 82, 117, 121, 143, 163,
    195
Erhard, Ludwig, 74, 84, 87–8, 91, 220
Eucken, Walter, 6, 62, 65, 71, 82, 83–4, 87,
    147, 220
European Economic Community, 87–8; *see also*
    European Union
European Union, 133, 135, 188

Fabian Society, 55–6, 96
Family Allowances Act, 146
Finer, Herman, 67
Fisher, Antony, 91, 102
Fisher, Irving, 102
Foucault, Michel, 10, 11, 14, 216
Foundation for Economic Education, 223

Four Year Plan, 62
Freiburg Imperative, 83
Freiburg School, 81–2
French Revolution, 30
Friedman, Milton, 6, 63, 71, 75, 103, 105,
    216–17, 219, 221–2
    and American Constitution, 171–3
    and global economy, 133–4
    and liberalism, 101
    and monetary policy, 93–4, 96, 101–2, 222
    and private ownership, 203, 209, 211
    and social policy, 149–51, 154, 157

Galbraith, John Kenneth, 98
German League for Free and Economic Policy, 65
Germany
    and cartels, 39, 60, 81–3, 86–7, 107, 211–12
    and capitalism, 30, 39–40, 52, 82–7
    Constitution, 28, 174–7
    and corporatism, 60–2, 151
    and liberalism, 7, 8, 14, 22, 27–31, 38–40,
        82, 220
    and nationalism, 30, 38–40, 60–2, 67, 82,
        130, 133, 147, 176, 211, 219–20; *see also*
        National Socialism
    and private property, 199–201, 211–12, 220
    and social reform, 144–5, 147–8, 153–4, 155
    and state power, 27–31
Gold Standard, 133, 184
Goldwater, Barry, 102–6, 221, 223
Great Depression, 41, 49, 56, 58, 60–1, 67, 102,
    145
Green, David, 152–4
Green, T. H., 36, 42, 217–18
Grossmann-Doerth, Hans, 83

Habeas Corpus Act, 169
Harris, Ralph, 91–2, 96
Hayek, F. A, 6, 23, 64–75, 83, 89–90, 91, 93,
    101, 103, 106, 116, 119–20, 121–9,
    131–3, 136, 216
    and American Constitution, 172–3, 186
    and capitalism, 66, 85, 132–3
    and classical liberalism, 48–9, 121, 219
    and collectivism, 63, 69, 123–4, 133, 149–50
    and conservatism, 99, 219
    and democracy, 168, 174, 180–2
    and history, 48–9, 50
    and international order, 132–4, 136, 187–8
    and law and legislation distinction, 177–9
    and liberalism, 168, 174, 180–2, 218–19,
        222–3

245

Hayek, F. A, (cont.)
  and model constitution, 184–7, 188
  and National Socialism, 39, 40, 66, 171, 219–20
  and private property, 192, 199, 202
  and *Rechtsstaat*, 28, 85, 125, 174–7, 179–80, 219
  and slavery, 199
  and socialism, 48–9, 51, 65–6, 69–70, 148–5, 180
Hazlitt, Henry, 71
Heath, Edward, 91–3, 95, 97
Hegel, G. W. F., 7, 9, 68
  and property, 199, 200–1
  and the state, 28–9
Heritage Foundation, 7, 102, 106, 160, 223
Hitler, Adolf, 39, 62, 63
Hobhouse, John, 7, 36–7, 42, 51, 56, 217
Hobson, John, 7, 36–7, 51, 56, 217–18
Hong Kong, 133–4
Hoover, Herbert, 32, 42, 58, 223
Hoover Institute, 102, 106, 221, 223
Howe, Geoffrey, 74, 91, 95–6
Humboldt, Wilhelm von, 29, 200, 216, 220
Hume, David, 34, 121, 205, 212, 216

ideology, 9–14
  boundaries, 10, 217
  genealogy, 10, 11, 216
  Marxist approaches, 9
Individualist Group, 65
International Monetary Fund, 116, 135
Institute of Economic Affairs, 6, 91–6, 102, 152, 159, 171, 220, 222–3

Jefferson, Thomas, 32, 172, 198, 216
Jewkes, John, 68, 71, 89–90
John Birch Society, 100, 104
Johnson, Andrew, 198
Johnson, Lyndon B., 98, 104
Joseph, Keith, 74, 91, 95–8, 115, 156, 220–1
Jünger, Ernst, 40
justice, 16, 141, 201
  negative, 193, 204–6, 212, 218
  social, 86, 119, 150–2, 220

Kant, Immanuel, 28, 43, 199–200, 212, 216, 220
Keynes, J. M., 7, 48, 49–52, 53, 55, 59, 148, 221
Keynesianism, 57, 59, 64, 66, 68, 74, 86, 96, 102, 105, 115, 146–7, 156–7, 163, 183–4, 222–3

Kirk, Russell, 100, 221, 223
Knight, Frank, 71
Kristol, Irving, 101–2, 156, 221, 223

Labour Party, 38, 56, 65, 146, 156
Laffer curve, 160
laissez-faire, 5, 14, 23–4, 35, 36, 41, 42, 49–56, 65, 82, 85, 90, 125, 142–3, 154, 173, 201, 221
Laski, H. J., 38, 57, 170–1
law, 16, 28
legislation, 16
Lewis, Russell, 91
Liberal Party, 25, 38, 56–7, 65, 144
liberal progressivism, 7, 8, 40–3, 43, 58–60, 98, 172, 217
liberal traditions, 21–35
liberty, 23, 25, 28, 35, 62, 84
  individual, 16, 24–5, 26, 27, 29, 32, 33, 36–8, 42, 64, 68, 72, 94–5, 101, 103, 106, 116, 118, 122, 125–6, 130, 133–4, 137, 141, 149, 151, 167–8, 178–80, 192–3, 198–9, 203–6, 218–19
  negative, 144, 195–6, 218
  social, 24, 36–8, 41–2, 56
Liberty and Property Defence League, 26
Lippmann, Walter, 58, 63–4, 173
Locke, John, 7, 34, 41, 43, 194–5, 197, 203
Lockean liberalism, 7, 8, 31–2, 33, 198, 216

Machlup, Fritz, 71
Macmillan, Harold, 90, 92
Madison, James, 183
Magna Carta, 169
Malthus, Thomas, 23
Manchester School, 25–6, 27, 82
Mandeville, Bernard, 117
markets, 4, 13, 23, 115–37, 140, 142, 150, 160, 163, 167–8, 172, 184, 195, 201, 203, 209, 218
  and bureaucracy, 15, 127–8, 131
  and capitalism, 49–50, 52–4, 59, 94, 120, 129–30
  and competition, 16, 62, 84–5, 87, 93, 97, 101, 104, 106, 118, 127, 130–2, 147, 150, 220
  and free enterprise, 25–6, 33, 39, 53–4, 55, 60, 62, 64–6, 68, 83–5, 88–9, 91, 94–7, 104, 106, 115–18, 121, 124–5, 130–4, 147, 193, 202, 213, 218, 223
  global, 132–6
  and knowledge, 121, 123, 129, 218

INDEX

and monopoly, 15, 72, 126–7, 210–12
and neo-liberalism, 15, 115–16
and regulation, 15, 53, 57–8, 64, 83, 87, 116, 121, 127–9, 131
and spontaneous order, 15, 86, 115, 121–2, 124, 130, 134, 192, 218
Marshall, Alfred, 119–20
Marshall, T. H., 152
Marx, Karl, 52, 68
Marxism, 67, 71, 120, 135, 202, 217
Maude, Angus, 91
Mead, Lawrence, 154
Menger, Carl, 120
Microsoft, 210–11
Mill, James, 24
Mill, John Stuart, 24–5, 36, 43, 53, 118–19, 196
Mises, Ludwig von, 5, 6, 53, 63, 64, 71, 101, 116, 120–1, 136
and property, 192, 202–5, 207
Modern Age, 100–1
monetarism, 97
Mont Pelerin Society, 1–2, 6, 7, 14, 69–75, 80, 88, 91, 93, 96, 107–8, 136, 217, 222, 224
and collectivism, 1–2, 48
founding of, 71–3
and liberalism, 73–4, 80, 221
statement of aims, 72–3
Montesquieu, Charles de Secondat, 169
Morrison, Herbert, 56–7
Müller-Armack, Alfred, 6, 62, 84–5, 95, 220
Murray, Charles, 151–2

National Economic Development Council, 90
National Health Service, 132, 146, 149, 159, 161
National Insurance Act (1911), 144
National Insurance Act (1946), 146
National Labour Relations Act, 58
National Review, 100, 103
National Socialism, 38–40, 43, 55, 60–2, 66–7, 130, 176, 211, 220
Nazi Party, 39, 62, 63, 65, 67, 84, 133, 147, 176, 220
negative income tax, 154
neo-conservatism, 156, 220
and neo-liberalism, 223–4
Neumann, Franz, 174–5
New Deal, 41–2, 58–60, 65, 98–100, 102, 105, 145, 146, 159, 172, 217, 224
new liberalism, 6, 7, 8, 36–8, 40, 51, 56, 217, 219
New Right, 5, 15, 81, 84, 92, 96, 106, 157, 159–60, 162–4, 171, 217

New Statesman, 38
Newsweek, 105
Next Five Years Group, 56
Nixon, Richard, 105, 157
Novak, Michael, 102

Oakeshott, Michael, 89–90
Omega Report, 153
One Nation Group, 91–2
ordo-liberalism, 16, 81–9, 95, 125, 147, 153–4, 176–7, 211–12, 222; see also Social Market Economy
Orwell, George, 66–7

Paine, Thomas, 33–4
Pensions Act, 144
Philadelphia Society, 223
planning *see* collectivism
Plato, 68
Polyani, Karl, 48, 50, 53–5, 129
Polyani, Michael, 66, 71
Poor Law Amendment Act, 142, 145
Popper, Karl, 67–8, 71, 91
Powell, Enoch, 74, 91, 94
privatisation, 131–2, 137, 159–60, 161
property, 5, 13, 16, 23, 32, 83, 101, 192–213, 218
common and private distinction, 201–3, 205, 207
and ownership, 192, 194–6
and the public interest, 209–10
rights, 135, 137, 172, 197–200
and Roman law, 193–4, 201–2, 212
public goods, 23–4, 35, 55, 117, 128, 142, 150, 174, 210
Public Interest, 101
Public Sector Borrowing Requirement, 131

Radcliffe Report, 92
Reagan, Ronald, 103–7, 131, 155–7, 159–61, 163, 221, 223
Rechtsstaat, 4, 6, 16, 27, 29, 30, 83, 108, 125, 168, 174–7, 179–80, 189, 200, 204, 220, 222; see also rule of law
Reformation, 27
Republican Party, 103–6, 157, 221
republicanism, 32–3, 58, 103, 105–6, 172, 197
Ricardo, David, 23, 34, 118, 142
Robbins, Lionel, 6, 71, 72, 75, 91, 119–20, 216
Robinson, Joan, 50
Roosevelt, Franklin D., 41, 58–9, 98, 105, 145, 147, 217

247

Röpke, Wilhelm, 6, 64, 71, 82–3, 88, 211–12, 222
Rosenberg, Hans, 61
Rougier, Louis, 64
Rousseau, J.-J., 28
Rueff, Jacques, 64, 72
rule of law, 4, 16, 28, 125, 167–8, 170, 176–7, 179–80, 223
Rusher, William, 103
Rüstow, Alexander, 4, 6, 63, 64, 65, 82–4, 87, 220

Say's Law, 50, 116
Schlesinger, Arthur, 98
Schmitt, Carl, 40, 176, 180
Schumpeter, Joseph, 48, 50, 51–3, 55, 206–7, 221
Seldon, Arthur, 91–2, 159
self-help, 27
Sewill, Brendon, 96
Shanks, Michael, 92
Sherman, Alfred, 96
Shonfield, Andrew, 92, 129
Silicon Valley, 211
Smiles, Samuel, 142
Smith, Adam, 7, 23–4, 25, 34, 117–18, 122, 141–2, 144, 157, 180, 195, 216
Social Democratic Party, 89
Social Market Economy, 15, 28, 82, 84–9, 95, 147, 153, 176–7, 220; *see also* ordo-liberalism
social democracy, 57, 95, 155
social policy *see* welfare
Social Security Act (Britain), 158
Social Security Act (United States), 58, 145
socialism, 38, 48, 51, 53, 55–7, 63, 65–70, 74–5, 94, 101, 103, 156, 193, 196, 202, 216
Society of Individual Freedom, 65
Soviet Union, 68, 97
Spencer, Herbert, 25, 29, 35, 82, 119, 196
Spengler, Oswald, 40
Stein, Herbert, 102
Stigler, George, 71, 103, 222
Sumner, William Graham, 35
supply-side economics, 132
Supreme Court, 173–4

Tawney, R. H., 38
Thatcher, Margaret, 96–7, 131, 155–6, 158, 163, 171, 220, 223
think-tanks, 6, 15, 74, 80, 91–2, 94–7, 100, 102, 106, 152, 160, 220–1, 223–4

Third Reich *see* National Socialism and Nazi Party
Thorneycroft, Peter, 91
Tocqueville, Alexis de, 34
Townsend, William, 53
trade unions, 61, 72, 81, 92–3, 108, 131
Treitschke, Heinrich von, 29
Truman, Harry, 59
Tullock, Gordon, 6, 182–3

United States
  and capitalism, 32, 34, 41–2, 59–60, 98, 100, 108, 130
  and collectivism, 58–60
  Constitution, 6, 32, 33–4, 100, 171–4, 183, 188, 196–8
  and democracy, 32, 33, 198
  and liberalism, 14, 31–5, 40–3, 58–60, 98–9
  and libertarianism, 5, 101
  and neo-liberalism, 3, 22, 35, 65, 94, 99–107, 131–2, 220–1; *see also* New Right
  and private property, 196–9
  and social policy, 143–5, 146–7, 151–2, 154–5, 156–7, 159–62
  and slavery, 198–9
utilitarianism, 7, 8, 24–5, 34–5, 36, 41, 143, 196, 201, 212

Virginia School of Economics, 182–4, 221

Wagner, Robert, 183–4
Walras, Léon, 120
Walters, Alan, 6
Wattenberg, Ben, 102
Weber, Max, 31, 39, 52
Weimar Republic, 38–40, 61–2, 175–6
welfare, 5, 13, 15, 57, 59, 81, 86, 89, 97, 98, 132, 140–64, 218
  and charity, 143, 145
  and citizenship, 152–5
  and equality, 150–2
  and public expenditure, 103, 107, 142, 149, 156, 158–60, 161–2
  state, 98, 104, 140–1, 145–6, 148–50, 153–4, 155–62, 175, 222
Whigs, 27, 32, 33, 198
'winter of discontent', 156
Wittgenstein, Ludwig, 12
Wootton, Barbara, 56–7, 63
World Bank, 116, 135
World Trade Organization, 135

Rueder 231
laissez-faire continuum 125

* Geoffrey Hodgson 138 n 43, 44
* Hayek on social minimum — 150

Hayek — overall views 121-25
66